Graphic War

Graphic War

Jewish Women Drawing Contested Spaces

LAINI KAVALOSKI

Rutgers University Press
New Brunswick, Camden, and Newark, New Jersey
London and Oxford

Rutgers University Press is a department of Rutgers, The State University of New Jersey, one of the leading public research universities in the nation. By publishing worldwide, it furthers the University's mission of dedication to excellence in teaching, scholarship, research, and clinical care.

978-1-9788-3099-8 (cloth)
978-1-9788-3098-1 (paper)
978-1-9788-3100-1 (epub)
978-1-9788-3101-8 (webpdf)

Cataloging-in-publication data is available from the Library of Congress.
LCCN 2025020704

A British Cataloging-in-Publication record for this book is available from the British Library.

rutgersuniversitypress.org

In memory of Susan Stanford Friedman, a wonderful scholar and mentor, who encouraged me in this journey of ideas. She will be deeply missed.

Contents

Acknowledgments

There were many people who had a hand in bringing this project to light. I am grateful to all of them. First, thank you to Miriam Libicki for early inspiration and permissions to use her work, including the cover image. My deepest gratitude to graphic artists Julia Alekseyeva, Nora Krug, Leela Corman, Amy Kurzweil, Sarah Glidden, and Bernice Eisenstein for their wonderful work and generosity of spirit.

The National Endowment for the Humanities provided support during the summer of 2022: Thank you to the Engaging Geography in the Humanities Institute leaders Angel Nieves, Serena Parekh, and Liza Weinstein at Northeastern University for encouragement and title suggestions. My heartfelt gratitude to Michelle Neiman for her astute feedback and coaching in the last stages of the writing process. I could not have managed the images without star librarian Joe Malek. The anonymous readers at Rutgers provided incredibly useful comments and questions: Thank you. I could not have completed the book without the enthusiastic support and patience of my editor, Nicole Solano at Rutgers University Press.

Graphic War was in its early stages at least twelve years ago (unbeknownst to me at the time). The *Graphic Details* art exhibition and *Communities of Experience? A Symposium on Autobiographical Comics by Jewish Women* that took place in London in 2014 provided a valuable space for feedback and conversations with the artists and writers on sections of what would become chapter 1. A special thank you to organizers and curators of *Graphic Details* Sarah Lightman and Heike Bauer for their enthusiastic support for the resulting article in the special issue of the journal *Studies in Comics* (vol. 6, no. 2). Presenting parts of some of the chapters at several MLA conventions (2014–2022) also allowed me to hone many of the ideas that made their way into this book.

My deepest gratitude to the steadfast Lisa King, Lauren Lacey, Sayeeda Mamoon, and Ashley Byock for providing valuable feedback and support over the years. Many thanks to my family for the support, especially to my children, Elisheva and Lianna, who were patient during the many weekend and evening hours that I spent writing. Finally, I would not have been able to complete this work without the enthusiastic encouragement and support of my adviser and mentor Susan Stanford Friedman, to whom this book is dedicated.

Graphic War

Introduction

Jewish In/security and Graphic Borders

> Before we mistake a shift of scale for a qualitative shift of perspective, we need to develop more accurate cartographies, to stay focused on the potential for qualitative changes . . . not just quantitative proliferations.
> —Rosi Braidotti, "Affirming the Affirmative"

In the current political climate, national boundaries are increasingly militarized or closed, immigrants and refugees are criminalized and incarcerated, and vulnerable lives are often framed as disposable in state rhetoric. This book focuses on the effects of policed boundaries on women's bodies, identities, and psyches. Twentieth-century Jewish identities have been overwhelmingly influenced and defined by experiences of conflicts, genocide, and war, including the Holocaust, the Soviet occupation, the Israeli War of Independence in 1948, and subsequent and persistent Israeli-Palestinian conflicts. Forces like cultural memory, state-based Holocaust memorial practices, and state rhetorics work to compound and obscure the long-term costs of war-based identities on psyches and bodies. In addition, representations of violent conflict, exile, and genocide have historically been male-centered, obscuring narratives of women in those processes. The graphic works in this project make visible the consequences of borders, nationalist spaces, and state rhetorics on women's bodies.

While an intellectual understanding of the Jewish exilic position often claims that Jews speak from a unique position outside of state and dominant cultural locations,[1] Jewish communities have continued to seek out secure territories and nations precisely because of their often-precarious exilic position.[2] Indeed, the role of the nation-state has taken center stage in the wake of World War II and with the establishment of the state of Israel in 1948.

Graphic War examines the comic form as a means to theorize political and affective histories, militarized boundaries, and cultural narratives of violence. Stories of space and movement and their impact on social structure, stories of identities, and collective and individual bodies are crucial to understanding contemporary North American Jewish identities.[3] As hand-drawn visual stories, comics uniquely engage with border discourse and related perceptions of violence and memory. As Hilary Chute suggests, "the comic form is poised to make an intervention in the literary and historical fields because its formal possibilities are so rich as to be able to accommodate, and even redefine, this doubled act of narration and expression" (*Disaster Drawn* 34). I use the term *graphic border poetics* to refer to the spatial forms that represent boundaries such as walls, ghettos, and war zones together with the artistic renderings of affective histories, gendered experiences, and cultural narratives that make visible the long-term consequences of conflict on bodies and political futures. Representations of Jewish territorial positions are not only metaphoric but also an active force in determining the effects of boundaries—political and cultural—on Jewish lives. Spatial configurations of border conflicts refracted through graphic narratives open new ways of viewing narratives of conflict.

Through an archive of contemporary memoirs that grapple with Jewish experiences of war (1981–2019), *Graphic War* illustrates women's complex relations to nationhood, security, and gender: The devices in these texts reorient bodies and histories in time and space and, in doing so, reveal the ways that boundaries of nationhood and gender are untenable and often dangerous for those caught in the frames of war.[4] The graphic border poetics in these texts reveal broader power relations through which identities are co-created within and beyond militaristic practices and thus allow the reader to excavate the emotional strata of landscapes that animate the political realms.

My work makes three interlinked claims that align with the three sections of this introductory chapter. First, the representations of the female body in these graphic memoirs illustrate the locational position of women within national and affective environments. The space the body occupies in these works represents the environment in which we feel protected or precarious or both. The focus on graphic border poetics in a feminist context makes visible the consequences of state structures, militarized environments, and nationalisms on the female body and, in doing so, illustrates the danger for those caught in these frames. Likewise, these comics highlight the emerging legacies of Jewish joy and social action that shape twenty-first-century identities. Second, *Graphic War* claims that Jewish identity is undergoing seismic cultural shifts in the twenty-first century. Jews around the world are grappling with the atrocities of October 7, 2023, in Israel and subsequent wars in Gaza and Lebanon; the controversy of BDS (Boycott, Divestment, and Sanctions); widespread concern and protest about the militarism of the Israeli state; the rise of anti-Semitism; and the loss of elder survivors of the Holocaust—and thus the loss of living Holocaust witnesses. *Graphic War* argues that Jewish graphic narratives address these cultural pressures on dominant narratives of Jewishness[5] and gesture toward a constellation of emerging identities that embrace self-awareness, responsibility, and activism across national borders. Third, the graphic border poetics in these works focus on a critical politics of location[6] that enables a methodological response to various nationalist, empirical, and gendered ideologies produced in specific geographical locations.[7] Visual devices in graphic works echo lines and boundaries of maps to draw attention to cartographic colonizing practices and often subvert these borders through creative alternative mappings. The lines on maps are not just visual boundaries but delineate physical, controlled spaces like militarized zones, occupied territories, and state structures together with deeper emotional and psychic strata that illustrate the flows or pathways in which war and oppression are often enacted, solidified, dissipated, or transformed.

The power dynamics of contested and colonized spaces in the graphic medium are particularly fascinating to explore.[8] Due to the pictorial rendering of border discourse, spatial interpretations of contested spaces in graphic narratives have the potential to both mimic and subvert the very terms on which national boundaries are predicated. The ways that representations of geographical location and space on a page are manipulated using various graphic devices may be instructive for refiguring bounded, static, and unproblematized constructions of space.[9] Through the creative reorganization of space, borders, and representations of bodies on the page, graphic texts move beyond common constraints of identity politics and boundaried nationalisms and toward new constellations of Jewishness.[10]

The focus on what I call graphic border poetics is a way of knowing and theorizing visual structures and devices. This term refers to graphic representations of material borders between political and national spaces and their visual intersections with religious, gendered, affective, and cultural borders. Poetics here refers to the literary theory and practice of seeing form and structures in a text that collide to create meaning. The word *border* is instructive, as graphic memoirs have the peculiar ability to engage with bordered discourse on the terrain of the page—that is, the creative organizations of space using borders, panels, bleeds, overlays, and so forth create effects such as temporal layering and historical juxtaposition that illustrate the ways that gender and insecurity are determined by factors such as multiple nationalisms, physical and ideological discontinuities, and simultaneous contradictory narratives of history.[11] Graphic narratives are also a fertile medium for understanding and depicting the position of the body in fraught environments; the territory and space that characters inhabit become extensions of the body affecting, for example, its movement, its precarity, and its sense of belonging. The space around the female-identified body shapes the self in its complex formulations of identity, but space and territory around the body are also the air and earth that allow one to feel protected or precarious or both simultaneously.[12] Indeed, the narrative of disposable Jewish bodies throughout history makes the investigation of territory an important site of identity and political formation. Graphic border poetics in these works engage with the ways that state boundaries impact stories and experiences of gender, sexuality, race, memory, and the repercussions of these entanglements.

Locating Women's Bodies in Graphic Narratives

As an American and an Israeli citizen living in and between national spaces, I have discovered connections between my own personal narratives of nationhood and identity and the dominant cultural narratives of the nation-state: As I sit in a café in the center of Jerusalem, seventeen rounds of automatic weapon fire shatters my birthday dinner; I sleep on the floor of my daughter's room with several blankets over my head trying to escape the incessant staccato of helicopter blades; the phone rings over and over again, echoing in the 7 a.m. quiet of our Jerusalem apartment, bringing reports of two friends who were on the bus blown up this morning. As these events illustrate, I am bound to environments, political events, and narratives that compel me to question the constructions of my own nationalisms and identities. Living in these spaces, I feel my very body and those of my children are in danger. In effect, the landscape on which we live has become a very threat to our survival.[13]

Precarious environments, affective spaces, and cultural narratives shape our perspectives and our sense of our own bodies. When I entered my PhD program after moving to the United States from Israel, feminist spatial theory resonated with my own experiences of violence and war. Feminist writing and theory have long grappled with the ways that national boundaries and violence shape women's lives. As this book will argue, the spatialization of situated experience and representations of bodies in art and literature are crucial to understanding women in the context of violence and war. Conflict and violence take place on territories that contain geographical boundaries, nodes of tensions, layers of colonialism and nationalism—some of which are not readily visible. How then do we understand the effects of those multifaceted spaces?

A material feminist approach to the creative organization of space in comics makes visible the *processes* of transnational oppressions, intersectional identities, and multidirectional memories.[14] By focusing on locationality as a lens through which to discern the proximities of stories to one another, I connect this project to the work of feminist theorists such as Adrienne Rich, Gloria Anzaldúa, Kimberlé Crenshaw, Audre Lorde, Sara Ahmed, and Rosi Braidotti.[15] These feminist scholars focus on the politics of location, orientation, identity, and gender. Centering locationality in comic studies facilitates cross-categorical thinking across national boundaries, or what Braidotti calls "assemblages of knowledge." These assemblages illustrate ways that "power is a multilayered and dynamic entity, and . . . as embedded and embodied, relational, and affective subjects, we are immanent to (immersed or embedded in) the very conditions we are trying to change" (Braidotti, "Theoretical" 42). Comics that depict these embodied assemblages "think through" these issues in their very form; the visual devices are a way of theorizing political and gendered histories in the larger contexts of war that include Jewish memory of the Holocaust, German memory of World War II, the Israeli-Palestinian conflict, and the Soviet occupation, among others. The women artists in this study illustrate the contexts and environments that shape their lives.

A focus on spatiality and location, or what Susan Friedman calls locational feminism, is a feminism that considers ways "in which rhetorics from the outside"—particularly those produced by war, diaspora, exile, and transnational migration—"transform those inside" ("Locational" 17). While some of the artists in *Graphic War* experience violence and war directly, others are affected by the burden of the inherited memory of war and a family history of displacement. These texts illustrate the precarity of bodies in the context of war and cultural memory. The graphic devices in the comics I examine depict the "rhetorics from the outside" in relation to the contemporary lives of the subject. Material feminism, like its name, is "devoted to a critical analysis of actual conditions of existence" and their effects on the body and political structures (Coole and Frost 25). The visual devices in comics, including the serial form of the panel in these works, illustrate interlocking systems and their consequences on bodies. The artistic renderings of war and other violent structures allow us to perceive forces that are not always readily apparent, including "the forces, energies, and intensities" that configure individuals as well as social and political worlds (Coole and Frost 13).

Attention to the spatial rhetoric of location allows us to see the power relations that occur in those spaces and the ways that gender interacts with other culturally constructed systems and institutions. While temporal rhetorics are often linear, progressive, or isolated in their relation to other systems of power, a spatial rhetoric of location gives attention to the shifting power relations that exist in a location and across time (Friedman, "Locational" 20). This situated approach is related to what Adrienne Rich calls a feminist politics of location—and aligns with the concept of situated knowledges (Haraway; Harding). As discussed earlier, comic spaces are deftly suited to thinking about space and situated social production.

In graphic narratives, pages, lines, borders, and panels divide spaces, but they also show the ways that contested spaces work to violate bodies, haunt families, and shift political discourse. Unlike the geographical maps and political boundaries that they mimic, they can insert representations of memory, emotion, and bodily experience that reveal otherwise obscured stories of space. In its visual messiness, the comic form helps us imagine and feel the ways that spatial production affects women. One individual image or a series of images together can create this locational rhetoric through artistic devices like the juxtaposition of past and present, the use of symbolism, and creative territorial mapping—political and otherwise. Within the graphic form, panels or pages connote the passage of time, while the graphic devices that constitute the images and panels "locate" the subjects within a history, an affective space, or an imagined environment. For example, the cover image of Miriam Libicki's *jobnik!* provides a mapping of Miriam's experiences on her Israeli army base during the Second Intifada. In the cover image, Miriam walks among jets and stars as she walks away from the male barracks buttoning her army shirt (fig. 1.1). The symbols and precarious spaces in this image create a visual rhetoric that shows intersections of cultural, religious, national systems of power and their relation to Miriam's life and body. Her very body becomes a part of the violent and misogynistic environment around her—making it difficult for her to find the close relationships that she craves or to feel the patriotism for the homeland she has come to defend. This complex locational rendering of her life in the Israel Defense Forces (IDF) in her work illustrates her fierce patriotism to Israel and its connection to her Jewish identity on the one hand and the devastating consequences of that same patriotism and army service on her body and psyche on the other hand.

Personal distance to cultural narratives is important for women, as female bodies have been historically objectified, overlooked in the literature of war, or by default gendered male (Horowitz 368). According to Sara Ahmed, orientation is the way "we inhabit space," or how we find our bearings "in a world that acquires new shapes, depending on which way we turn" (*Queer Phenomenology* 1).[16] In his famous *The Production of Space*, Henri Lefebvre describes orientation as "a sense" or "an organ that perceives, a direction that may be conceived, and a directly lived movement progressing toward the horizon" (423). Ahmed reminds us that orientation not only is a sense or direction but also includes our proximity to objects, places, landscapes, and cultural narratives. Proximity suggests our distance from or nearness to an object or narrative. The focus on objects in Ahmed's work emphasizes the importance of the material world and the affects that reside within it. Orientations can reveal the limitations of our interactions with our world: hierarchies and power structures that shape and define the space in which we reside. Objects are not always familiar, and we don't always understand what we are looking at. In comics, the aesthetics within the images and frames are made visible to the reader: They *speak* to the bodies, allowing the reader to see inside the frame and to understand another's orientations, pathways, and limitations. The visibility of orientation also allows us to notice what resides within the frames of our own lives, to perceive the landscapes and objects that we live in proximity to every day—and indeed to understand the paths and direction that we ourselves are facing.

Graphic artist Nora Krug articulates feelings of national shame through objects associated with the German national project. The series of objects that she draws in her work reveal structures of nationalism and national shame that are not always readily visible or acknowledged by Germany. The objects she draws in multiple sections titled "From the Notebook of a Homesick Émigré: Things German" are imbued with Krug's feelings of pride about Germany. She problematizes her own attachments to national objects in these sections, creating a tension between the personal and nationalist narratives of attachment. The tensions between the multiple narratives of object attachment in the sections titled "From the Notebook of a Homesick Émigré: Things German" begin to sketch out the complex contemporary structures of nationalist shame and the lingering reactivity to that shame. The Leitz notebook is a particular symbol of efficiency and organization—words largely associated with the methods of extermination in the death camps during the Holocaust. She writes that the Leitz is designed to "establish order" and that it is the "German consulate binder of choice" (*Belonging*, chap. 4). Krug even encases her memoir within the image of a German notebook or Leitz—literally placing her writing and ideas within a nationalist object. By using the Leitz to symbolically bind or hold her memoir, she suggests that her own work and life are inextricable from nationalist German symbols and feelings. Instead of relegating affective environments and objects to the background, graphic narratives bring to the fore emotions that matter to the ways we understand intersections of political, geographical, and historical narratives.

By applying the concepts of orientation and proximity to comics, our readings and understanding may shift focus. One's sense of direction or loss of bearing affects the ways we turn next. If we turn toward objects of loss and fear, our direction is determined by a search for security and protection. Emotions are essential to understanding the constructions of state narratives, the culture around us, and the larger systems of violence. These often invisible forces that affect female-identified bodies go undetected or obfuscated by dominant narratives. In her scholarship, Rosi Braidotti describes a symbiotic interdependence where humans are dependent on the forms around them. If the body is coextensive with the territory and environment around it, then it cannot thrive in an environment of violence and hostility. The orientation of emotion, layered histories, absent or obscured stories, and unspoken oppressions in comics are revealed in creative organizations of space like layering, collage, use of lines and borders, maps, spatial metaphors, and so forth that make visible transnational oppressions, intersectional identities, and multidirectional memories (Bedad; Braidotti; Crenshaw; Rothberg). By paying attention to the artistic devices that illustrate the relation of bodies to objects and cultural narratives, we can recognize the ways that graphic poetics in the works track emotions that circulate between generations and geographies and their impacts on our futures; the graphic border poetics in these texts create a way of knowing, a method of understanding or making visible the often invisible narratives that are central to our collective futures.

Affect or emotions are often feminized and thus tend to be overlooked in serious discussions of war and memory, while more masculinist narratives of warfare, strategy, and violence dominate media stories, films, TV shows, and even video games. Far from separate, the emotions and dominant cultural narratives of violence are inextricably intertwined. As Sara Ahmed writes, "'being emotional' comes to be seen as a characteristic of some bodies and not others. . . . In order to discover how this process works, we need to discover how emotions operate to 'make' and 'shape' bodies as forms of action" (*Cultural* 4). Indeed, emotions are inextricable from the human body as well as the national body—and historically have been gendered male and positioned to stand in for the national body; bodies that are gendered female have been deemed unremarkable by a culture that values action and power. This has also been true historically for Jewish bodies. For example, the body of the victimized Jew in World War II was often feminized, portrayed as "soft" and without agency, especially in Israel. In contrast, nationalist narratives in the new Jewish state sought to reverse the affective depictions of the Jewish body as victim. The narrative of the "new Jew" in Israel was reinvented as a strong, militarized body that stood in for the nation-state, one that could ensure that the slogan "Never Again" would hold true.[17] The discussion of women's bodies recenters the lives of those who have been overlooked or dismissed in the wake of World War II and the new state.

War is of course devastating to human lives and bodies. The scale and methods of the destruction of lives/bodies in the Holocaust—in laboratories, in camps, in mass graves—are important to recognize. As Jerome Kohn reminds us, individual people were made irrelevant by transforming them into "'inanimate' matter to fuel the engines of extermination" (Arendt, *Responsibility and*

Judgement xix). Hannah Arendt claims the Nazi practices of making the object of their killing machine invisible in World War II were particularly insidious. People were taken out of the sight of the community and the public and put into concentration camps, killed in forests, taken away in gas vans, and buried in mass graves. Such methods that removed human beings from the realm of the visible—or of the known—literally made their bodies invisible, and seemingly irrelevant, to the dominant populations (in *The Origins of Totalitarianism* and *The Human Condition*). Graphic artists Leela Corman and Bernice Eisenstein use images of the mutilated and missing body as tropes in their works, again making the disappeared visible.[18] Corman uses a severed arm to represent traumatic exile and the loss of family in the Holocaust, while Bernice Eisenstein thematizes the trope of the missing limb and the prosthesis to articulate the painful absences that result from her family's Holocaust experiences.

By paying attention to the bodies that are rendered invisible by the processes of war and genocide and by looking at them as part of our moral responsibility, we can change the exclusionary reality. Comics use the realm of the visible to address this dangerous absence. Arendt describes invisibility as a phenomenon that arises from within the political sphere. She writes, "The presence of others who see what we see and hear what we hear assures us of the reality of the world and ourselves"; she insists that the expulsion of Jews from the German political arena is an exclusion from an established reality, a collective agreement (*Human Condition* 50). Thus, what threatens the collectively chosen "reality" is made invisible or hidden. Those who become invisible in the chosen "reality" are then set outside of politics—in this case, excluded, pushed outside of biopolitical borders, and murdered. The comics in this study center the lives of those who were murdered, oppressed, or made invisible. In works like Leela Corman's and Bernice Eisenstein's, for example, murdered family members frequent the spaces on the page, making visible their continuing painful absences as well as the joy and healing their memories bring in the present. Graphic narratives use the realm of the visible to make the disappeared and the missing known once again, to give voice and shape to lives that had been relegated to the realm of the abject or invisible. In this sense, graphic narratives push back against the totalitarian project of disappearing those deemed undesirable by giving voice and space to those people as individuals. These graphic works present these bodies as visible, dynamic, and in complex intersections with diaspora, memory, patriotism, and the homelands past and present.

The postwar environment in Europe was marked by denial and a culture of hidden atrocities, which led to the continuing repression of war narratives and culpability in European communities. Nora Krug, a non-Jewish German artist, uses the graphic medium to reveal the culpability of her own family in the Nazi Party and to illustrate the ways that coveted products/objects in contemporary Germany tie back to the war machine of the Holocaust. Krug's own life is tied up in the obscured histories of her family and in her own attachments to German objects and their proximity to national pride. Her discussion of her uncle's involvement with the Hitler youth stands in stark contrast to the silence and invisibility of the disappearances of Jews and others; Krug gives voice to the hidden narratives of genocide that lurk beneath the surface of everyday life in Germany. While Krug explores the ways her own life has been indelibly marked by these histories, she simultaneously questions the ways nations and communities take responsibility for the oppression of others. She excavates archives and family albums in order to uncover family secrets that were buried eighty years earlier. Her family's multigenerational disengagement with responsibility is not unique but a problem Krug implies is relevant to all Germans. Krug's work—particularly when read alongside Amy Kurzweil—implies the importance of asking questions about how a shared responsibility might shift the burdens of identity and the victim-perpetrator binary that has come to define cultural memory after World War II.

Jewish Identity and Twentieth-Century War

In his 2024 Oscar acceptance speech after winning Best International Feature, filmmaker Jonathan Glazer condemned the war in Gaza and connected it to the legacy of the Holocaust, spurring an explosion of online responses. His film *Zone of Interest* tells the story of Rudolph Hoss, a Nazi commander who lived with his family next to Auschwitz. Glazer spoke to the audience, saying, "All our choices were made to reflect and confront us in the present, not to say look what they did then, rather look what we do now. Our film shows where dehumanization leads at its worst. It's shaped all of our past and present. Right now, we stand here as men who refute their Jewishness and the Holocaust being hijacked by an occupation, which has led to conflict for so many innocent people" (qtd. in Siegel and Ritman). The media world blew up in response. Glazer's speech drew a barrage of responses, partly due to his jilted cadence and the unclear syntax[19] but also due to the loaded content of his speech. Social platforms like Twitter/X and Instagram were flooded with reprimands as well as praise, though most responses centered on the contemporary ethical uses and abuses of the Holocaust narrative. A letter of condemnation was swiftly created in response to Glazer's words and signed by over 400 Hollywood luminaries (Rahman). Despite the controversy over the meaning of the speech, one thing is clear: Glazer made a direct connection between the actions of the Israeli state and the narrative of the Holocaust. The media controversy in part reveals the way the narrative of the Holocaust continues to dominate and reverberate in contemporary Jewish life, in U.S.

politics, and indeed on the larger world stage. The Holocaust is not past; it shapes political and affective cultural narratives of the present.

Current cultural changes that include the loss of the last Holocaust survivors and their living testimony; controversies around support for Boycott, Divestment, and Sanctions (BDS); an increase in international disapproval of the Israeli state's military actions;[20] and a rise in anti-Semitism in the United States signal major seismic shifts in Jewish identity—yet also leave an opening for a potential unburdening of identity. While Jewish identity is becoming more fluid due to the shifting values of a younger generation and the increasing use of digital platforms and archives, the dominant narratives of Jewish institutions and the Israeli state are still mired in deeply reactive narratives of fear and destruction associated with war and genocide.

Leela Corman explores the question of Jewish identity in her short comic "The Irreducible Essence of Jewishness." Leela laughs with a group of Jewish coworkers about the "irreducibles" of being Jewish or "those things that you find inside yourself that can't be boiled away, no matter how assimilated you might be." With bright colors and a tongue-in-cheek tone, she describes some of these Jewish irreducibles such as eating gefilte fish, walking with a Yiddish Vaudeville shuffle, kvetching, black humor, and perhaps most saliently, "the constant fear and preparedness for disaster that results from the deep identification with the horrors of Jewish exile and WWII" (Corman, "Irreducible"). Though Corman's depiction of Jewish identity is humorously self-deprecating in this short comic, her commentary on the impact of the Holocaust on contemporary Jewish identity is devastating.

The impact of Holocaust memory is evident in wider twentieth-century American culture as well. Ewa Stanczyk suggests that the Holocaust became an important touchstone in American historical memory starting in the 1980s in part due to the popularization of the graphic narrative *Maus* and TV series like *The Story of the Family Weiss* (1978), which contributed to the Americanization of the Shoah (Stanczyk 1). In 1993 the United States Holocaust Memorial Museum was built on the National Mall in Washington, D.C., moving it to the center of American culture and history. The spatial positioning of the museum and its proximity to other iconic American symbolic monuments such as the Washington Monument, Lincoln Memorial, Vietnam Veterans Memorial, and Martin Luther King Memorial solidify its status in the American national story.[21]

War, exile, and diaspora have had an immense influence on the Jewish experience and on the ways Jews and Jewish communities see themselves.[22] An overidentification with the Holocaust continues to shape articulations of public and personal Jewish identity. The experiences of war and the resulting displacement, oppression, loss of community, and fear of annihilation continue to cause persistent trauma for many Jews. Wars and occupations that affected huge Jewish populations in the first part of the twentieth century alone include the Russian Revolution, the Russian Civil War and subsequent Soviet occupation, two world wars that resulted in millions of deaths including the systematic murder of six million Jews, and wars in Palestine. In the second part of the twentieth century, wars in Israel and the larger Middle East in 1956, 1967, 1973, 1982, and 2006, including two intifadas,[23] created an atmosphere of fear and terror. These events fueled an impetus for the Jewish state to bolster its military and shore up borders.

As many scholars have suggested, the residues of atrocity in the twentieth century continue to shape those born after the Holocaust.[24] Children and even grandchildren of Holocaust survivors are marked by an "unlived Holocaust in their lives" and often suffer a stigma of shame and suffering (McGlothlin). The children and grandchildren of Soviet Jews continue to write about their own and their parents' and grandparents' harrowing experiences under leaders like Stalin, Lenin, Khrushchev, and Putin—including the experiences of World War II narratives in their lives.

As living Holocaust survivors pass away, their stories are often taken up by their grandchildren. In the last decade or so there has been a surge of storytelling by third-generation family members in various public media. Colloquially called the "3G," third-generation Jews are taking an interest in the experiences and memories of their grandparents and great-grandparents. Groups like 3GNY (Third Generation New York) have emerged in cities across the United States.[25] Some grandchildren have taken on their grandparents' Holocaust scars quite literally. In Israel some of the third generation have tattooed their grandparents' camp numbers on their own arms, making the link with the past indelible in ways the second generation did not.[26] Dana Doron's documentary film *Numbered* (2012) includes interviews with approximately fifty Holocaust survivors, some of them with their tattooed grandchildren. Rachael Cerrotti's memoir and popular podcast *We Share the Same Sky* (2021) and her subsequent podcast *Along the Seam* (2024) were inspired by the discovery of boxes of journals documenting her grandmother's experiences during World War II and led her on a journey to trace her grandmother's footsteps in Europe. Other grandchildren write about the ways their families defied the horrors of war. Dan Grunfeld writes about the place of basketball in his survivor family and in the life of his father, Ernie Grunfeld—a professional player for the Knicks—in *By the Grace of the Game: The Holocaust, a Basketball Legacy and the Unprecedented American Dream* (2021). Grunfeld writes, "Being two generations removed, I have some distance which helps alleviate some of the trauma," which allows him to reflect on his family trauma in a different way than his parents; nevertheless, he admits the trauma "stays with you" (Amatenstein).

Popular media about the Holocaust in the form of podcasts, films, YouTube videos, TV series, and books have soared in recent years. Dara Horn's popular collection of journalistic essays, *People Love Dead Jews: Reports from a Haunted Present* (2022), points to the fetishism of war and tragedy. Her book reports on anti-Semitism that is often articulated in the fetishism of the destruction of Jews and Jewish communities in the United States and elsewhere.[27] Ken Burns, Lynn Novick, and Sarah Botstein's PBS series *The US and the Holocaust* was released in 2022. Popular TV series and films like *The Way Home* (2023), *Russian Doll* (2019), *A Small Light* (2023), *The Tattooist of Auschwitz* (2024), Oscar winner *The Zone of Interest* (2023), *The Commandant's Shadow* (2024), and *A Real Pain* (2024) point to a renewed interest in Holocaust narratives.

Many of the works in the following chapters attest to the toxicity of war memory and give space to narratives of Jewishness and war that are less burdened and constrictive.[28] As Dana Mihăilescu suggests, examining comics like Amy Kurzweil's shows the ways that memory and politics intersect in graphic texts and may help open a dialogue about memory practices in the United States and Europe "whilst going beyond the narrowly defined and politicized forms of war remembrance that have dominated the commemorative cultures of East and West" ("Mapping" 110). Mihăilescu argues that memory influences the ways one reacts in the present, not just in our personal lives but also in the public sphere. Memory of the Holocaust includes sedimented and circulating emotions that affect our actions in the present.

As many of the graphic narratives in this book illustrate, a threat to one's body does not have to be immediate or even in the present; rather, a threat can be embedded in affective spaces and memories. Memories of war and trauma haunt many of the women in this study even though they are removed a generation or two from directly experiencing violence or war. The graphic texts I examine challenge the weight that Jewish identity has taken on in the postwar years. As Miriam Harris suggests, though some might see it as blasphemy, these works perhaps show brave truths: "The Holocaust has become a cornerstone of identity for many Jews, even those whose families were not in Europe during the war" (132). Graphic artists like Bernice Eisenstein and Amy Kurzweil show the individual pain of that inheritance as well as the cultural consequences of Holocaust fetishism. What are the repercussions of the specters of war, genocide, and oppression in the lives of those who come *after*? How do the terrors of the past affect the decisions and politics of the present?[29] The graphic texts discussed in *Graphic War* make visible the consequences of narratives of fear and genocide and often tackle their cultural and personal significance head-on by pointing toward a more varied, complex narrative of Jewish identity in the twenty-first century.

Graphic War addresses a unique archive of women's graphic memoirs (what Sarah Lightman calls confessional comics) that focus on the way that new constellations of Jewish female experience are shifting perceptions of war and nationalism. Historically, Jewish women's writing has been underrepresented in Holocaust studies, memory studies, and comic studies (Lightman; Chase; Hirsch). Lightman suggests that female-identified Jewish comic artists are almost absent in the discourse (38), while Alicia Grace Chase observes that comic exhibitions have included male artists almost exclusively, citing several comic exhibits in Europe and North America ("Draws like a Girl," qtd. in *Graphic Details* 3). *Graphic War* not only brings women comic artists to the fore but also argues that their work makes a unique contribution to visual studies, comic studies, Jewish literary studies, and feminist theory. Recent publications that address women's comics, Jewish comics, and comics of war have gained wide readership and popularity in the last fifteen years. Works that address graphic narratives by women include Hilary Chute's *Graphic Women* (2014), Deborah Elizabeth Whaley's *Black Women in Sequence: Re-Inking Comics* (2015), Monalesia Earle's *Writing Queer Women of Color: Representation and Misdirection in Contemporary Fiction and Graphic Narratives* (2019), and *Monstrous Women in Comics* (2020), edited by Samantha Langsdale and Elizabeth Rae Coody. Recent monographs in the field of graphic novels and war include Laurike in 't Veld's *The Representation of Genocide in Graphic Novels: Considering the Role of Kitsch in Graphic Novels* (2019), and Hilary Chute's *Disaster Drawn* (2016), which traces a history of representations of war in comics and emphasizes the importance of comics as a form of witness (*Disaster Drawn* 17).

Texts that address Jewish women and comics have increased in the last decade. Tahneer Oksman's *How Come Boys Get to Keep Their Noses?* (2016), examines seven artists' work, arguing that "Jewish identity means negotiating between inherited and invented structures, between rejections of, as well as attachments to, communal, individual, and historical actions of self and identity" (4), while Victoria Aarons's *Memory Spaces: Visualizing Identity in Jewish Women's Graphic Novels* (2023) examines ways that Jewish women cartoonists use the verbal-visual medium to show how history, ritual, myth, and memory contextualize and shape identities (2). Kevin Haworth's single-author study *The Comics of Rutu Modan: War, Love, and Secrets* (2019) traces the history of comics in Israel and Modan's place in that oeuvre. The collection *Graphic Details: Jewish Women's Confessional Comics in Essays and Interviews* (2014), edited by Sarah Lightman, brings to light a constellation of Jewish artists who write about various pressures in their own lives.[30] *Jewish Women in Comics: Bodies and Borders* (2022), a collection of interviews and essays, explores the graphic work of women across a wide range of experiences and borders. Karolina Krasuska's *Soviet-Born: The Afterlives of Migration in Jewish American Fiction* (2024) illuminates the often overlooked works of Soviet-born Jewish American writers and graphic artists. Whereas these works illustrate important histories and representations of women in comics across a variety of experiences, *Graphic War* uses a theoretical approach that highlights the effects of policed boundaries on identities, psyches, and women's bodies.

This project too responds to Benjamin Schreier's call "to approach identity as a *problem*—a problem around which Jewish literary study needs to deliberately and critically organize itself" (23). Jewish identity, as Schreier suggests, often "functions as a police form in the ethnographically limned historicist study of identifiable groups," or said in another way, "Jewish American literary studies and the habits through which its practitioners operate . . . sometimes looks very much like a golden ghetto" (3). In its authorship and focus, *Graphic War* examines the visual and textual tendrils that move beyond identity categories to include actions, emotions, and groups historically outside of how "Jewish" is often defined. The authors of the graphic works critique dominant historically legible locations of Jewishness and think and write across national and positional boundaries. Like the Jewish American literary studies that Schreier helps to relocate if not redefine, these texts begin to shape a more open concept of Jewishness that is recombinant, flexible, and interwoven with other minority positions in the United States.

While questioning the ways that violence and war have shaped Jewish identitarian politics, *Graphic War* critically examines cultural tropes associated with Jewish trauma and memory. Graphic artists Amy Kurzweil, Sarah Glidden, and Miriam Libicki, for example, explore ethical issues that include the role of Holocaust narratives in conflicts in Israel. So too the works of Bernice Eisenstein, Amy Kurzweil, and Nora Krug question the weight of the responsibility that Jews have taken on; they probe the second and third generations' roles in the perpetuation of Holocaust trauma as well as the shared responsibility of the grandchildren of the Nazis who committed those crimes.[31] By looking across national and identitarian spaces (as in Kurzweil's and Krug's work), we may open a dialogue around memory practices in order to "move beyond the narrowly defined and politicized forms of war remembrance that have dominated the commemorative culture of both the East and West" (Mihăilescu 108).

Comics and Spatial Theory: Graphic Border Poetics

Graphic War examines the effects of war and policed boundaries on identities, psyches, and women's bodies. The authors of these memoirs illustrate how narratives of war affect their own lives, physical bodies, families, and collective futures. For example, the women in these works are impacted by the ghetto spaces of the Holocaust, bounded nationalist territories in Israel, borders of geopolitical control like checkpoints and walls in Israel-Palestine, landscapes of contemporary German nationalist memory, and spaces of Soviet control in Russia and Ukraine. The graphic texts discussed in *Graphic War* make visible the consequences of narratives of fear and genocide and often tackle their cultural and personal significance head-on by pointing toward a more varied, complex narrative of Jewish identity in the twenty-first century.

Mapping Graphic Border Poetics

The term *graphic border poetics* allows for a visual representation of the consequences and the long-term legacies of war and violence and is a means of theorizing the collision of spatial and artistic elements in graphic narratives that make up the multivalent meanings. Within comics, the panel (or page) becomes the map that creates the story. The mappings of violence on bodies and environments within the visual parameters of the comic form mimic the affective, physical, and collective worlds we create for ourselves. Boundaries on landscapes and maps are often determined and drawn by those in power to control a geographical location or a people. The Nazi Party, for example, used maps and boundaries to facilitate the occupation of countries like Poland and France, using lines that created militarized zones, occupied territories, and concentration/death camps. Cartographic lines like these are not just boundaries but delineate physical, controlled spaces. These enclosed or monitored spaces in turn control populations; in the case of World War II spaces, ghettos and camps dehumanized or delineated people into biopolitical categories—those deemed unworthy of life. A focus on graphic border poetics, then, allows us to see the ways that individuals are affected by configurations of war and thus to recognize the impact on the world we build and inherit. Maps have helped to facilitate the exile, othering, and murder of Jews, gay folks, communists, intellectuals, and many others, often confining them within the cartographic lines and territories that defined the physical spaces of oppression. In National Socialist Germany, for example, the party's boundaries of sexual identity, gender expression, ethnicity, and religious affiliation determined who lived and who died. Graphic border poetics focus on the ways that boundaried spaces—identitarian, carceral, and affective spaces—are complicated or subverted within the comic form. The term *graphic border poetics* builds on terms like *countermapping*, the practice of resisting dominant mapping via spatial interventions "to assert alternative, potentially decolonizing geographies" (Hunt and Stevenson 373).[32] Comics are a fitting medium through which to express experiences of war, feelings of insecurity, inherited memory, and their repercussions on bodies and lives.

Graphic border poetics in this project take a neoformalist approach to geographical borders and wars, highlighting the ways that comic devices and graphic modes of resistance are positioned as directly representational of bordered spaces in the larger world. The visual affordances of graphic narratives then provide a rich palette through which to study borders and to develop an emerging vocabulary of graphic representations of geopolitics. Unlike strictly topological representations, comics allow for the integration of narratives of affect, resistance, and residues of war into the discourse around conflict and the nation-state. Border discourse in graphic narratives works differently than in prose texts. Instead of the single plane constituted by combinations of letters and numbers that prose occupies (left to right in English), the graphic form uses a two-dimensional plane to represent cultures, religions, and of course power relations in spatial terms. Images in graphic narratives work to represent the event or social construction in terms that allow for spatial articulation and play. Artistic devices used in comics might include diagonal slicing, panel overlays, and bleeds or borderless panels that show an expansion of a personal feeling, political event, or idea. The graphic poetics within a panel may suggest different strata of meaning or the complex locations of identity. As Tahneer Oksman has suggested, "the medium can open up relational considerations of identity by considering the manifold entangled layers that inform a person's sense of self" (22). Thus, objects or objects-as-metaphors are locations in physical space that interact and *speak to* other images in that narrative space.

Graphic narratives can map new power relations and connect to the material world through images and visual rhetorics, but they also mimic the material world in important, imaginative ways—including the hierarchies of power and logics of security that play out in these media.[33] Architectures of form are powerful tools for restructuring the logics of security and violence through their formal affordances. Spatial forms and architectures (walls, checkpoints, tunnels, bounded territories) are an inextricable part of the rhetorical divisions of people and landscapes—that is, formal structures inform and change the ways bodies engage with stories of belonging and violence.

The spatial approach to graphic narratives in *Graphic War* builds on the scholarship of philosophers, feminist thinkers, and cultural geographers who have argued for a critical geography that spatializes social and historical narratives and their related systems of power. Cultural and postmodern geographers like Elizabeth Grosz, Doreen Massey, Henri Lefebvre, Edward Soja, David Harvey, and Yi-Fu Tuan, among others, have already established that the social production of space is intertwined with, and inseparable from, the spaces where that production occurs. Historically, a focus on temporality, social life, and theory submerged and decentered the geographical and spatial imagination (Soja, *Postmodern Geographies* 131). In the 1980s and '90s, geographers focused on the palimpsestic qualities of state geography as inherent to understanding territoriality and sovereignty. The production of space examines geopolitical factors and tools of the state including the delineation of borders and territories, the development and destruction of neighborhoods, the occupation of tribal lands, and so forth. Theoretical frames like these have a sizable impact on the ways we perceive and move through space—and a direct bearing on the practices and policies of warfare. Visual arts such as comics show horizontal and vertical planes of meaning—not just across lines on the surface of a landscape but also beyond Cartesian forms to make visible the emotions, bodily pressures, haunted landscapes, and lurking cultural narratives. The spatial border poetics in graphic narratives center feminist frameworks and critical geographies to excavate seemingly static geographical or Cartesian space.

Graphic texts use visual devices that echo the artistic devices of maps to draw attention to cartographic colonizing practices and the limitations of geopolitical mapping; in doing so, they can subvert these borders through creative alternative mappings.[34] Within graphic narratives, the colors, mediums, overlays, and lines are creative ways of expressing what Cartesian spaces often obfuscate. Emotions become visible: Physical spaces overlap with metaphorical spaces, making emotions like fear, anger, ambivalence, and patriotism visible inside and outside of militarized spaces. For example, Sarah Glidden's watercolor maps blur national borders, bringing attention to the constructed nature of these boundaries and at the same time invoking the ways that cultural stories and memory bleed across physical or political boundaries in the context of the Israeli-Palestinian conflict.

Graphic devices like collage, the layering of images, the blurring of lines and borders, and creative mapping assist in the articulation of these processes, setting affective environments in proximity to depictions of everyday life and bodies. Proximity, a theoretical concept that is visually spatialized in graphic form, is central to understanding the ways that bodies and psyches are affected by war and by movement across and through geographical spaces. Proximity, a term used by Sara Ahmed (*Queer Phenomenology*), shows distance between bodies, objects, symbols, and borders, illustrating the intersections of one's geographical location, gender identity, religious belief or practice, and other cultural influences as central to the ways that violence, occupation, war, and the memory of these narratives affect women.

Comics may also be thought of as a space outside of territories and national borders, a space that incorporates a flow of ideas from outside of the constructions of national definitions and lines. In recent collective memory, Jewish experiences of destruction, exile, and refugee status loom large. Our connections to a place depend on our experience of being inside and outside of a place, including citizenship status, feelings of stability, and conditions of safety and security, among others. Siegfried Kracauer, a Jewish intellectual, suggests that the stripping of his citizenship rights in Germany and his later migration to France and then the United States "left him feeling personally adrift in space and time" (qtd. in Hart 14). As Matthew Hart suggests in his work on extraterritoriality, "an extraterritorial person is not simply located outside a territory: she is poised between places and potencies" (15). Comics depict betweenness or liminal spaces in visual terms. Amy Kurzweil, for example, depicts the escape route through which her grandmother leaves the ghetto; a crack in the ghetto wall allows her grandmother to survive the war and to pass as a non-Jewish citizen in Poland (fig. 2.7). The hole in the ghetto wall in Kurzweil's work is an in-between space, a life-giving space of escape situated in the wall of the ghetto; the crack in the wall then becomes a visual metaphor through which Amy repurposes a piece her grandmother's terrifying story into an artistic tool in her own life. Cracks or openings in boundaries are a trope in Kurzweil's work, representing an extraterritorial space, a way out of the deathly spaces of the Holocaust, and at the same time an exit metaphor that Amy uses to escape her own narrative of inherited fear. Graphic border poetics highlight artistic devices like these to make visible the national, social, and emotional interactions on the page; they illustrate spaces of territoriality within the nation-state while allowing for a movement and articulation of space that defies confining national definitions/prescriptions.

A Lineage of Border Poetics

The term *graphic border poetics* comes from a lineage of artistic and philosophical sources. These scholars include Homi K. Bhabha, Georg Simmel, and Craig Saper, who use the related term *sociopoetics*. According to Simmel's 1903 dictum, "the boundary is not a spatial fact with sociological consequences, but a sociological fact that forms itself spatially" (142). Borders are narrated. While borders shape political and cultural narratives of space, political and cultural stories also impact real spaces and borders. The focus on borders in visual texts and comics employs a spatial approach to cultural studies that examines topographical spaces together with the spaces and theories of culture. Borders then can be understood as "performative renegotiations of nations and their narration" (Rosello and Wolfe 2). Geopolitical boundaries both shape and are shaped by the narratives we tell about them.

My work is also indebted to theorists like Walter Benjamin, Michel Foucault, Gilles Deleuze, Rosi Braidotti, Donna Haraway, and Eyal Weizmann,[35] who have worked toward models of materialist intervention in the hierarchies of power inherent in bounded territories and military practices. Braidotti, for example, advocates for what she calls a "symbiotic inter-dependence" where the human body is coextensive with the territory and environment around it ("Affirming"). The space within and around comics provides a representational palette that necessarily includes environments, objects, and affects as inextricable from the form of the body. Theories of sociopolitical space have a history of addressing carceral forms specifically. Foucault's work on disciplinary society and institutional control of populations, Deleuze and Guattari's use of nomadic theory and rhizomorphic and arborescent forms to deterritorialize space and knowledge, and Agamben's focus on concentration camps and bios and zoē shape the ways I approach comic spaces.[36] My work builds on these theories by arguing that spatial assemblages allow us to access and understand the affective and historical narratives that belie the violent structures of the present. Scholarship like Weizmann's opens new conversations about the implications of the flow of theory into real spaces. So too, it draws much-needed attention to questions of the ethical use of philosophical frameworks in military contexts. His work brings focus to the ways that material structures that contain bodies or that symbolize occupation and control affect the landscape and surrounding populations. These structures and concepts are often visible in the comic form, creating a cross-disciplinary conversation about the ways that spaces, structures, and borders shift how we perceive security and safety—and their dangers for long-term peace and security.

Graphic border poetics shares a theoretical foundation with the emerging field of border aesthetics, which examines border representation at the intersection of territorial and aesthetic works to show how "figurations of borders in cultural expressions matter for social, political, and historical processes of bordering" ("Border Poetics / Border Culture").[37] Borders do not just separate spaces but also imply interaction and connections that occur on and between borders. The discussions of borders in *Graphic War* are not abstract but rather focus on the proliferation of dangerous borders in political and social life. Like cultural geography, border poetics research examines "borderscapes," or the dispersed and dislocated regimes, practices, and assemblages that make up the complexity of borders (Rajaram and Grundy-Warr).[38]

Chapter Outlines

Although this study is far from a complete investigation of comics by Jewish women or of comics about women and war, it acts as a touchpoint for discussions about how creative forms in graphic narratives reveal the cultural dynamics that animate larger stories of communities and nations. The scope of the book focuses specifically on the ways that graphic border poetics can be used as a means of reading complicated dynamics that reside in bodies, landscapes, and cultural narratives. In this introductory chapter, I lay out the contemporary political and social shifts that are affecting the dominant trajectories of Jewish history and culture and argue that while these challenges pose significant risks to the stability of Jewish identity, they may also allow for an unburdening of identity. These cultural challenges include the loss of the last Holocaust survivors and their living testimony, an increase in international disapproval of many of the practices of the Israeli state, and a rise in anti-Semitism in the United States. While Jewish identity is becoming more fluid due to the shifting values of a younger generation and the increasing use of digital platforms and archives, it remains mired in narratives of fear and destruction associated with war and genocide. By highlighting the feminist geographies or graphic border poetics in Jewish graphic narratives, I suggest that war continues to shape twenty-first-century Jewish identities, articulations of gender, constructions of nationalism, and geopolitical futures.

Chapter 1, "Militarized Bodies and Contested Homelands in the Works of Miriam Libicki and Sarah Glidden,"[39] argues that Miriam Libicki's *jobnik! An American Girl's Adventures in the Israeli Army* and Sarah Glidden's *How to Understand Israel in 60 Days or Less* serve to reorient religious, nationalist, and sexual identities in the context of the Israeli-Palestinian conflict. Through a spatial exploration of contested homelands, Libicki and Glidden engage with complex graphic depictions of ambivalence toward Israeli power in spatial terms, which connects national violence to sexual violence as well as to cultural memories of the Holocaust. The renderings of memory and contemporary violence in Libicki's work, for example, create a second story of identity that suggests a connection between gendered identity in the IDF and larger systems of violence and territorial division.

In chapter 2, "The Implicated Subject and World War II Identity in the Twenty-First Century," the juxtaposition of Amy Kurzweil's *Flying Couch* and Nora Krug's *Belonging* reimagines the shared legacy of World War II memory and identity from both Jewish and (non-Jewish) German perspectives. Arguing that Jewish identity and texts cannot be separated from other proximal histories and identities, this chapter looks at two works that address the effects of Holocaust and Nazi memory on contemporary women's lives in the twenty-first century. These two graphic memoirs give voice to the inherited burden of memory for women, showing the ways that the self is affected and formed by the discursive powers of memory of World War II. Through Krug's and Kurzweil's work, I theorize the power of artistic form as a way to address reactionary memory and to move toward what Michael Rothberg has called the implicated subject—a position that is neither victim nor perpetrator and that facilitates a more politically productive memory.

The third chapter, "'The Drug of H': Holocaust Addiction, Pulp Horror, and Jewish Identity," examines the post-Holocaust graphic novel through Bernice Eisenstein's work, suggesting that Holocaust memory continues to shape twentieth-century Jewish identity and thought in significant ways in the twenty-first century. The centering of the Holocaust in Jewish culture and memory is what Eisenstein calls "the drug of H," a metaphor for articulating Holocaust memory as a cultural addiction. Eisenstein centers important twentieth-century Jewish thinkers and artists like Charlotte Salomon and

Hannah Arendt as part of crucial conversations we need to have about the legacy of the Holocaust and its impact on survivors' families and on Jewish culture and history more generally.

Through Julia Alekseyeva's *Soviet Daughter: A Graphic Revolution* and Leela Corman's short works (2013–2021), chapter 4, "'Work for the Future, Not Only for Memory': Agency, Activism, and Joy in the Works of Leela Corman and Julia Alekseyeva," illustrates the ways that the memory of diaspora, genocide, and anti-Semitism orients identities and cultural constructs of contemporary Jewish life. Alekseyeva's work introduces the Soviet Jewish experience into the book's constellation of war and violence in Jewish memory. Alekseyeva's and Corman's texts articulate the importance of specific geopolitical locations and gendered experiences of war in forming the identities of three generations of survivors. By connecting to transnational identities in Europe and beyond, they forge positive identities with landscapes and people that are associated with the oppression and murder of their families.

The archive of graphic works in this project points toward the profound ways that women experience war, emotion, and bodily feeling as intersecting—not as discrete—events. By illustrating overlapping and often contradictory personal and political locations, these graphic narratives suggest that the current dialectical positions that construct bordered, gendered, and colonized spaces become untenable in their rhetorical constructions. *Graphic War* argues that a material feminist analysis of these works is pertinent to illustrate (1) the personal and political consequences of cultural identities that are based in narratives of war and victimhood, (2) the possibilities for decolonizing nationalist narratives within visual and geopolitical assemblages, and (3) models for reorienting the overdetermined memories of past atrocities within a more productive ethics of comparison. *Graphic War* focuses on assemblages of affect and spatial precarity in these works in order to highlight pressures that sustain the discourses of contemporary (in)security and militarism. An examination of the graphic border poetics facilitates a recognition of the complex affects that produce bounded territory and, in doing so, challenges us to narrate borders and identities differently.

1

Militarized Bodies and Contested Homelands in the Works of Miriam Libicki and Sarah Glidden

Like the identities of many other nation-states, the identity of Israel is informed by boundaries, both literal and otherwise. Exclusive notions of cultural belonging, religious notions of biblical promise, and the cultural memory of victimization are all central to building a cohesive story of membership as an Israeli (Segev; Zertal). The repeated historical attempts to create untenable divisions of space, histories, and peoples in the geographical locations of Israel/Palestine are revealed here as attempts to both fix and separate that which is always flexible, impermanent, and inextricably intertwined. This chapter explores the ways that contemporary graphic representations of these landscapes have begun to rupture and transform earlier static notions of homeland and contested terrain. Miriam Libicki's graphic memoir, *jobnik! An American Girl's Adventures in the Israeli Army* (2008), is an attempt to synthesize her imaginary conceptions of Israel as homeland with her lived knowledge based on her experiences in the Israel Defense Forces (IDF) during 2000 and 2001. Her army diary notes were first worked into a short story "Rituk" and later were used as the basis for *jobnik!* (Libicki, "Jewish Memoir Goes Pow!" 261).

Libicki was born in the United States and is a Vancouver-based cartoonist and illustrator who focuses on nonfiction narratives. In addition to *jobnik!*

(originally a comic book series), her publications include *Toward a Hot Jew* (2016), "How the Soviet Jews Changed the World" (2021), the essay "Jewish Memoir Goes Pow! Zap! Oy!" in *The Jewish Graphic Novel: Critical Approaches* (2010), and the story "A Kind of Resistance" in the award-winning anthology *But I Live: Three Stories of Child Survivors of the Holocaust* (2022). Currently, she exhibits at galleries and comic conventions and lectures on cartooning across Canada and the United States. In her essay about Jewish memoir in graphic form, "Jewish Memoir Goes Pow! Zap! Oy!," Libicki notes that the comics based on her life in Israel were not accepted at the local Jewish Community Center gallery because, she was told, her "love for Israel is not evident" in them, and she would "break the Holocaust survivors' hearts" (272). More recently Libicki was not permitted to sell or display her memoir *jobnik!* at the Vancouver Comic Arts Festival (VanCAF) and was then banned from the comic festival due to her "prior role in the Israeli military and their subsequent works which recount their personal position in said military" (VanCAF board, qtd. in Libicki "I Was Banned").[1] What the Comics Arts Festival board did not say in their statement is that Libicki's graphic memoir works to destabilize the often-binary rhetoric of homeland and return that surrounds the Israeli-Palestinian conflict, questioning her own position in the IDF and the occupation more generally. Her short essay "I Was Banned from the Comic-Con!!" (2024) recounts this experience.

Sarah Glidden's first book, *How to Understand Israel in 60 Days or Less* (2010), also depicts her ambivalent relationship with the border policies and practices of the state of Israel through unique rendering of graphic border poetics. The first chapters of her book were self-published as minicomics. In addition to *How to Understand Israel in 60 Days or Less*, Glidden has published *Rolling Blackouts* (2016)—a full-length graphic nonfiction narrative about a trip she took with journalists through Turkey, Syria, and Iraq—along with shorter works, including "Monuments" or "Drawing a Line" (2013) and "The Art of War" (2018). By depicting political boundaries in the watercolor medium, Glidden questions state-drawn lines and walls that divide landscapes. Her creative graphic work engages with the spatial terms of military boundaries, suggesting a subversion of formal territorial spaces.

Starting from two very different political positions in relation to Israel, Miriam and Sarah both question their original assumptions about Israel during their experiences visiting the country. Miriam's political and personal identity positions shift from a Modern Orthodox nationalist position to one that questions and even rejects parts of the Israeli state project, while Sarah's position shifts from one of deep suspicion of the Israeli state to one in which she begins to feel strong ties to Israel that cause her to question that suspicion. Through a sustained reading of Miriam Libicki's graphic narrative *jobnik! An American Girl's Adventures in the Israeli Army* together with a comparative sampling of select images from Sarah Glidden's *How to Understand Israel in 60 Days or Less*, I trace a passage through multivalent territory—both on the page and in geographical space—that attends to the formal disintegration and realignment of boundaries between personal, gendered, and national-militarized spaces.

After the Holocaust, the practical question of a Jewish homeland took on monumental significance. Many Jews looked to the ancient land of Israel as a place of potential safety and security. Indeed, Jews lived in Palestine in the 1940s, some residing there for many generations while others came as a part of the Zionist movement in the nineteenth century. Though many scholars have theorized the role of homeland in diaspora and migration,[2] few have explored the ways that Jewish pictorial narratives represent the intersections of the homeland of the imaginary[3] with the homeland of lived experience. Tahneer Oksman's recent work *How Come Boys Get to Keep Their Noses?* reads Libicki's work as a travel narrative that challenges the idea of homeland in the context of Jewish American identity,[4] while Nina Fischer examines *jobnik!* through the lens of the Jerusalem landscape, arguing that the absence of encounters with and images of Arabs in Libicki's text reveals the sharp divisions and distance between Arabs and Jews in the political landscape (292). How might the graphic border poetics or creative organizations of space complicate binary nationalist discourse and illustrate the precarious borders between the private and public? In what ways do pictorial representations of contested space challenge the ways that we think about conflicting narratives of gender, memory, and national belonging?

Diaspora and border theory are contingent on conceptions of homeland and return, both practical and imaginary. Yet home is not such a simple place to conceptualize. Homes may be domestic spaces, physical locations, or even groups of people; however, home does imply a sense of belonging and safety. What happens, then, when the home becomes a site of violence or violation? If, as Susan Friedman claims, "longing for home is the body's desire—a feeling of homesickness experienced viscerally in the flesh" ("Bodies on the Move" 191), then Miriam's experiences rupture the narrative of bodily longing and allow her to see beyond the narrative of Israel as a militarized homeland to the suppressed narratives beneath. Likewise, Sarah Glidden's graphic work moves across geographical spaces to connect different colonialisms to create a homeland that is vastly more nuanced and complicated than she anticipated at the start of her Birthright trip.

Spatial configurations of border conflict refracted through graphic narratives like Libicki's and Glidden's open new ways of viewing narratives of conflict. Literary narrative in graphic form is a particularly fascinating medium with which to explore the power dynamics of contested and colonized spaces. Because of its pictorial rendering of border discourse, spatial interpretations of contested spaces in graphic narratives have the potential to both mimic and subvert the very terms on which national boundaries are predicated. Such an analysis allows for an articulation of geography in an interpretive framework that is itself spatial. Further, the representations of geographical location and space on a page using various graphic devices may be instructive for refiguring bounded, static, and unproblematized constructions of space.

In a graphic image that becomes telling for the rest of the memoir, the back and front covers of Miriam Libicki's graphic narrative *jobnik!* open up to create a two-page, full-color illustration of an exclusively militarized Israeli space within which Miriam grasps her unbuttoned and untucked Israeli army uniform shirt as she walks away from the male barracks, stars and jets careening overhead in a carnivalesque light show (fig. 1.1). The white stars and jets that hover above Miriam's head invoke militaristic and biblical narratives that have both informed the Israeli-Palestinian conflict. While the stars suggest the biblical promise to multiply Abraham's descendants like stars in the sky and to bequeath them "these lands" (Genesis 26:4), the jets are an unsettling contemporary representation of Israeli militaristic power in a surreal, fun house–like backdrop. Above Miriam, jets careen in a Ferris wheel–like formation, suggesting a subversion of military power. The graphic representations of narratives of biblical territorial promise and military actions mingle together in a single panel to illustrate the complex and often competing narratives that create bounded spaces. Symbols commonly associated with the stories of a Jewish Promised Land fill the space in the panel as Miriam looks on in surprise and buttons her uniform. Miriam moves between gendered locations—the male and female barracks—in her army base (a precarious zone to be sure, as suggested by her unbuttoned uniform), while the complex intermingling of historical and political narratives is represented literally above her head. This image functions on several levels, making manifest the intersections of nationalist, historical, political, religious, and gendered narratives and their repercussions on Miriam's personal life.[5]

Miriam, an American Modern Orthodox Jew with powerful allegiances to Israel, volunteers in the Israeli army for a period of two years. Once in Israel, her experiences of unsettling violence—both militaristic and sexual—create an insightful dissonance between her identity as a patriotic Israeli and her increasing distress over the surrounding representations of aggression. While the character of Miriam clearly supports the state of Israel, the nationalist narratives of the government and army are often ruptured by depictions of political events and by representations of her serial misogynistic relationships. These simultaneous spatial representations of memory create textual friction that reveals Miriam's difficulty reconciling state violence with her intersecting

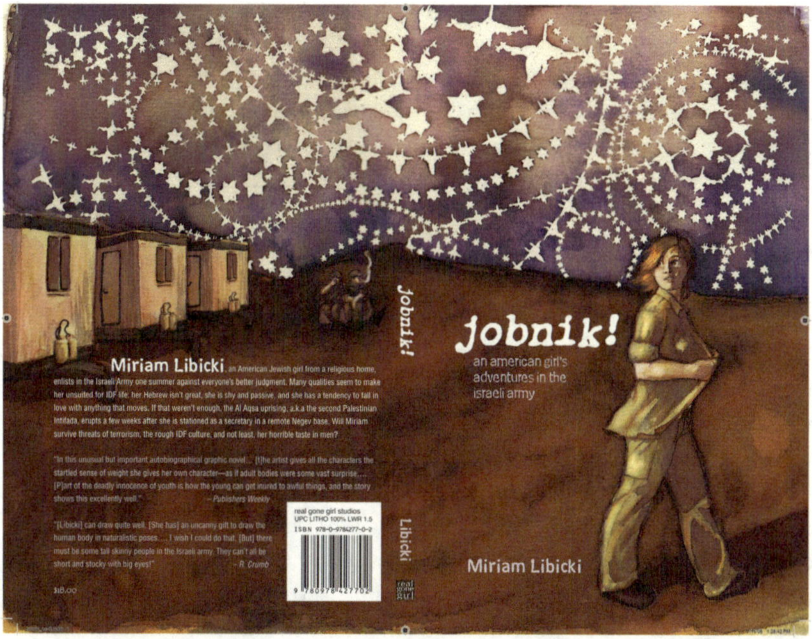

FIG. 1.1 Back and front covers of *jobnik!*

identities. Her position as a woman, a low-status "jobnik" in the army, an American, and a non-native Hebrew speaker puts her in a situation of relative powerlessness in a system that values physical strength, maleness, military status, and native language ability. While she does position herself as a member of a nation-state—of both the United States and Israel—the complex graphic renderings of her ambivalence toward Israeli power in spatial terms create a second story of identity that suggests a connection between her own gendered identity position in the IDF and the larger systems of violence and territorial divisions.

Graphic Form in *jobnik!*

Despite the recent attention to both graphic narrative and representations of geographies and spatiality in literature and comics,[6] few scholars have explored graphic narrative's peculiar ability to depict fraught landscapes, to engage through its very form in land-based conflict and occupation on the space of the page. Recently popular graphic novels such as Joe Sacco's *Palestine* (2001) and *Footnotes in Gaza* (2009), Ari Folman's *Waltz with Bashir* (2009), Sarah Glidden's *How to Understand Israel in 60 Days or Less* (2010), and Rutu

Modan's *Exit Wounds* (2007) and *Jamilti and Other Stories* (2008), among others, explore the fraught terrain of Israel-Palestine. These depictions of spatiality engage with and depict embodied apprehension of historical, religious, and cultural narratives of diaspora, homeland, and identity that are often absent in dominant cultural narratives. I suggest here that a close examination of the enunciative act of comics (Marion)—the effects of lines, contours, and colors and their relation to narrative—offers a model for understanding the complexity of border conflict via graphic narrative.

Reading practices that engage the spatiality on the page allow for a certain tangible engagement and understanding of the ways that space can be both limiting and multilayered. Libicki's narrative uses various methods for making borders and historical spatial violence visibly evident to the reader. Her use of different mediums, scale, repetition, nonlinear panel arrangements, and uneven or folded temporal landscapes among other artistic devices allows for nonconventional interpretations of static landscapes. For example, the construction of scale—that is, the size of images of territory or bodies in relation to other images—incorporates power "whether through material practices or rhetorical practices of individuals, groups, and institutions" (Leitner 238). Thus, the hierarchical standard of scale in geography needs to be rethought by making scalar representation transparent (e.g., the use of size and space) and by taking into consideration the significance of the body, gender, and home. In part, the hand-drawn, self-reflexive medium of comics draws attention to its own status as artifice in its use of scale.

The graphics within a panel—a condensed representation of a limited environment—represent artistic choices that privilege certain landscapes and narratives over others. We might ask, for example, What representations are absent on any given page? As Scott McCloud reminds us, "The comics creator asks us to join in the silent dance of the *seen* and *unseen*. The *visible* and *invisible*" (92; emphasis in original). For example, the pages of the text in Libicki's *jobnik!* are taken up largely by representations of Jewish Israeli space, while pages in Joe Sacco's *Footnotes in Gaza* are filled almost exclusively with depictions of Palestinian spaces. This divergence might not be noteworthy except for the fact that they take place in roughly the same geographical location. When read relationally, these manifestations of divided and embodied spaces not only reflect the geopolitical positions of the writers, their subjects, and their identifications but also reveal the increasingly stark state-constructed divisions between Israeli-Jewish and Palestinian landscapes and their residents.

Within Libicki's and Glidden's work, the spatial configurations bring to the foreground the ways that the space of the page can engage with and "speak to" our perceptions of physical environments, landscapes, and structures/buildings. For example, the text might challenge the borders of nation-states by using intersecting, shifting, or overlapping borders and lines on the space of the page, visually making present the ways that we imagine and produce nationalist space, as in Libicki's cover image (fig. 1.1). These literary and visual techniques, or what I call *graphic border poetics*, emphasize the ways that territorial contestation and asymmetrical power relations affect the people who live within those environments and the lasting traumatic repercussions on both people and environment. Libicki and Glidden probe the boundaries of graphic texts and, in doing so, explore the aesthetics of space that construct national and personal identity, definitions of homeland, and the repercussions of this psychic-social space on personal and political motivations.

Intersecting Borders in *jobnik!*

As Miriam experiences physical violation of her own body and of the body of the country she identifies with as her homeland, she grows to question the narratives of obligatory service to that homeland and the exclusionary and violent border politics that define it. She, in some sense, has become an outsider in her own narrative—a subject of violation and dislocation. Likewise, her own narrative cannot exist without the incursions of the Second Intifada's violence. That is, the terms of victimhood and power on which the state's existence is predicated allow for the validation of the militarism in which she participates; instead of a sense of home and belonging, Miriam finds a more complex narrative in which she is implicated as both perpetrator (as an army soldier, a keeper of borders) and victim of the homeland for which she longs.

Miriam's multiple subject positions are laid out on the first page of the prologue as a layered collage of Miriam's identity in September 2000. These are portrayed retrospectively. It begins, "It's been over a year since I've written in this. I am still Miriam Libicki" (*jobnik!* 4). The text copy tells us that she is a citizen of the United States and Israel, an Israeli soldier, and a sexually active young woman (4). Five black-and-white sketches of imagined Polaroid photos depicting Miriam's sexual encounters are set over a drawing of Miriam sitting in her army bunk writing in her diary (4). These Polaroid-like illustrations of past sexual experiences quite literally cover over the image of Miriam in the present-tense narrative (fig. 1.2). These overlays create a collage effect that foregrounds her sexuality as intertwined with her identity as a soldier, particularly her low status as a *pkida*, or low-level administrative assistant. Throughout the text, graphic depictions of unsatisfying intimate relationships along with one instance of anal rape act as ruptures in the narrative of Israeli nationalism at the diegetic level of the plot.

The narrative layering technique in this introduction to Miriam's personal and nationalist identity is telling for the rest of the text, not only because it

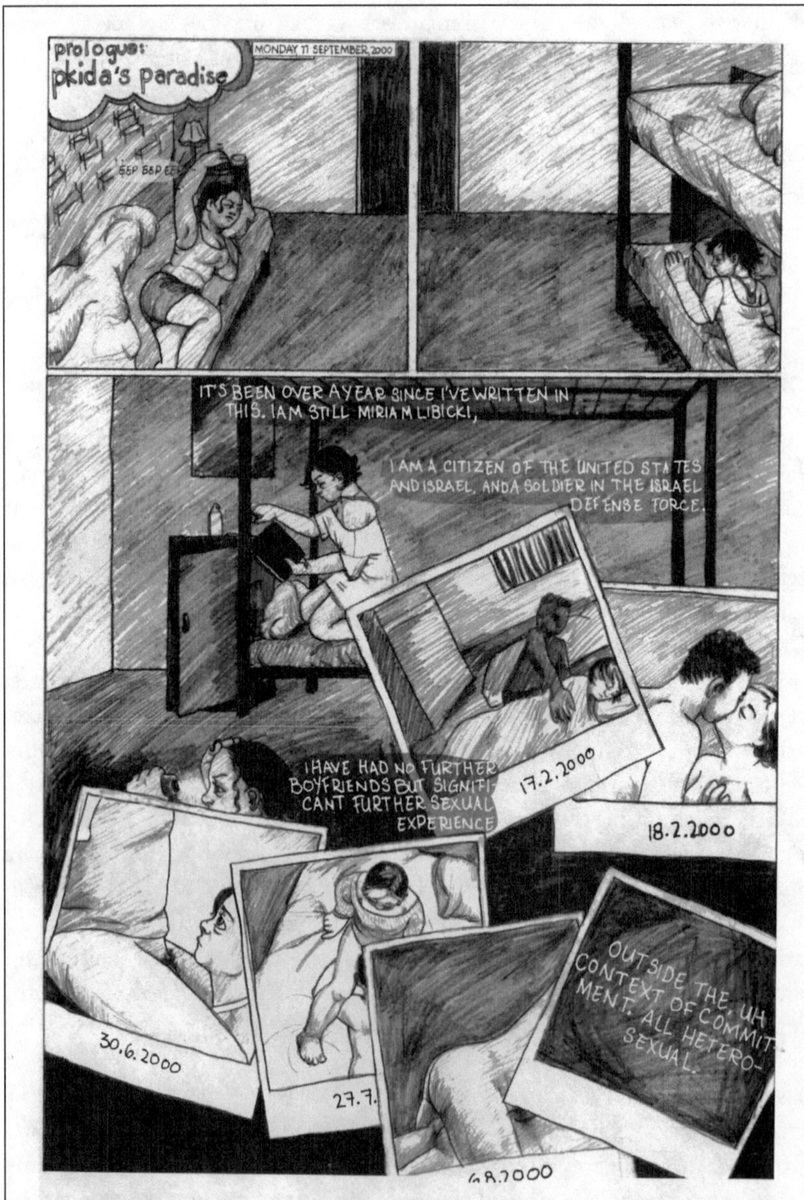

FIG. 1.2 Layered collage of Miriam's identity in the prologue.

represents her intimate encounters within the context of the Israeli military, but because it demonstrates an identity connected to specific historical moments of collective cultural memory. By using techniques of narrative layering and temporal juxtaposition to create depictions of historical memory concurrent with the present-tense narrative or by collapsing and expanding representations of time, graphic narratives have the potential to recast and complicate limiting notions of Jewish identity. Overlapping images of events and places create dynamic spaces that elude the static boundaries of colonized places and expose the multiple narratives that reside below the surface of the constructed place; this technique allows us to see multifaceted stories of identity and place, narratives that may otherwise remain invisible. Comics' subjective renderings of experience and history do not attempt to re-create the trauma or event as such but seek to self-consciously recontextualize memory—both individual and collective. Historical memories are rendered as active cultural narratives that affect present-tense narratives of militarism, nationalism, and Miriam's own feelings of patriotism.

Historical narratives in graphic form allow us to perceive history and time in spatial terms. If comics or graphic narratives use a hybrid form that represents the verbal and the visual in two separate narrative tracks (Chute, "Comics as Literature?" 452), then spatial layering creates multiple simultaneous narrative tracks. Layering techniques effectively register temporality in spatial terms, not only conveying slowed-down or sped-up time but allowing for different times and events to be presented at once. This technique is used in Amy Kurzweil's work as well (chap. 2) to suggest the ways that Holocaust trauma is handed down through generations. Both works show the ways that memories can coexist spatially alongside or in between present-tense narratives, recasting the past as an inextricable component of the present moment. Within such graphic mediums, we may see history and the present simultaneously or scan back and forth between nonsynchronous events, making meaning as we do so. "Reading" in this sense requires us to (re)order and (re-)create the narrative while interpreting multiple modes of representation. When we encounter vertical or overlapping panels, for example, the linear progression of the narrative becomes ambiguous; we experience events in a spatial depth and volume unavailable in a strictly textual work. Particularly in representations of traumatic or politically contentious histories, such visual techniques challenge traditional historical narratives, allowing for more permeable and creative thinking about history and conflict by refiguring representations of the past. Libicki depends on such techniques in order to register her retrospective explorations of Jewish national patriotism, Israeli military power, and the personal repercussions of nationalistic identity.

Spatial Occupation

Understanding the ways that images inhabit the blank space on a page may be useful for thinking about fraught geographical spaces. In graphic narratives, the terrain of the page becomes occupied space; panels and images recreate the space into defined and limited places. Lines and gutters (the spaces between panels) divide a page into separate spheres and locations. A panel is itself an additional representation of a confined space, a condensed representation of a limited environment. Such lines and boxes on a page physically create borders and represent corresponding locations as bounded. The images themselves represent artistic choices that privilege certain landscapes and narratives over others. We might ask, for example, what representations are absent on any given page. In Libicki's text, her panels represent Jewish Israelis and Israeli space almost exclusively, and Palestinians are only given panel space in news footage. The occupation of space in the text and the clearly separate narrative spheres between Israelis and Palestinians[7] are indicators of the larger narrative and spatial boundaries of the nation-state. The patterns, sizes, repetitions, and absences of images and panels reveal the invisible dynamics that are always present in the politics of space.

Spatial patterns not only mimic but also have the potential to subvert the power relations that they describe. For example, multiple locations may intersect or overlap on a page to illustrate the collapse of geographical boundaries. Panels illustrating Miriam's formational experiences in Israel often employ techniques of overlapping historical and cultural narratives. Libicki's use of spatial proximity includes rogue images that cross panel borders (such as the stone thrower in fig. 1.4) to signal the breakage in seemingly clean, linear narratives of nationhood. Other artistic devices used in Libicki's work include shading, shifting the size of panels and characters, slowing down time with small multiples, and zooming in on or out of images.

Images in graphic narratives work to represent the event or social construction in terms that allow for spatial articulation. The devices used in graphic art might include diagonal slicing, panel overlay, or slowed moment-to-moment panels. Thus, objects or objects-as-metaphors are locations in physical space that interact and speak to other images in that narrative space. Within comics, the panel becomes the map that creates the story. We see the imaginary in pictorial terms (metaphorical and spatial), which allows the reader to take into consideration, among other things the strong but often invisible influence of contested historical memory; in the case of *jobnik!*, biblical narratives and the fear of displacement and homelessness permeate the nationalist spaces.

The graphic interactions of the current events (in the year 2000) in dialogue with historical memory lay bare the constructs of Miriam's outward patriotism, a central component of her identity in *jobnik!* While Miriam is participating in an army memorial service for Yitzhak Rabin in 2000, she remembers hearing about his murder while still a student in the United States in 1995. Her memories are visually inserted into the present-tense narrative (Libicki, *jobnik!* 73). Her pride in being a member of the IDF at this moment is evident as these historical moments collide in the visual medium. The largest drawing on the page depicts Miriam as an almost indistinguishable part of her unit standing silently as another woman soldier sings "Ein Li Eretz Acheret," a popular song by the well-known nationalist singer Naomi Shemer (fig. 1.3). The refrain translates, "I have no other country / even if my land is aflame / just a word in Hebrew / pierces my veins and my soul" (Libicki, *jobnik!* 72). This image of Miriam's army unit observing Rabin's *yarzeit* or death anniversary is juxtaposed with her memories of Rabin's death in 1995 and with representations of an aerial map showing Israel from farther and farther away in four sliver-like diagonally positioned frames. In the final sliver frame, we are left with a picture of the globe in which Israel is indistinguishable. When read from top to bottom, these drawings work to show the minute size of a seemingly vulnerable Israel in a larger world and universe (fig. 1.3). But when read left to right on the diagonal, the construction of Miriam's patriotism—that is, her actions as a Jew who chooses to make *aliyah* or immigrate to Israel and to join the military—becomes more transparent. The side-by-side frames of a diminishing Israel and Miriam's immigration to Israel in 1998 together with her reflection on her mother's grief at Rabin's death in 1995 show a desire to protect a country positioned as vulnerable—literally in danger of disappearing in the larger world. At the same time, it depicts her own desire to live in and take responsibility for the survival of (what she positions as) the only "real" Jewish homeland. The narrative slicing illustrates her fierce loyalty in the face of her fear of Israel's disappearance in the wake of the prime minister's murder; the murder, however, was committed by the young Jewish Israeli settler Yigal Amir, a Jew who is circumscribed within the space of Israeli citizenship. This series of memories and the cinematic-like aerial shots of Israel lead her to conclude, "I don't belong *in* Israel as much as I belong *to* Israel. Every year on Rabin's yahrzeit I know it's not even a choice" (Libicki, *jobnik!* 73; emphasis in original). Her nationalism here is constructed as an obligation she must incur, not as a choice. If nations are often figured as domestic genealogies, as Anne McClintock argues (357), then Miriam's struggle is figured as a result of her desire to be part of a family constituted by nationalism.

Slowed-down time and interjections of memory in the form of what I call temporal slicing are graphic devices that help articulate Miriam's sense of obligation to the idea of homeland as a familial obligation in times of national mourning and internal strife. The palimpsestic spatial representations expand a moment in time to emphasize the complexity of Miriam's constructions of patriotism as identity. Clearly, within her present-tense narrative, her

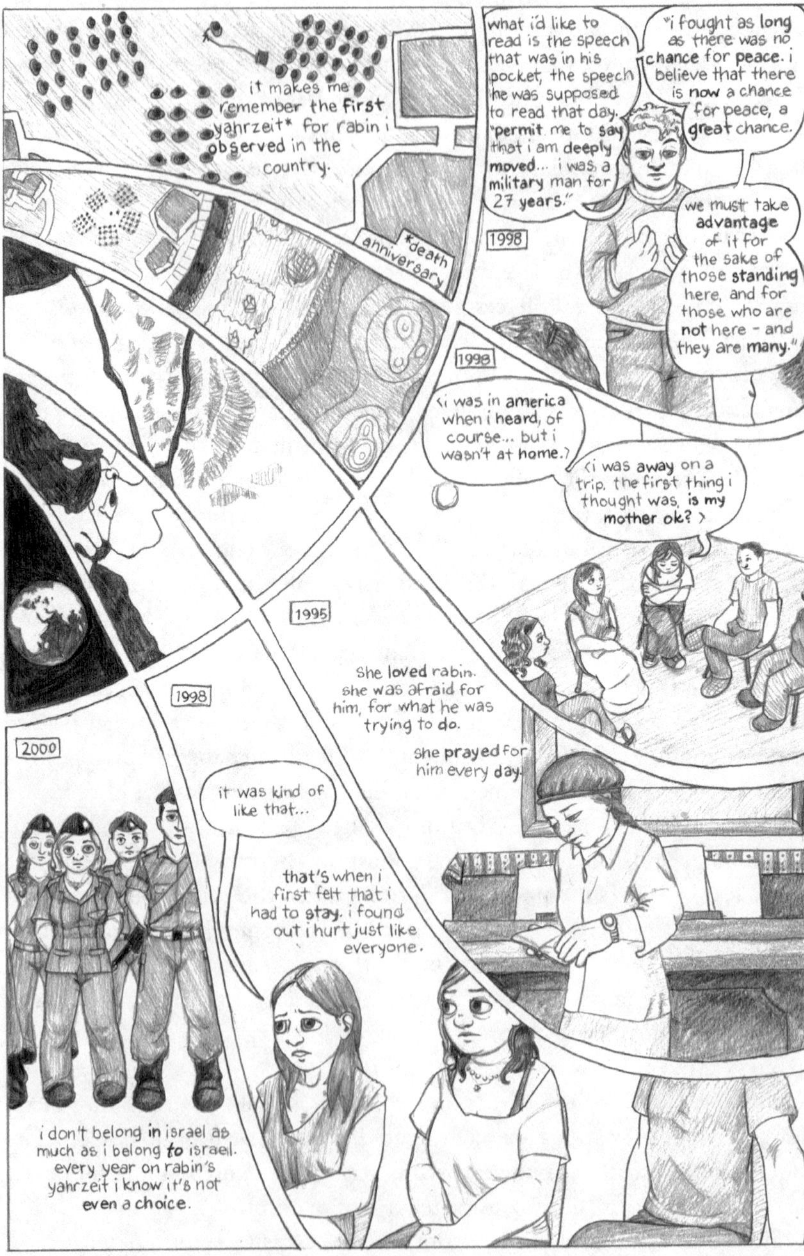

FIG. 1.3 Temporal slicing illustrates Miriam's memories of Rabin's death (*lower right set of panels*) with her feelings of patriotism toward Israel (*upper left panels*).

memories of Rabin's death become germinal in her decision to move to Israel, and her service in the army becomes a way to actively exercise her patriotism. Thus, her memories have become a part of her narrative about her sense of belonging "to Israel" and about her cognizance of her subsequent difficulties engaging with various forms of violence that increasingly invade her narrative. The surrounding text, which tells of Miriam's personal experiences of subordination and abuse in the context of the army, illustrates that Miriam's patriotism is not an unquestioning allegiance but an identity position that is thrown into question as the political narrative progresses.

Her geopolitical location within Israeli society, in effect, allows her to recognize her own vulnerability within a patriarchal militaristic institution and thus to occupy a subject position that permits her to see the vulnerability of the Palestinians as targets of this same institution. While she does indeed position herself as a member of a nation-state, the complex graphic renderings of her ambivalence toward Israeli power create a second story of membership that produces a different rhetorical position: Miriam's graphic narrative disengages from the narrative of the Second Intifada, while Libicki's retrospective narrative—that is, the reflections on Miriam's position—troubles the often unquestioned Jewish national allegiance to Israel as home.[8] Her geopolitical location within Israeli society, in effect, allows her to recognize her own vulnerability within a highly militarized patriarchal institution and thus to occupy a subject position that permits her to see the vulnerability of those positioned in similar precarious narratives of both homeland and nationhood.

Domestic Home and National Violence

Creative depictions of violence in the form of reproduced media images and their relationship to Miriam's body on the space of the page generate an additional narrative that shows Miriam's struggles with—and her disassociation from—the Second Intifada. These interruptions are heightened in the chronological plot of Miriam's army service beginning on September 28, 2000, when Ariel Sharon announces his visit to the Palestinian-controlled Temple Mount (Libicki, *jobnik!* 36). Sharon's tour of this religiously and politically fraught area became the central tipping point for the beginning of the Second Intifada. Graphic panels of Sharon in sunglasses, masked Palestinian protesters throwing rocks, and Israeli police in riot gear surround images of the silent Miriam as she rides the bus to her apartment in Jerusalem for Rosh Hashanah, the Jewish New Year (fig. 1.4). Libicki draws this page of panels in collage form (rather than with traditional square or rectangular panels in rows), tying together seemingly disparate events as intimately connected. Miriam's inner circle of home, though doubtlessly separated from the panels depicting the intifada (shown in double-lined panel divisions), is situated within the larger

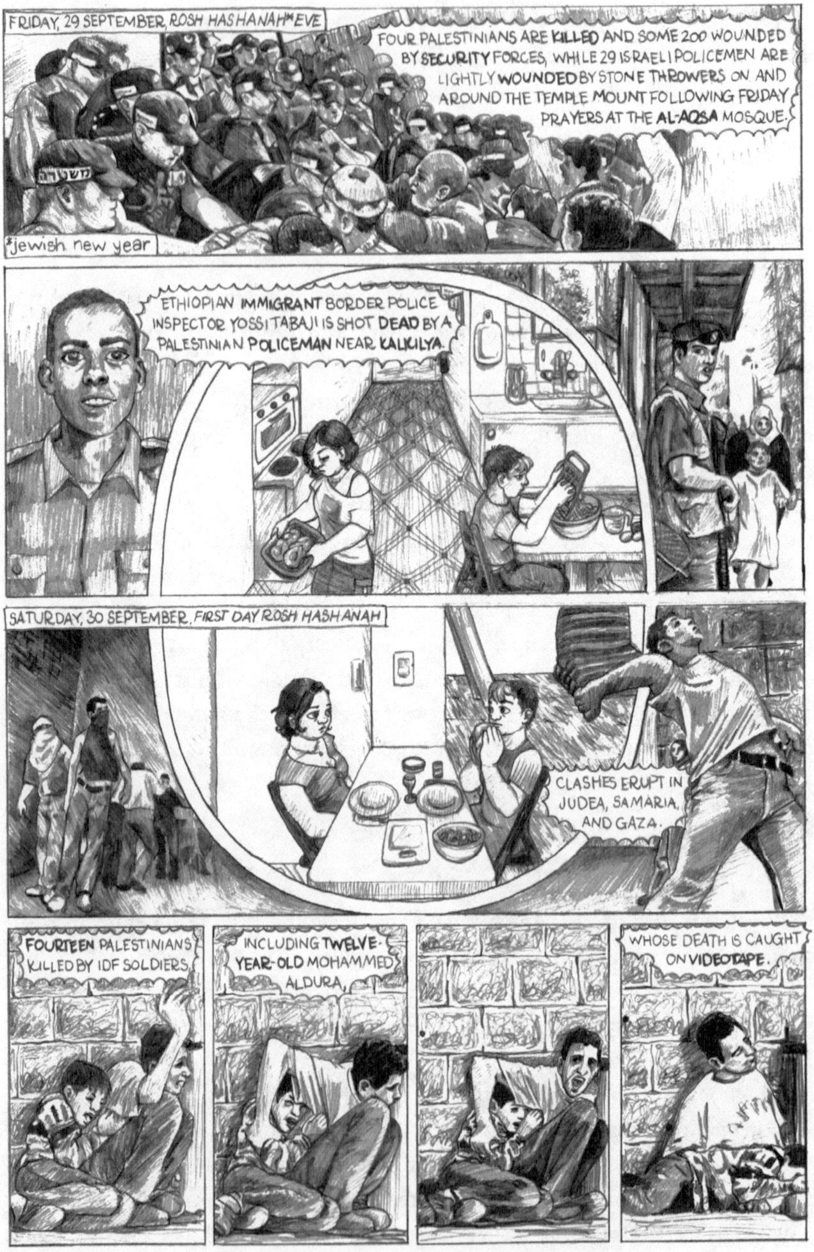

FIG. 1.4 The arm of a Palestinian crosses over the panel into Miriam's world. The bottom four panels show a temporal slowing in the shooting of Mohammed and Jamal al-Dura in Gaza.

context of political space. Despite the close spatial arrangement of these images, Miriam is repeatedly represented as detached from these events by the gutters and spaces between panels. Miriam silently goes about her daily life, cooking, eating a Rosh Hashanah meal with her sister (Libicki, *jobnik!* 37), or riding the bus. The only visible reaction to these events is a short sentence written below the panel, which reads, "Then everything goes wrong" (36). The graphic techniques become the vehicle for both Miriam's voice and Libicki's retrospective insights. In this set of panels, Libicki creates broad, white, arc-shaped divisions between the images of Miriam and the images of violence. This literally removes Miriam from the realities of the intifada; indeed, her life seems to continue quite normally despite the dramatic political downturn. The close proximity of the panels of violence to Miriam's more mundane life, however, reveals a different story. By putting the images of violence and the frenetic pace of the news's copy in juxtaposition to Miriam's silence in the surrounding frames, Libicki suggests that Miriam, though seemingly numb to these events, is unable to escape the escalating violence, the military actions of the intifada, or her silent complicity in them.

In one scene, for example, the arm of a Palestinian youth throwing stones wanders into the next frame of Miriam silently preparing for Erev Rosh Hashanah, the first evening of the Jewish New Year (Libicki, *jobnik!* 37). This rogue image, or picture that crosses over the gutter spaces that separate out temporally and spatially divided events, creates an unexpected rupture of the panel borders and, hence, the borders of Miriam's personal experience. By using graphic devices of overlay and gutter separation (lines or spaces that create physical separations between panels), Libicki depicts Miriam's emotional distance from the violence of the intifada; however, when an arm crosses over the space that divides panels and enters Miriam's silent world, the political climate becomes an undeniable part of her own experiences and her shifting political awareness (fig. 1.4). Though Miriam sits at the table eating a festival meal with her sister, her surrounding world blows up in violence, shaking the safety of her own domestic space. The panel borders between the events that start the Second Intifada and Miriam's serene kitchen are penetrated—showing not only a growing awareness on Miriam's part but a recognition of the interdependence of these two narratives: her own commitment to Israel (or, as she articulates earlier, "belonging to" Israel) and the explosion of violence in the surrounding landscape.

A five-panel sequence showing the death of twelve-year-old Mohammed al-Dura in Gaza on September 30, 2000, becomes a continuation of this visual incursion of the intifada into Miriam's personal life (fig. 1.4, bottom panels). A moment-by-moment depiction of the IDF shooting of al-Dura—taken from France-2 video footage that was aired on the Israeli news—spatially lengthens the action, prolonging the representations of al-Dura's suffering. The series of four images at the bottom of the page show the Palestinian father, Jamal, pinned against a wall with his young son. While the IDF initially accepted responsibility for the death of al-Dura, it later retracted responsibility, saying that the event had been staged. The French courts claimed in May of 2008 that the killing was orchestrated ("Court Backs Claim"), while Hamas leaders claim that al-Dura was indeed killed by IDF gunfire ("Media Analyst"). The ambiguous truth status of this incident and the surrounding controversy represent the complex and long-waging disagreements that shape the Israeli and Palestinian conflict. The validity of the actions of the IDF becomes suspect in Miriam's narrative in this temporally slowed rendering of violence against civilians. The proximity of these panels creates a narrative where the Al-Aqṣā riot leads to stone-throwing and finally to the death of a father and child. The visual detachment of Miriam's domestic activities from these political scenes suggests that Miriam has difficulty reconciling these events with her own investment in her daily life and feelings of home. Jamal's arm is shown stretching back in an act of defiance against the throngs of police depicted in the panels above him. The arm enters Miriam's dining room as her sister says *Ha Motzi*, the ritual blessing over the bread: Blessed are you our God, King of the Universe who brings forth bread from the earth. The juxtaposition of the quiet moment of prayer and the act of resistance embodied in the arm creates a tension that illuminates the ways that Miriam is implicated in the politics, if not the physical violence, of the conflict. Despite her best attempts to ignore the political violence and injustice that increasingly invade the spaces of her visual narrative, the violence becomes inextricably connected to her experiences, her sense of self, her identity, and her budding sexuality.

Gendered Violence

The narrative of Miriam's sexual experimentation in *jobnik!* rivals the thematic importance of the political violence in the text; indeed, it becomes an inextricable part of her army narrative. The pictorial representations in the text make visible Miriam's complex geopolitical identity as a non-native Israeli, a desk worker, and a woman in this militarized and patriarchal space. The first-person narrative voice that is present in the prologue is conspicuously absent throughout most of the memoir. Dates, news copy, and dialogue between other soldiers are common enough; however, Miriam's written thoughts are scarce. Libicki instead uses the dissonance between the graphic images and the text copy to convey her retrospective narrative voice. Her verbal silence in the present simultaneously shows complicity with the patriarchal narratives of nationalism that she encounters and reveals the divisiveness of these narratives for those in subordinate positions in this system. The prevalence of Miriam's multiple unfulfilling sexual encounters with male soldiers illustrates how the narrative of militaristic violence that Miriam attempts to shut out becomes an internalized experience in her intimate relationships. The site of Miriam's body might be read as an extension of the national violence that is visible throughout the rest of the graphic text and, like the violence of the intifada, remains largely uncommented upon except in pictorial terms.

Miriam's geopolitical location in a militarized culture determines much of her experience in the army. Interestingly, being an American-born citizen (an identity that in other contexts is often equated with power and strength) in this context positions her as an outsider. Though Jewish, she is a non-native Israeli and immigrant and, therefore, perceived as a relative outsider in the close-knit hierarchy of the Israeli army. Because her Hebrew language skills are poor (she tells us), Miriam is not allowed to do important office work, a job many women are assigned. As Susan Sered writes, most women in the Israeli army are groomed as menial workers; rare is the woman combat soldier. In a telling comment, Colonel Gershon HaCohen announced to a group of future army conscripts in Israel that "traditionally men are warriors and women are prostitutes, and that most of what women do in the IDF can be replaced with office machines" (Sered 80–81). Miriam's status as a woman in an institution that values male-centered combat puts her at a disadvantage. Even the psychological profile that she is given by a male officer who gives her a cursory précis through a Rorschach inkblot test, diagnoses her as "overly emotional, disconnected from reality, possessed of anxieties (especially social), unable to form interpersonal bonds, sexually conflicted" (Libicki, *jobnik!* 4). The overlapping cards of inkblots are a disturbing mirror image of the Polaroids of Miriam in sexual positions in the prologue. When read together, the army's inkblots represent an institutional erasure of any personal identity that Miriam establishes on the earlier page. She is diagnosed and defined by the huge black-and-white images that hover above a miniaturized Miriam, who hunches over her sketchbook in the corner of the panel (Libicki, *jobnik!* 5). The army psychiatrist's diagnosis includes "ambiguous sexuality" (something Miriam herself does not discuss in this novel), which lowers Miriam's profile yet again. As Alon Raab points out in "Ben Gurion's Golem and Jewish Lesbians," for many years anyone suspected of having homosexual tendencies in the Israeli army was viewed as unreliable and thus not allowed to serve in important positions like the intelligence units (228). Miriam's geopolitical locations are determined by heteronormative patriarchal values within the militaristic mechanisms of the Israeli army.

Throughout *jobnik!* the nationalist narratives of Miriam's experiences in the army are continually paralleled by her serial misogynistic relationships. These narrative interruptions create a textual dissonance that reveals Miriam's inability to reconcile state violence with her intersecting identities; her vision of Israel as a homeland has been ruptured. Miriam's position of powerlessness within a system that values physical strength, maleness, military status, and native language ability becomes clearer in the brief sexual encounters that Miriam repeatedly hopes will develop into relationships.

In one scene Libicki uses graphic representation of news copy from the local paper to push Miriam toward Asher's bedroom, illustrating the ways that militaristic violence is translated to bodily violence. In this scene, Miriam reads *Maariv*, an Israeli newspaper, as news text swarms around her body. Just after Yom Kippur 2000, an escalation in violence is reflected in the barrage of news copy. The newspaper—which tells of political demonstrations, tank incursions into the West Bank, and both Palestinian and Israeli casualties—takes up sixteen frames, crowding Miriam's physical space (Libicki, *jobnik!* 63). Her immediate reaction to the horrors she reads is to find Asher (presumably for comfort), one of the soldiers with whom she has repeated sexual encounters. After a brief sexual encounter, she leaves his bunk clutching her sketchbook. Her sketches are her primary means of self-expression and the place where she is able to render an interpretation of these experiences in graphic form—perhaps the very one we read in *jobnik!* As she leaves the male barracks, she looks up again at the night sky, loses her balance, and falls onto the ground. She lies there silently staring upward with wide eyes. Three slanted frames give the reader a sense of Miriam's vertigo (65). The juxtaposition of the graphic devices in these scenes links violence in the media, Miriam's sexual encounters, and her vertigo. The narrative in visual form shows that Miriam is haunted by state violence in the form of media reports of Palestinian deaths as she simultaneously works to serve the mechanism of militarization. Indeed, she takes part in the dominant heteronormative narrative of the Israeli army, servicing soldiers at the expense of her own psyche as her body gives way beneath her. The patriotism that leads her to move to Israel and support the military becomes irreconcilable with the violence and injustice she continues to see around her.

Miriam's complex experience of homeland and identity may be framed as an experience of double vision. In his discussion of Caribbean diasporic identity, Stuart Hall claims that peoples who have been forced into diaspora experience both continuity with the past that allows them to create a cohesive "oneness" from their experiences and profound discontinuity in the wake of diaspora (Hall 235). This doubleness of identity[9] may be useful in thinking about Jewish identity as steeped in the desire for a homeland both in the wake of the diaspora and the genocide of European Jews during the Holocaust. Miriam's experience of dissonance can be framed in terms that parallel Hall's. She goes into the army in order to experience the continuity of the past and to bring this imaginary "oneness" into being. What she experiences is incongruous with her expectations of unity. As an immigrant, albeit an immigrant to her perceived homeland, she finds herself positioned as an outsider in the closed, patriarchal world of the Israeli military. Historically, Jewishness has been positioned in transgressive terms in the diaspora. The establishment of the state of Israel, then, repositions Jews both inside and outside of Israel in a bind of double identity—both as victims of oppression and exile and as oppressors. This Jewish doubleness resonates with Miriam's experiences as a religious American Jew in the Israeli army, for rather than a place of safety and stability for women, home (a smaller, domesticated version of homeland) is "a place constructed by power and inequality" (McDowell 15). Miriam's experience of homeland then is not the "home" she has imagined; her disruption of the cohesive narrative of the nation here is significant. If a nation is an "imagined community because regardless of the actual inequality and exploitation ... the nation is always conceived as a deep, horizontal comradeship" (Anderson 7), then Miriam's experiences create a significant rupture in the allegedly unified narrative of nationhood.

Spatializing the Memory of the Holocaust

During Miriam's extended initiation into Israeli army life, the multiple systems of cultural violence become more apparent. Libicki's explorations of Jewish Israeli cultural memory of the Holocaust work to undermine Miriam's initial conceptions of Israeli power. The memoir represents Miriam as inducted into Israeli army life through an act that associates her metaphorically with the ovens of the death camps in 1940s Europe. The very first task she is given in the army is to burn classified materials in an incinerator. The soldier who gathers the paper materials intended for burning in a large postal bag turns to her and asks, "Remember the Nazis? 'member where the dead Jews went?" (Libicki, *jobnik!* 14). A rigid Miriam stares out at the reader from an all-white background in the following frame. Her silence and shocked expression show her horror at this Israeli soldier's casual reference to the death camps. Even more disturbing is her potential association with the Nazis in this soldier's black humor. The graphic panels on the following pages invoke the landscape of the death camps superimposed onto the Israeli landscape through the use of signifiers associated with the Holocaust.[10]

Collective Jewish memories of the death camps in the form of recognizable symbols create new hybrid landscapes where past stories are rendered as active cultural narratives (fig. 1.5). Close-up views of a Star of David on the side of the military vehicle, a guard tower in the distance, stripes from the corrugated metal shelter, and smoke and flames billowing out of the incinerator (Libicki, *jobnik!* 20) create a double rendering of history; these symbols easily invoke the spaces of both the Israeli military and Holocaust Europe. The double metonyms on this page create a spatial environment that is a multitemporal, multidirectional depiction of history. The Star of David, for example, invokes

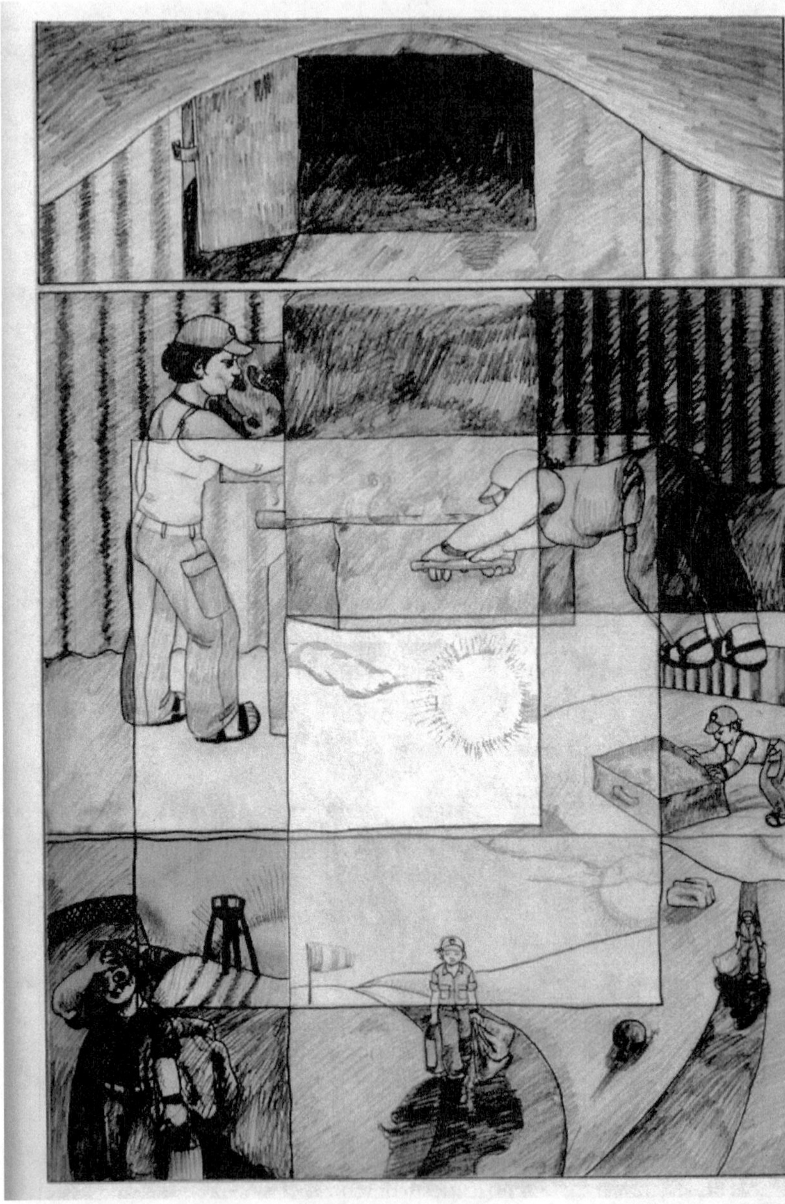

FIG. 1.5 Cube-like illustration of Miriam burning classified material and walking back to base under the shadow of the guard tower.

the traditional symbol of the Jewish people but also suggests the Magen David Adom of the Israeli ambulance service and the yellow star that was mandated for Jews living under the Nazi regime. Similarly, the guard or military observation tower of the IDF stands in for an ideology of the Israeli state, *Homa Umigdal*: the quick-build wall and tower structures that were erected for purposes of land reclamation and security in the pre-state landscape.[11] Simultaneously, the visual association of the tower with the gaping incinerator in these panels transforms the tower into a Nazi guard tower, similar to those surrounding camps like Auschwitz-Birkenau. So too the stripes of the corrugated metal outbuilding easily shift to invoke the infamous stripes of the prisoners' uniforms in Auschwitz. These symbols haunt the space around Miriam's body, and as such, they affect Miriam's feelings of patriotism in *jobnik!* and at the same time shift the present-tense narratives of nationalist identity, Israeli militarism, and historical violence.

In a full-page sketch that collapses historical time, an ash-covered Miriam is depicted tending the oven from different angles and then walking back to the headquarters alone under the shadows of the guard tower in the unbearable heat of the Israeli sun. Miriam is left to complete the burn and empty the ashes from the incinerator herself (fig. 1.5). The graphic renderings on the page are wordless (22–23), allowing the reader to focus attention on the complex images. When she returns to the office covered in sweat and ash, she is greeted by one soldier with "God, you smell bad" as her supervisor shouts from the other room, "I give you permission not to do anything else before you go back to the barracks and *have a shower*" (24; emphasis in original). This event physically dirties Miriam and makes her repulsive to her fellow soldiers. It is difficult not to read the emphasis on *shower* in this context as an association with the showers of Zyklon B and carbon monoxide gas used in the Nazi death camps in the 1940s. Through the act of burning papers, Miriam is situated within a larger system of power that resonates with historical atrocities wreaked upon the Jews, while the references to the showers connect her to the victims of historical atrocity. The surrealist rendering of the Israeli landscape together with a macabre European landscape blurs the lines of a fixed geographical position, creating an in-between space that makes manifest the tension between historical memories of trauma and Miriam's experiences of the state of Israel as homeland.[12] Perhaps Miriam's position edges toward the implicated subject that Rothberg describes, a multidirectional position that recognizes complex histories while taking responsibility for violence against another. In this representation of an inverted power relationship, Libicki implicates both the patriarchal militarized system that has facilitated Miriam's position of powerlessness in the hierarchy of the IDF and Israel's suspect moral position as a military power.

The larger surrounding text, which tells of Miriam's personal experiences of subordination and abuse in the context of the army, illustrates that Miriam's patriotism is not an unquestioning allegiance but an identity position that is thrown into question as the political narrative progresses. Her geopolitical location as a woman, an immigrant, and a non-native speaker within Israeli society, in effect, allows her to recognize her own vulnerability within a patriarchal military institution and, thus, to occupy a subject position that permits her to see the vulnerability of others who fall outside the circumscribed parameters of institutionalized expectations.

As she experiences physical violation of her own body and of the body of the country she "belongs to," she grows to question the narratives of obligatory military service to that homeland and the very terms that define it. Miriam, in some sense, has become a subject of violation and dislocation in her own narrative. In these graphic renderings, her personal narrative is inextricably connected with the representation of the incursion of the Second Intifada's violence and with stories of historical Jewish trauma. Instead of a sense of home and belonging, Miriam finds a more complex narrative in which she is implicated as both an army soldier / keeper of borders and a victim of the homeland for which she longs.

The colliding visions of homeland in Libicki's work are inextricably connected to both biblical narratives of promise and Jewish experiences of exile and return. As discussed in the introduction, when the homeland of the Jewish imagination took on territorial form in 1948, the diaspora-homeland binary became an extension of the territorialist nationalism that has been integral to Western ideologies (Sternhell 51). Miriam's experiences in graphic rendering resist the diaspora-homeland formulation and indeed resist any simple closure of the diaspora story. Instead, the story facilitates an "openness" to narratives of those who stand outside of the traditionally circumscribed Israeli state. As Sidra Ezrachi notes, one of the greatest challenges in literature about Israel is "to keep images from becoming icons, archeology from becoming eschatology, 'arrival' from becoming the terminus of a vengeful excess of memory, the eros of an unconsummated journey from being extinguished in the killing fields of exclusive visions" (23). Instead of a feeling of ultimate arrival, an end to diaspora and uncertainty, Libicki's representations of multivalent and transhistorical hand-drawn images depict a feeling of unarrival that allows the reader to see beyond "the killing fields of exclusive visions."

Glidden's Blurred Boundaries

In contrast to Miriam's early assumptions where she explains her feeling of obligation to serve in the IDF as part of her Jewish identity, Sarah Glidden enters the same landscape hoping to justify her skepticism about Israel's militarism in *How to Understand Israel in 60 Days or Less*. Though these authors begin their journeys from very different political and ideological positions, they both grapple with the geopolitical landscape via graphic devices. Glidden uses the affordances of the watercolor medium to suggest her shifting relationship with Israel's contested spaces. As she says goodbye to her boyfriend Jamil at the start of the story, she tells him that her extensive readings on the Israel-Palestinian conflict have prepared her for "whatever propaganda they try and throw at [her]" (Glidden, *How to Understand* 6). Her book is a tongue-in-cheek memoir that ends with Sarah reeling from a dizzyingly complex view of Israel. Despite Sarah's acceptance of the free trip to young adults of Jewish descent through Birthright,[13] throughout the text she remains highly skeptical of the agenda of the trip's sponsors and decides to take the trip only to confirm her convictions that "Israel was the bad guy" (103). The watercolor medium through which Glidden chooses to portray her subject suggests an ambiguity of space and of political position by extension. In particular, the watery paint-washed maps that frame the context of each chapter heighten the ambiguity of both borders and narrative truth (fig. 1.6).

Glidden begins each chapter with a different rendering of a map showing the locations she visits on each leg of her Birthright tour. The representations of landscapes and borders, though, are not simple here. The diluted paints of the map suggest a running together of spaces, but also a temporary, impermanent reality. Glidden's map (fig. 1.6) does show lines of landscape division such as the separation wall and the West Bank, yet borders are fuzzy. The first map depicts central Israel, including the West Bank and the political border with Jordan (Glidden, *How to Understand* 5). The subtle green lines that Glidden uses to outline the West Bank (or Green Line) recede into the map in contrast to the bright-red lines of Sarah's bus route. Similarly, the separation wall is represented by a faded gray dotted line.[14] The faded pastels fail to circumscribe the sharp geographical boundaries of the political map or the checkpoints and walls on the landscape (30–31, 40). The pink and faded lavender areas that represent the Palestinian-controlled and Israeli-controlled territories in the West Bank become blurred as the paints merge. On the one hand, these maps depict a naive superficial view of the state and its territories (Sarah does not enter the territories except to speak to Jewish settlers); on the other hand, Glidden's maps show a sophisticated understanding of the impossibility of stark divisions on territorial and cultural landscapes. As Glidden's watery maps propose, political boundaries are not fixed nor do they define the landscape but rather maps and lines are created according to the ways we imagine geopolitical boundaries and places; paradoxically, those lines define us and our locations, our definitions of inclusive and exclusive space, and our relationships to one another. Such depictions respatialize "fixed" histories and our resulting perceptions of the present, thus portraying space, time, and social

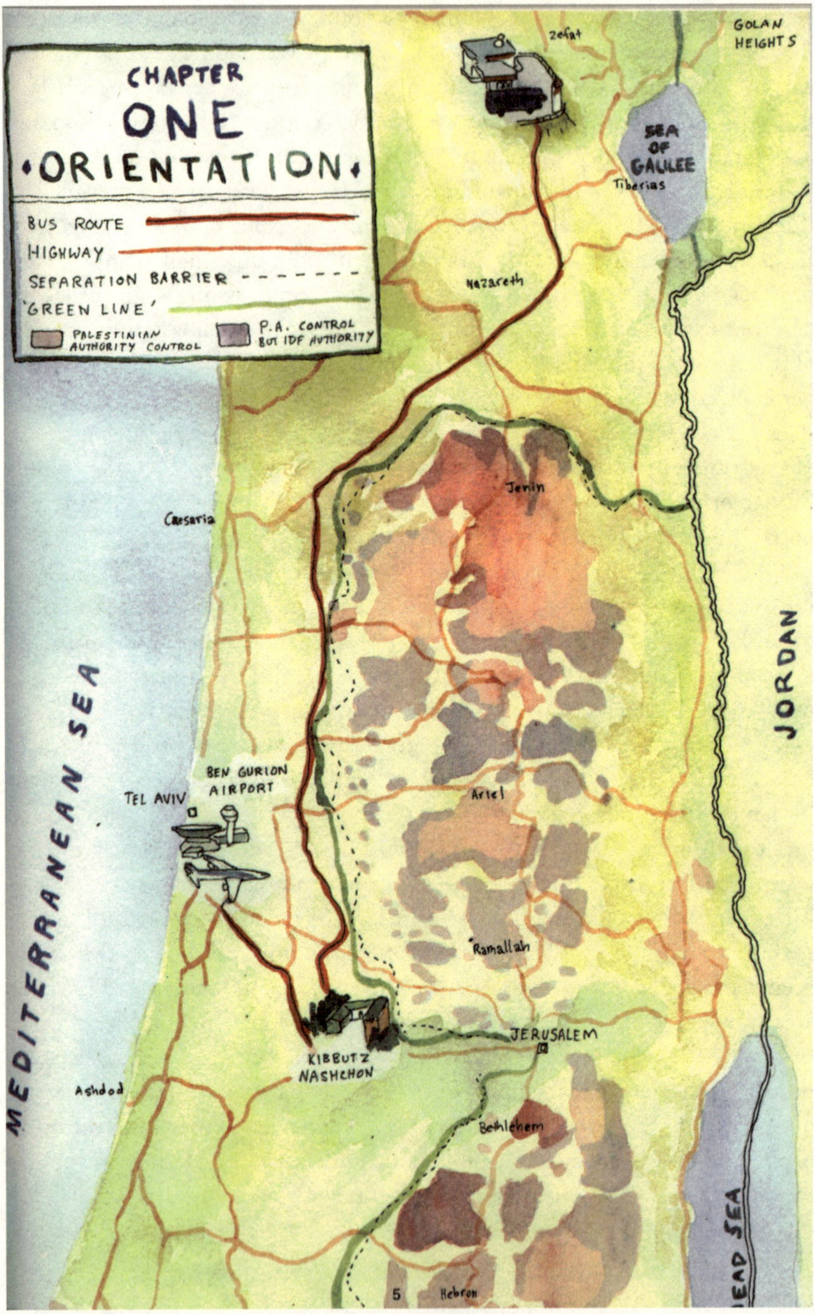

FIG. 1.6 Glidden begins each chapter with a watery map of the area she visits.

being as intertwining entities that inform and create one another. Glidden's watery maps and panels suggest the ambiguous and porous boundaries that affect her perception of the land and its people.

While official state and geographic maps are documents that support and create colonization,[15] graphic texts like Glidden's use the map form to draw attention to cartographic colonizing practices and to subvert borders through creative alternative mappings. While the accuracy of geographical maps is based on the premise of precise lines and divisions of space, Glidden's choice of medium suggests an *impossibility* of precision and highlights the lyrical flow of landscapes through the use of the watercolor medium. Glidden's artistic strategies give a vivid visual sense of both the constraints and the graphic possibilities of restructuring bounded territory, occupation, and perpetual conflict.

Sarah Glidden's work engages directly with political barriers as fraught visual representations in her text. In addition to her creative use of the paint medium, Glidden's use of panel size and placement becomes a running commentary on occupied space and on her physical relationship to that space. At the start of her official Birthright bus tour of Israel, Glidden's panels momentarily put the reader in the position of the tourist on the bus. As Glidden positions Sarah's body in relation to these constructed boundaries, the reader too has an experience of confinement and restricted ocular vision. Glidden uses conventionally sized panels—or what Scott McCloud calls democratic panels—to depict her first glimpse of the "security wall" on her Birthright trip to Israel (fig. 1.7).

Though only small pieces of the wall are visible in each panel, she creates a string of panels that, when read across the entirety of the open two pages, create a single barrier across the reader's visual field of the text. The representations of the tall, cement barriers work to obscure Sarah's vision of the natural landscape she describes a few panels earlier. The reader, along with Sarah, is left on one side of the wall, temporarily unable to access any other vision of the land (fig. 1.7). This wall acts as a physical and cognitive marker for Sarah of the "truth behind this whole mess" (Glidden, *How to Understand* 6) that she hopes to uncover on her trip. The wall then not only becomes a physical boundary on the space of the page but represents the boundaries that Sarah (and the reader) faces—both on the landscape of Israel and in her cognitive expectations of the space and her understanding of Israel. While the wall represents clearly defined boundaries and territorial borders, the visual track of the panels works to create a feeling of confinement. Upon recognizing the structure for the first time, Sarah wildly waves her hand demanding an explanation for the wall. The explanation she receives from Gil, her tour guide, is clearly unsatisfying and unsettling to Sarah, charting a small part of her complex and nuanced journey through narratives of history, conflict, and border division.

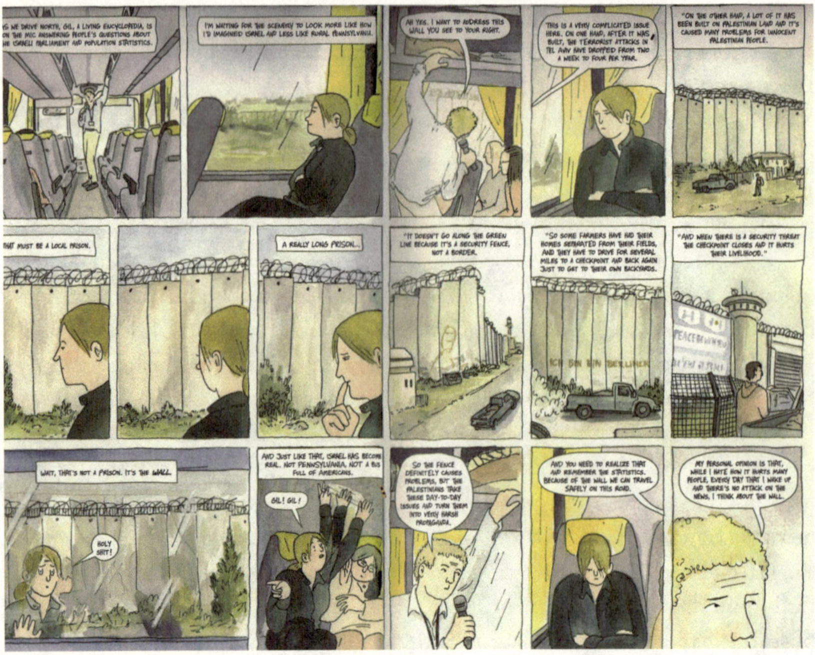

FIG. 1.7 Glidden questions the spatial and rhetorical structure of the wall as she passes it.

One way that Glidden expresses Sarah's complex feelings about Israel is by moving her in and out of alternate geographies and histories to explore the conflicting emotions she grapples with in the book. In one scene just after Sarah visits Independence Hall, where the establishment of the State of Israel was declared in 1948, she is emotionally overwhelmed by the conflicting narratives of war that she passes on her walk. As she walks through the streets of Tel Aviv, she pictures a scene from the Holocaust: A Nazi soldier kicks a Jewish man in a concentration camp as emaciated figures watch from behind. In the next panel, Sarah walks by the border or security wall she questions earlier in the text as an Israeli soldier points his gun at Palestinian women and children. In the culmination of the panel series, violence swirls together in a chaotic collage: An image of a bombed bus is set beside a soldier pointing guns at civilians, a masked terrorist with a gun looks out at the reader, and crying parents stand over a dead child. Sarah cries as she passes these scenes of violence (Glidden, *How to Understand* 100). The compelling histories of the Jewish past blend with contemporary violence (bus bombing) that resonates with the pain of the Holocaust and at the same time underscores the need for the safety of all citizens, Jewish and non-Jewish. By the end of the text, Sarah questions her earlier opinions about Israel's political policies and practices. The nuanced histories, land ties, overlapping borders, and affective connections or feelings she cultivates for Israel run together like the paint medium and memory collages she uses to depict these scenes, creating a more complex and confusing state narrative for Sarah. The precarity and violence depicted in the collaged space show the impossibility of a secure landscape, at least in the shadow of past histories of genocide and in the reactive violence of various actors in Israel and Palestine. Sarah is faced with a conundrum.

As she becomes overwhelmed by the rhetoric and violence around her, Sarah confides in her group leader Nadan, "You're gonna think I'm crazy. I just thought I knew what I felt about this place and now I'm all messed up" (Glidden, *How to Understand* 102). Later in their conversation when she confesses that she feels a connection to Israel despite her earlier convictions, she adds, "How can I feel a connection to a place that causes so much suffering?" (104). She has shifted her position or at the very least feels confused by the things she sees and the people she talks to. In the process, she doubts her own feelings, thinking that she may be brainwashed—as Jamil's father predicted (104). By the end of the text, Glidden suggests that Sarah feels unsure about the strong opinions she had when she began the trip. After Sarah leaves Israel, she spends a day touring Istanbul. When Sarah tells a group in her Turkish youth hostel that she has been traveling in Israel, someone asks, "What's the deal with that place, anyway?" (206). The last two panels of the memoir show Sarah with a confused expression on her face, suggesting she is not quite sure how to answer. The last word of the text is, "Well . . ." (206) with no further explanation. Glidden's exploration of Sarah's emotions and the rhetoric she encounters are mirrored in the comic devices. The conflicting emotions and shifts in convictions are reflected in the pauses in these panels and reinforced in the bleeding watercolor maps and the historical images that permeate the panels of Sarah's Birthright trip.

The space of the page in Libicki's and Glidden's work is territory with high stakes, at once representing the personal, artistic space of the creators and the wider geopolitical terrain of their emotionally charged investigations. Such nuanced, precarious spatial representations of historical memory unsettle often polarized, binary liberal/conservative responses, particularly around the conflict in Israel and Palestine, while they open space for identifying commonalities. Spatial representations like this challenge our own thinking about rhetorically entrenched identity positions and their relation to dangerous conflict. In each of these works, the protagonist shifts their perspective on the political landscape of Israel and their own position in relation to the country as a result. In the context of war in Israel and Palestine, the binaries that divide those that support one side or another are untenable. By seeing the conflict through the eyes of women who question, think through, and shift political positions, a model emerges for more humane visions of war and of dangerous entrenched positions.

My aims for theorizing the complex geopolitics via the graphic border poetics in Libicki's and Glidden's graphic narratives are threefold. First, the images of historical and contemporary violence in these two works show the ways that war and retaliation are inextricably tied up with feelings of Jewish insecurity and past atrocities such as the Holocaust, historical Jewish statelessness, and earlier wars in Israel and Palestine. Conflict and violence do not *end* as such; rather, the affective power of fear and insecurity fuels a protective stance based on militarization. Second, I illustrate the role of graphic border poetics in depicting contested national locations; that is, creative organizations of space may complicate binary nationalist discourse and illustrate the precarious borders between the private and public and between victim and perpetrator. Third, I aim to foreground the role of gendered discourse in discussions and theories of diaspora and border theory in Jewish American literature. Because Jewish history has become a central paradigm for diaspora studies, it is imperative to make visible the ways that Jewish women have been members, but also objects, of the nationalist imagination. My hope is that a focus on the graphic border poetics in texts like these might challenge our own thinking about rhetorically entrenched identity positions, cultural notions of homeland, and dangerous conflict.

2

The Implicated Subject and World War II Identity in the Twenty-First Century

> I sense that Krug created *Belonging* not only for someone like herself, but for someone like me. I am also a writer and artist. I, too, feel wistful on Brooklyn rooftops. My grandparents . . . lost homes, jobs, years, whole families, because of the Holocaust. . . . I wrote a book not unlike Krug's in form and feeling about the inheritance of these stories.
> —Amy Kurzweil, "From the Notebook of a Fellow Graphic Memoirist: An Illustrated Review of Nora Krug's *Belonging*"

Amy Kurzweil's review of Nora Krug's memoir *Belonging: A German Reckons with History and Home* (2018) points to the connections that exist between Kurzweil's memoir *Flying Couch* and Krug's text: the former a graphic memoir written by the granddaughter of Holocaust survivors and the latter by the granddaughter of Nazi Party members. Though Krug and Kurzweil enter this conversation from two different positions culturally and geographically, both texts reveal an unbearable burden of history—a burden that threatens to overwhelm the lives of young women living almost seventy years after the traumatic events that they write about. When read together these works critique the often narrow and very separate memories of Jews and Germans in the Holocaust, becoming transparent and self-critical reflections on the ways the past has held each of the women in its grip.

Within Jewish studies and Holocaust studies, scholars have been cautious not to equate or even relate the victim's narrative with that of the perpetrator. Michael Rothberg claims that the narrative of the uniqueness of the Holocaust serves a purpose but that it also creates a "hierarchy of suffering" (*Implicated* 8–9). Rothberg suggests instead that we might think of ourselves not as victim, perpetrator, or bystander but as an "implicated subject" so that we might "develop an ethics of comparison that can distinguish politically productive forms of memory from those that lead to competition, appropriation, or trivialization" (*Implicated* 9). Krug and Kurzweil engage in deep analyses of the dominant cultural narratives within which they are positioned. They question the burden of Holocaust memory on their lives as well as their complicity in perpetuating those narratives. Together, their texts work to disrupt cultural narratives of memorialization that justify violent nationalism. My aim in looking at these memoirs together is not to compare histories or to create a hierarchy of suffering but rather to recognize the weight of the memory of atrocity on future generations and to imagine a productive, responsible way forward.

Within twentieth-century Holocaust scholarship, there is often a perception that a focus on gender or women is peripheral to the memory of atrocity.[1] In part because the genocide of Jews was based on race, gender is often erased as a category of analysis (Ringelheim 348). When women are portrayed in Holocaust literature, they are often depicted as helpless, fragile, or even erotic.[2] Ironically, within the domestic sphere, women have often been positioned as the keepers of family tradition and memory, the child bearers and the storytellers, yet in the dominant culture their stories are not seen as central to those memories. As shown in previous chapters, texts by women are often attentive to the female body and to womanhood; for example, both Krug and Kurzweil tie menstruation to their experience of Holocaust memory. While both authors explore the home as domestic realm, they position the community, city, and nation as part of that realm. Their personal experiences and memories are intertwined with larger cultural and national narratives. In this sense, texts like Kurzweil's and Krug's disrupt the dominant male-centered memory of the Holocaust, putting women's memory of the Holocaust at the center of understanding the long-term consequences of war that crosses boundaries of religion and geographical location.

When read together, these two graphic memoirs give voice to a burden that the Holocaust poses for women in particular, showing the ways that one's sense of identity and being in the world can be affected and formed by the discursive powers of memory and war. In doing so, Krug's and Kurzweil's visual reckonings with their pasts theorize a dual structure of sense (Butler): a cultivated sense of agency within their overwhelming identification with family histories of World War II, an embodied account of two young women grappling with unwieldy family burdens. A feminist analysis that is attentive to structures of sense is pertinent to illustrate the personal consequences of memory of the Holocaust on individuals as well as larger political consequences of cultural identities based in narratives of war and victimhood. The visual and experimental artistic devices in these texts might also serve as models for reorienting the overdetermined memories of past atrocities within a more productive ethics of comparison that moves across the victim-perpetrator binary. The question of how inherited Holocaust memory affects personal and cultural identities is addressed in both graphic works, though Krug's text is understandably more explicitly focused on her relation to her nation of birth and Germany's position of responsibility for the Holocaust.

Since its publication in 2018, scholars have pointed out the ways that *Belonging* is shaped by Krug's proximity to German Holocaust guilt and memory—and Krug's subsequent complicated relation to *Heimat* or feelings of being at home.[3] For example, Matt Reingold argues that through her exploration of feelings of disconnection from her German identity, "Krug is able to develop a stronger and more nuanced relationship with her identity as a German and begins to feel at home and comfortable in her acceptance of her Nazi heritage" ("Heimat" 552). Tammy Clewell similarly suggests that Krug confronts her family's past in order to find a "renewed sense of German cultural identity" that is tied not just to guilt and pain but also to "comfort and pleasure" (463). One major issue that is not addressed in the contemporary scholarship of these works is the deep imprint that family memory has on these third-generation women seventy years after the war—and the larger cultural and political implications of these inherited memories. What "cultural work" does the memory of war and trauma perform in these texts? How do the unique visual devices and structures within Kurzweil's and Krug's work theorize a dual structure of sense or sense of agency that allows for the subject to respond to war and inherited memory in more productive ways?

The burden of guilt and trauma in Krug's and Kurzweil's narratives suggests that individual lives—as well as the larger cultural narratives of Jews and Germans—are still affected by the memory of the war. Marianne Hirsch suggests that much memorialization in the current era "supports nationalist, ethnocentric, and masculinist imaginaries" (*Women* 8). She points out that these gendered narratives of violence "risk strengthening rather than contesting the ethnic, racialized, and nationalist barriers that are responsible for the violent histories they are recognizing" (Hirsch, *Women* 9). Krug's and Kurzweil's works are intimate portraits of these cultural narratives; the extreme guilt that hides truth on the one hand (Krug) and overidentification that immerses the living in tropes of fear and death on the other (Kurzweil) resound and reside in communities, in national narratives, and even in political policies.

As I argue in the introduction and in chapters 1, 3, and 4, other female graphic artists such as Bernice Eisenstein, Julia Alekseyeva, Miriam Libicki, and Sarah Glidden also address the ways that war memory becomes destructive in the private and public realms. Women's relationship to trauma in these texts is a visceral, embodied experience that is often shown in proximity to nationalist stories of fear and shame. These feminist narratives seem particularly attuned to the position of bodies in war and culture. While texts like Libicki's and Kurzweil's may invoke stereotypical helplessness of the female body, the metanarrative of their location in relation to patriotism, Israeli nationhood, and Jewish identity reveals a female agency that gestures toward a more sustainable model of memory. Hilary Chute has written about the visual medium's ability to represent the body and trauma, arguing that graphic narrative is a "rich location for the work of documentation" that is also self-reflexive (*Disaster Drawn* 17–18). Krug's representations of family documents and archival photos are images that act as witness to her German family's past, but at the same time their proximity to her perceptions of her body allows her to trace the transversal components of selfhood in relation to shame, history, and structures of sense.

Kurzweil and Krug use creative graphic devices and archival reproductions to question, challenge, and rewrite dominant cultural narratives of history and identity. While Kurzweil's text often questions the repercussions of the weight of the Holocaust on Jewish identity and larger geopolitical forms, Krug explores the weight of historical responsibility for third-generation Germans. Kurzweil articulates one of the narrative complications that Krug encounters in the text: "Her family lived through uncertainty, poverty and loss. Her *Heimat*—defined as 'imaginary developed or actual landscape or location with which a person . . . associates an immediate sense of familiarity'—is scarred with historical disgrace. She is haunted and homesick and there is no comfortable label to absolve her" (Kurzweil, "From the Notebook"). The visual and spatial approach that I offer here argues for models of thinking through graphic works that are animated by cultural, personal, and historical memory and the repercussions of these memories on our bodies and our collective futures.

Location and geography are interwoven with a cultural and personal sense of identity in these texts. Matt Reingold usefully points out that the German word *Heimat* is linked to land ownership and physical space, itself a suggestion that "being at home" in Krug's text (titled *Heimat* in all editions outside of the United States) is spatial and land-based. He writes that "heim [connotes] a legal term for a privately-owned house or farm" ("Heimat" 556). Krug's written and visual exploration of German locations and objects addresses the relation between historically fraught national objects and her emotional connections to them. Instead of laying out a linear family history, Krug creates an artistic and emotional exploration of her reflections on her family's role in the Nazi Party, an exploration that grapples with the role of personal German memory and its connections to responsible futures.[4] Krug's and Kurzweil's graphic representations of self, geographical location, and domestic spaces help us to think through the spatiality of gender, violence, religion, race, and memory and the tolls they take on generations.

The graphic border poetics in these works give a vivid visual sense of the constraints as well as the graphic possibilities of reimagining bounded territory. Krug and Kurzweil use creative practices to push the static lines that make up maps and national borders. One way that they do this is by drawing attention to the constructed spaces within the comic form and refiguring that space as layered and asynchronous. In traditional colonizing maps, or maps that determined/delineate power and control over occupied lands, the printed line often has a corresponding militarized border, wall, or fence—a concrete consequence of the seemingly innocuous line on paper. Graphic texts can use visual devices that echo the devices of maps in order to draw attention to cartographic colonizing practices and to subvert them in creative alternative mappings. The graphic work reorients the geographic space in an interpretive framework that is space-bound by the limits of the page, the panel, and the two-dimensional figures; this process of reorientation becomes a commentary on geographical boundaries as well as on affective spaces, a meta-analysis of cultural, national, and institutional structures. Through the use of watercolors, boundary cracks, and mixed media, these artists suggest ways to decolonize the intrusive lines of predetermined maps and memories, challenging the static and exclusionary histories.

In their spatial configurations or graphic border poetics,[5] these narratives highlight the importance of proximity to historical narratives of fear, guilt, and shame that are connected to violence and militarized spaces—and their consequences on the body. The visual representations of orientation in the two graphic works creatively convey unspoken consequences of cultural memory, which include the long-term processes by which war and genocide create shame, gendered narratives, and fear in the body. Both Kurzweil and Krug consider and challenge boundaried or culturally defined Holocaust memory of the twentieth century, thus creating possibilities for new configurations of cultural and territorial identities on their own terms in the twenty-first century.

The Ongoing Burden of Memory in *Flying Couch* and *Belonging*

Amy Kurzweil's *Flying Couch* was published in 2016 and was Editor's Choice for *The New York Times*, a Junior Library Guild Selection, and one of *Kirkus Reviews*' Best Memoirs of 2016.[6] The graphic memoir moves back and forth between twenty-first-century California and 1940s Europe, weaving Amy's coming-of-age story together with her grandmother's (Bubbe's) Holocaust story. Growing up in Newton, Massachusetts, as a third-generation survivor, Amy lives an economically privileged life with professional parents and plenty of resources for her education. Amy has an especially close relationship with her maternal grandmother, a Holocaust survivor who tells Amy harrowing stories about her life during World War II. Despite her comfortable environment, Amy often struggles to separate her own life from her grandmother's stories of survival in the Warsaw Ghetto.

The memoir begins by tracing Amy's life from her childhood home, through her college years at Stanford, to Israel, and into her early adulthood in New York City. During Amy's formative years, her psychotherapist mother's high anxiety together with her bubbe's stories shape her life. Bubbe's World War II diary stories haunt the spaces around Amy's world, lurking in the backdrop of her childhood and keeping Amy in a grip of fear and anxiety. The visually intertwined stories of the Holocaust and Amy's contemporary life become indistinguishable, and as a result Amy has difficulty functioning due to the anxiety it causes her. As Dana Mihăilescu suggests, "acts of seeing . . . depend on one's vantage point or positioning in space and time" ("Mapping" 107). Amy clearly sees her world through the stories she hears and the anxiety she feels around her. She writes, "The women in my family have certain stories to tell. Why does it feel like I'm not the protagonist of my own life?" (Kurzweil, *Flying Couch* 245). Amy's constructed visual and affective world, in part, is a way of mediating her bubbe's trauma and precarity onto her own life. (Bubbe is also known by her first name, Lily.)

Amy Kurzweil's memoir opens with an image of her grandmother's diary (a book)—an object that shapes not only the memoir but Amy's life; the diary in this opening image seems to constitute the very house she grew up in (fig. 2.1). In a one-page series of images that acts as a prologue, the top image shows a book with Amy's grandmother's image on it and a note that reads, "Amy—here are Bubbe's stories." The ending of the note falls off the page in a scattering of letters that spell out "Love, Mom" along with more abstract configurations of letters that read "Bubbe's," "stories," and "some." The handwritten note that is signed "Love, Mom" concretizes the handing down of Holocaust memory through the female line of the family (from grandmother to daughter to granddaughter); indeed, men are largely absent from the story,

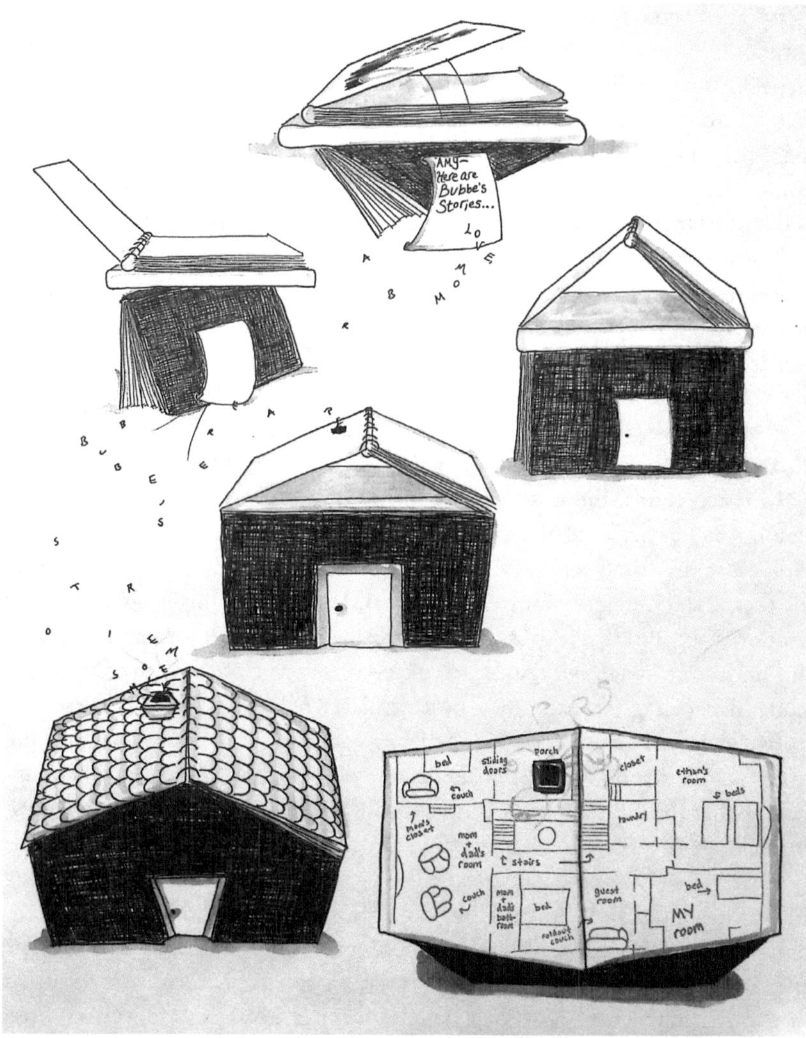

FIG. 2.1 Bubbe's diary opens to become a house.

suggesting a counterpoint to the largely male-dominated fields of graphic novels and Holocaust memoirs.

As the letter falls from the diary, the books open to create the shape of a house: one book takes on a triangular shape as it perches on top of another. In the fifth image on the page, the diaries have transformed into a tiled house complete with a smoking chimney: words and smoke intertwining as they exit (or enter) the chimney (see fig. 2.1).[7] Though the inherited memories are not her own, it is evident that the past has a significant impact on Amy's life:

The diary becomes the place in which Amy and her family reside. Visually, her mother's note becomes the door to the house, the way into the house and into Amy's psychological world that is created from her grandmother's stories. This framing metaphor suggests that Bubbe's/Lily's stories frame the domestic spaces of Amy's life and become the structural foundations of her childhood home. The subsequent chapters explore the ways the stories confine her as well as the tools they provide for her to develop her own agentic narrative.

Within the chapters of the memoir, the repercussions of the Holocaust stories on Amy's life are visible in the images that surround her during everyday activities. Amy expresses the feeling that "ordinary life was a ruse. Perilous drama hid under the surface of everything" (*Flying Couch* 23). Her young life is interrupted by her grandmother's stories of the Warsaw Ghetto, her mother's obsessive-compulsive tendencies (which she implies may be a result of Holocaust memory), and her own anxious fear that life is inherently unstable.

In visual terms, the postmemory of her bubbe's experiences threatens to encompass her personal and family space. As noted earlier, the horrors of the Holocaust are almost a seamless part of Amy's present life.[8] Throughout the text, watery images of towers, fences, and walls often linger outside Amy's windows, suggesting a fear of disappearing into her grandmother's Holocaust stories. In one image she stands on tiptoes trying to close the curtains on the scene of a young girl hurt by a mortar blast (*Flying Couch* 24). These war images are clearly from her bubbe's diary, as the next scene shows pages flying from the diary and out of Amy's bedroom window while she sleeps (25), suggesting that the harrowing stories of survival not only affect Amy but are present in the larger world outside of Amy's bedroom.[9]

Kurzweil's image track suggests that Amy's fears come to a head as a young adult visiting the Yad V'shem Holocaust Museum in Israel. During the Birthright trip, Amy wanders around the museum trying to understand the scope and horror of the Holocaust and its relation to her own story of identity. In another allusion to Art Spiegelman's *Maus II*, Kurzweil draws Amy in a striped concentration camp uniform as a part of the museum exhibit (*Flying Couch* 145). Spiegelman uses visual symbolism in *Maus*, including the stripes of the Auschwitz camp uniforms, to suggest the ways that the Holocaust continues to resonate in his present-day life in New York even though he did not experience the camps directly. Kurzweil draws Amy in a striped uniform as if she belongs in the museum exhibit, creating a comedic metanarrative based on her irrational fears. In one tongue-in-cheek image, Amy is shown drowning in the exhibit of the pile of shoes taken from prisoners in Auschwitz (144), and in another image, she becomes one of Janusz Korczak's Warsaw Ghetto orphans who are eventually deported to Treblinka in 1942 (145). Kurzweil shows how her grandmother's Holocaust memories dominate her early life and act as a barrier to her ability to function and develop a Jewish identity that moves significantly beyond World War II memory. In *Belonging*, Krug also illustrates the burden of World War II on her protagonist, who is held suspect by others for being German and plagued by the profound shame of her family's past.

Holocaust memory is not an isolated question within memory studies, but as many scholars have shown, it is intertwined with affective environments of place, politics, and even governmental policies. Memory helps determine the ways we define ourselves and the ways we build our futures. Theories about how Holocaust stories are "remembered" by the second and third generations after the war have been discussed by many scholars, including Marianne Hirsch, Shoshana Felman, and Cathy Caruth. Hirsch calls this phenomenon postmemory, a term that describes the relationship of the "generation after" to the trauma of those who came before, so that the memories of the next generation "seem to constitute memories in their own right" (*Generation of Postmemory* 5). Family memories continue to affect the children and grandchildren of survivors as well as the psyche of the larger culture. In the case of Amy Kurzweil's *Flying Couch*, the memories of her grandmother's experiences determine much of Amy's early life. One danger of such memories is that "to grow up with overwhelming inherited memoirs, to be dominated by narratives that preceded one's birth . . . is to risk having one's own life stories displaced" (5). Indeed, Kurzweil grapples with the ways her grandmother's Holocaust stories affect or overwhelm her own coming-of-age process. The visual devices illustrate Kurzweil's painful awareness of the weight of Holocaust memory on Amy's life; the metacognizance that she displays in the visual images eventually allows her to move beyond the enabling optimism of Holocaust memory.[10]

Krug's and Kurzweil's texts show many of the same problematic resonances of memory in everyday life, projecting and perpetuating affects like fear and shame into the future. In his work on multidirectional memory, Michael Rothberg suggests that different collective memories, like those of Germans and Jews, struggle for preeminence in a zero-sum game and argues that there are openings for more creative forms of memory-making. Comics are undoubtedly one of those forms. The graphic narrative form in these two memoirs suggests that a new generation of women is asking questions about the unwieldy burdens of war memory and forming new creative spaces and identities that allow them to move beyond the static affective fear and guilt of their parents' and grandparents' generations.

Nora Krug's 2018 graphic work *Belonging* (or *Heimat*) suggests that her own identity is affected, even tainted, merely by being born a German citizen in the wake of the Holocaust. She is also the author of *Diaries of Two Wars: Two Visual Accounts from Ukraine and Russia* (2023) and illustrator of *On Tyranny: Twenty Lessons from the Twentieth Century* (2021), a graphic adaptation of Timothy Snyder's book. Published in 2018 to critical acclaim, *Belonging* has won several awards, including the American 2018 National Book Critics Circle Award, the British Victoria and Albert Museum's Book Illustration Prize, and the German Youth Literature Prize. Krug's comic text is a creative curation of German World War II news archives, descriptions of flea market finds, historical photographs, personal reflections through which Nora grapples with her hidden family history and her own journey of self-discovery. Krug's tireless investigation into her family's involvement in the National Socialist Party implies an attempt to take a position of responsibility.

In contrast to Amy Kurzweil, who tells of her bubbe's stories about being a Jew in Nazi Germany, Krug confronts the history of her non-Jewish German relatives' participation in the Nazi Party during the same period. As a recent immigrant to Brooklyn, New York, Nora is spurred to question her background in the affective environment of Jewish New York. We learn later that Krug marries a Jewish man, adding more complexity and weight to her investigations of World War II. When Nora first moves to New York City from Berlin, she encounters what she frames as an epiphany about her own emotions as connected to the Holocaust. On the second page of her book, Krug uses a double-page spread to depict a rooftop view of New York City in blue and green watercolor (fig. 2.2). The hand-drawn text that describes the scene hovers in the watery clouds above the view of the city, creating an affective environment that permeates not only the visual space of one of Nora's first encounters in the city but also the very air she breathes. The text describes her encounter with an elderly Holocaust survivor who upon hearing Nora's accent asks, "Where are you from?" When Nora answers, "I'm from Germany," the woman replies, "That's what I thought." As it dawns on Nora that this woman spent time in a concentration camp during World War II, she writes, "A familiar heat began to form in the pit of my stomach. How do you react, as a German, standing across from a human being who reveals this memory to you?" (*Belonging* chap. 1).[11] The text of this encounter dominates the two-page spread in heavy blue-green clouds, overshadowing the New York City skyline; the words of the Holocaust survivor fill the airspace around the buildings, illustrating Nora's perception of the affective environment during this emotional encounter (fig. 2.2). Instead of seeing the wonders of the city on one of her first evenings, she instead is confronted with a question that haunts her for years to come. Krug's question "How do you react?" (to this encounter with a Holocaust survivor) along with the heat in her stomach leads her to undertake a years-long investigation into her feelings of shame and her family's role in the atrocities of World War II.

Krug charts her journey to discover her German family's tainted past through documents and found objects. In the face of crippling shame and guilt associated with Germany's role in the Holocaust, Krug decides to go beyond national responsibility to publicly uncover the details of her own family's

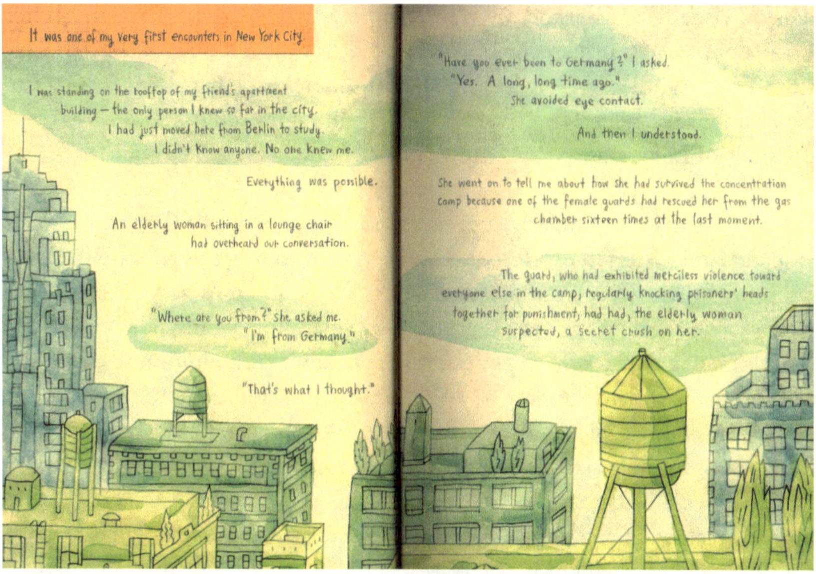

FIG. 2.2 The Brooklyn rooftop where Nora encounters feelings of shame that lead to her investigation of her family.

connections to the National Socialist Party. Her careful archival research follows her grandfather Willi's and her uncle Franz-Carl's involvement in the Nazi Party. Krug includes several documents related to her family, but the information she seeks is often beyond her grasp: Many of the war generation have died off, are too old to remember, or are reluctant to admit their involvement. The found archival images and objects that Krug includes serve as a counterpoint to the lack of information she receives from witnesses and relatives. Through a collage of personal stories, archival materials, and even German objects, Krug pieces together a poignant reflection on the consequences of the cultural memory of war and atrocity. As Victoria Aarons suggests, in Germany, "the shaping and transmission of memory is tied to collective, institutionalized expressions of guilt and accountability but also to the ways in which memories were and continue to be confronted in domestic space" ("Burden" 91). Krug's and Kurzweil's texts share a common desire to investigate the reasons their present is still so deeply affected by the past atrocities of World War II.

Within Kurzweil's text, the postmemory of her bubbe's experiences is a seamless part of Amy's present life. Not only do the images of her bubbe's experience hang outside of Amy's windows as a young child, but the stories in the diary punctuate the chronology of Amy's young adulthood, creating a disjunctive narrative telling that weaves her suburban coming-of-age story with her grandmother's trauma. During various stages in Amy's young adult life, the diary is visually present and often interrupts Amy's experiences: It sits on her nightstand at Stanford University (*Flying Couch* 154) and tells of the deportation of Lily's family (157), it appears several times during her Birthright trip to Israel, and it interjects itself into her and her mother's tour of Germany to tell the story of Lily's/Bubbe's story of survival during the war by passing as a non-Jew (190–201).

Nora Krug's text similarly suggests that her identity as a German woman is shaped and haunted by Holocaust memory. In contrast to Kurzweil's abundance of stories, Krug contends with an absence of family stories. Historian Robert Frie suggests that the German silence around family involvement in the Holocaust is a result of guilt and shame about the Holocaust as well as an attempt to "deny the past or avoid accusations and the loss of affections from their children or grandchildren" (9, 16). Krug's work takes up Frie's challenge to young Germans to uncover their own family's involvement in the National Socialist Party (Frie xiii). Krug's graphic narrative is the result of years of investigatory research in archives, visits to relatives, and probing questions about family involvement in the National Socialist Party. Within Krug's text, she includes a plethora of photographs, government documents, and family letters along with her own reflections on these findings. Krug weaves these archival materials, which are often related to her family's opaque past, with her personal journey as a way of expressing her ambivalent feelings toward Germany and toward her own identity.

A combination of historical and philosophical work, Krug's *Belonging* asks questions not only about personal and national responsibility in war but also about German attachments to national narratives, identities, and even objects. Throughout the book, for example, Krug presents several one-page sections titled "Things German," which include a large drawing and description of a German object (e.g., a binder, a mushroom, a bandage) wherein Krug details her deep attachments to these objects (fig. 2.3).[12] The "Things German" interludes are visual metanarratives that critique what she positions as her problematic love of German ephemera and commercial products. The juxtaposition of Nora's love for German commodities in "Things German" with the horrors they evoke in their described connections to the Nazi war machine creates a dissonant narrative of German patriotism that suggests a position of ethical responsibility.

Nora's feelings of guilt and responsibility as a German are of course personal to her, but they also invoke larger questions about responsibility and repair. Germany faces a unique challenge in remembering World War II.[13] How does a nation that committed the most systematic genocide of the twentieth century honor the dead and at the same time assume public responsibility for these crimes? Cecily Harris in her work on German memory writes that "Germans have been struggling for the past 60 years to . . . show deep remorse

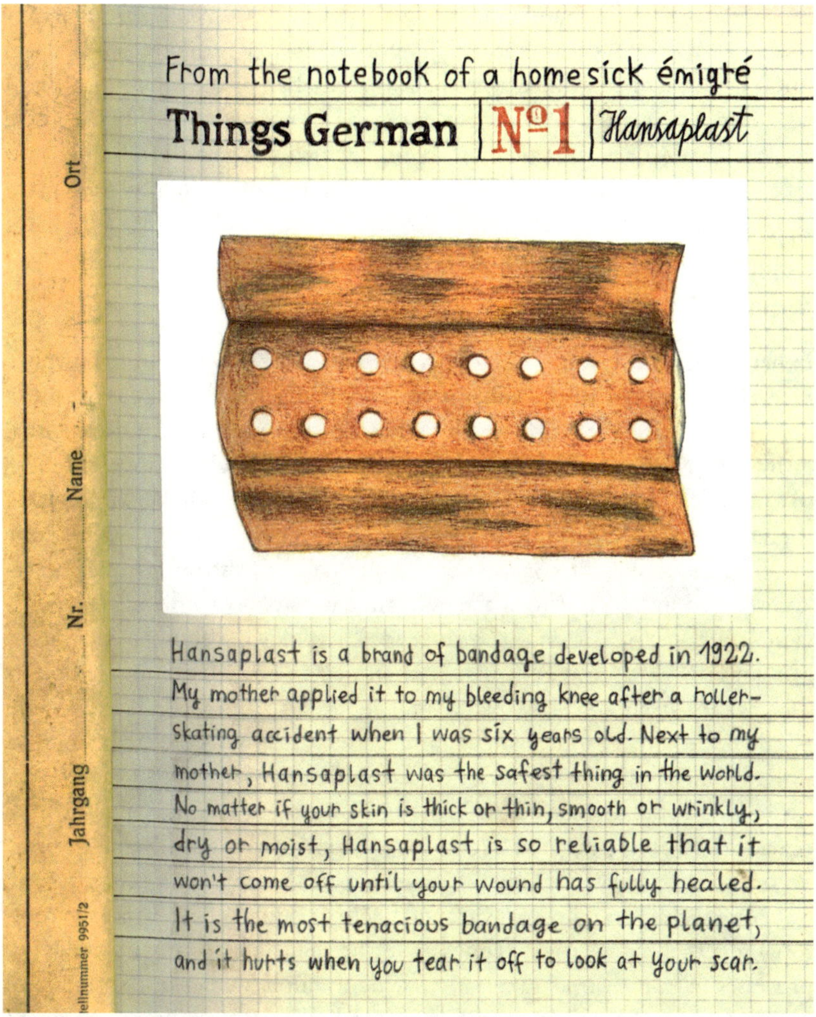

FIG. 2.3 The Hansaplast bandage: an example of Krug's use of the category "Things German." The image is visually encased in a Lietz folder (see fig. 3.5).

for crimes they themselves did not commit but by which they feel tainted, and through which the world often views them" (34). Germany invests in public remembrance projects—which include tripping stones, art installations, educational exhibits, and monetary remuneration—yet criticisms of these projects seem to imply that public reparative work is not enough. Krug's text suggests that she too struggles with the burden of her family history; on the one hand, she goes to great lengths to uncover documents in long-forgotten German archives, and on the other, she discusses her love of German products and ephemera and speculates on the ways that these attachments make her complicit in the narrative of Nazi power and history. Krug writes in a *New Yorker* interview that in *Belonging*, "it was especially important to weigh the text and images carefully in order to avoid a sense of sentimentality, or the impression that I was trying to create a false sympathy for the Germans" (Mouly). The visual track in her text acts as a medium through which she grapples with her own attachments to Germany and to German cultural narratives of superiority.

Object Nationalism and the Body's Proximity to National Shame

In her collage-like investigation of her German family's World War II involvement, Krug writes, "Throughout my childhood, the war was present but unacknowledged, like the heirloom lion's head tureen stored behind our usual dishware" (Krug chap. 1). Krug compares the obscured war narratives she seeks to a piece of hidden dishware—a gendered domestic object in her kitchen that is present but lurking in the shadows. Scholar Sara Ahmed writes that shame includes the desire for concealment; while collective shame is often unacknowledged in the present, at the same time it may surround and cover individuals "like a cloak or skin" (*Cultural* 102). Krug's work shows a complexity of shame and historical guilt that is often tied to everyday domestic objects such as the tureen, the Hansaplast bandage (fig. 2.3), and the Leitz notebook. While pride and patriotism are the initial affects that Krug recognizes in relation to some of these objects, the text reveals that patriotism acts as a cover for the lurking national shame. Krug's love of "Things German" is a visual symbol of national shame, a negative affect that is bound up in the body and its proximity to other objects (Ahmed, *Cultural* 103). The objects (e.g., the tureen, notebooks, glue) and the spaces around her (e.g., military base, Brooklyn rooftops) together with Krug's feelings about her female body and its biological processes (e.g., menstrual cycle) intertwine to implicate her in a structure of national shame. The narrative she creates in her book stems from a resonant absence in her own life.

The absence of information and discussion about the war—and Krug's family's place in it—prompts her to undertake this investigation. Krug is born many years after the end of the war and recognizes that her childhood was steeped in its reverberations. In "Chapter 1: Early Dawning," Krug displays a photo of her family's backyard, which sits next to a runway of a U.S. military air base. She writes that though she had no understanding of why there was an American base there, it served as a reminder that "something had gone terribly wrong" (Krug chap. 1). The photo from 1980 shows an American plane taking off above baby Nora's head, her mother standing nearby, illustrating the ways that repercussions of the war were an inextricable part of her everyday life, even if they remained unverbalized by those around her.

Krug did finally learn more about the Holocaust as a young teen in school. Her education of the war included documentary films like *Night and Fog* and somber visits to concentration camps (Krug chap. 1). Two small photographs in chapter 1 show students in her school class after their visit to Birkenau death camp (fig. 2.4). The photos show students sitting on a curb, one with head in hands, others with hands clasped uncomfortably in laps, faces downturned. Krug's adjacent text reads, "I remember the sense of gratification I felt when I developed the photos in my basement and saw the images slowly emerge in the acid bath: there was the evidence of our collective guilt" (chap. 1). The affective pain and guilt from her youth are made visible to her in the images she captures. Ahmed writes about the nation's relation to shame, explaining, "The very physicality of shame—how it works on and through bodies—means that shame involves the de-forming and re-forming of bodily and social spaces" (*Cultural* 103). The re-forming of these spaces is laid out visually for the reader. Using an informal scrapbook aesthetic, Krug shows skewed pieces of white tape tenuously adhering the snapshots of her classmates to green paper. Even the heading "After our visit to the extermination site, Birkenau" is written on a scrap of yellow paper that has been glued onto the green background. The layout of the page suggests a naive teenage rendering of a troubling class memory, an immediate and relatively raw reaction to a time-bound event that visually depicts Ahmed's idea of the "physicality of shame." The scraps of paper and tape themselves seem to be a part of Nora's and her classmates' visceral reactions to the camp and to German history. Speaking for her fellow classmates, Nora seems to be relieved to see how the bodies of her classmates—in the images all female-presenting students—are re-formed in the space of the death camp in this photograph, writing, "We felt history was in our blood, and shame in our genes" (chap. 1; see fig. 2.4).

Krug's feelings of shame surrounding her national past, in part, are tied to her shame of being female, suggesting that her national shame is gendered. She recalls learning about the Holocaust in school at the same time she got her first period. Recalling when her mother announced her new status to the family, Krug remembers, "For me the idea of being a woman seemed to be as shameful as being a German" (chap. 1). The sense of national shame that haunts Nora in her childhood, from the roaring sounds of the American air force base in her backyard to the absent family stories and the shocking visits to death camps, is intertwined with her feelings about her body. Through the text on the page, Krug ties her own menstrual blood with the shame of the nation, conflating the cultural shame of the gendered female body with that of a national atrocity (the Holocaust). Krug furthers this trope when Nora adopts the image of the Star of David with "Jude" drawn/written in the middle. Nora wears the star "out of solidarity with the Jews" until her mother tells her it is not a good idea (chap. 1). Nora's shame is a negative affect that is bound up not only with

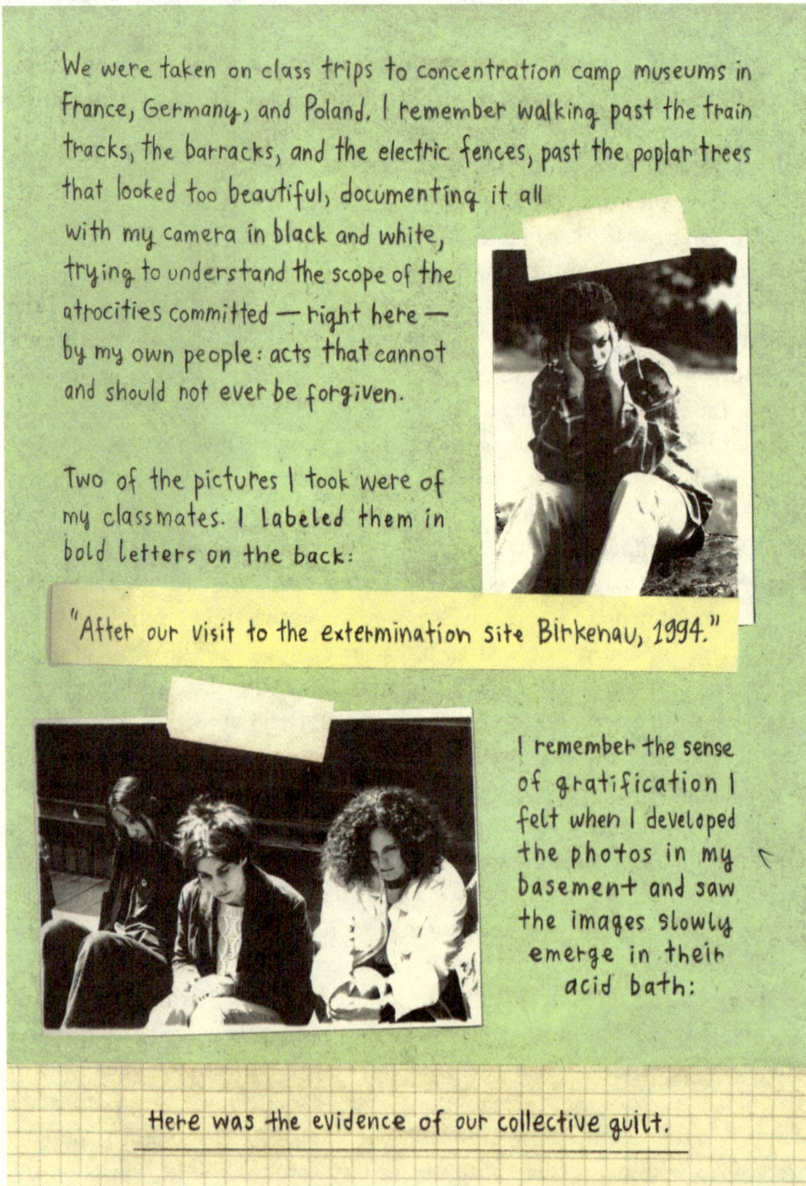

FIG. 2.4 Krug's photographs of her classmates during a visit to Birkenau.

how she feels about her female body but also with her perception of Jewishness. The naive attempt to associate herself with what she sees as an abject Jewish identity is perhaps a way to escape or cover over her shame-laden German identity. Ahmed writes that "individuals become implicated in national shame insofar as they already belong to the nation. . . . Shame impresses upon the skin as an intense feeling of the subject 'being against itself'" (*Cultural* 102–103). These feelings of "being against" herself, the shame of her German body and history, continue to follow Nora to New York several years later.[14]

When Nora moves to New York after college, her sense of shame influences her interactions, her marriage, and even the ways her body moves in space. Twelve years after her encounter on the Brooklyn rooftop, Nora still struggles with her fear of being equated with Nazi atrocities. Living in New York as an adult, Nora's shame seems to be as present as ever. She writes, "I still try to hide my accent . . . by covering my mouth while I speak, by keeping my answers short, by putting on a different accent" (Krug chap. 2). While in yoga class, she realizes, "My shame hasn't disappeared. I can't even stretch and hold my right arm at an angle" without thinking of the Hitler salute (chap. 2). The infamous Nazi salute haunts her body even though she did not live through the war. She equates the German National Socialist past with her bodily movements—and even with her female anatomical functions when she begins to menstruate. The guilt and shame that Nora inherits permeate her sense of herself as a German as well as her physical body. The shame of belonging to a country that is implicated in the atrocities of the Holocaust constrains Nora's thoughts and movements in space and overwhelms her daily life even into adulthood.[15]

Nora's sense of shame is heightened by the gaps and amnesia in her culture and in her family. She writes that German national culture was elusive in the absence of songs, stories, and histories, all associated with the mostly unspoken atrocities of the war. Krug explains that she did not learn what happened in her hometown during the war, did not learn the lyrics to the national anthem, and did not hum German folk songs (chap. 1). Likewise, she did not learn about her own family history. Though the title of Krug's book is *Belonging* in the U.S. edition, the U.K. and German editions, titled *Heimat*, suggest a sense of familiarity that is "imparted across generations through family and other institutions or through political ideologies" (chap. 1). This lack of feeling *at home* is precisely what Nora explores throughout this text. G. Schwab writes that in the face of a largely absent cultural narrative, the second generation of Germans patch together a history from stories, pictures, and letters. As Hirsch suggests, they understand trauma through the gaps, amnesia, and distortions of their families and surroundings (qtd. in Schwab 14). Krug's desire to feel a sense of familiarity with her culture and past is, in part, the result of missing information about her family's part in the war. Krug asks, "How do you know who you are if you don't understand where you come from?" (chap. 1).

In an interview on her website, Nora Krug reveals that these missing stories and histories provide the impetus for her book *Belonging* and, in doing so, align with the imagery of the *Hansaplast* or German bandage (see fig. 2.3). *Belonging* opens with an image and description of the *Hansaplast*, a German protective strip developed in 1922. She explains that the bandage "is so reliable that it won't come off until your wound has fully healed. It is the most tenacious bandage on the planet, and it hurts when you tear it off to look at your scar" (1). While reliable at covering and perhaps even healing wounds, it also conceals them. The bandage is a symbol of Krug's personal connection to the nation-state and at the same time stands in for the nation's complex relation to the Holocaust. Krug's connection to the bandage is visceral. She writes that her mother applied the bandage to her "bleeding knee after a roller-skating accident when [she] was six years old" (Krug prologue). Krug's bodily fluid is soaked in the bandage, suggesting an interconnectedness of national objects and vulnerable bodies. On the one hand, the bandage heals and covers Nora's open wound, and on the other, it is connected to more sinister national feelings. While Krug describes the *Hansaplast* as "the safest thing in the world," it is also connected to the story of a most dangerous national crime, not safe or reliable at all.

Krug's unique approach to uncovering her past includes using German objects like the *Hansaplast* to help explain her ambivalent feelings toward Germany's past. Krug offers the word *Vergangenheitsbewältigung*, which she defines as "not only coming to terms with one's political past," but "the process of *struggling* to come to terms with it" (chap. 1). For Krug, part of this struggle entails returning to her personal family history to make clear the foggy and unspoken narratives of her childhood. She writes that she hopes "to move beyond the abstract shame and ask those questions that are really difficult to ask . . . to go back to the beginning, follow the breadcrumbs, and hope they'll lead the way home" (chap. 2). Her book is the material evidence of *Vergangenheitsbewältigung*, the process of struggling to come to terms with her family's past.

Krug and Kurzweil are aware of the burden of cultural memory and its weight on their lives. This meta-awareness is visible in the graphic framing of each text. Both works begin with notebooks that connect them to the memories of the Holocaust, visually placing their stories squarely within the context of their pasts and at the same time tying them to traditions of writing and creative storytelling. While Amy Kurzweil frames her text with her bubbe's diary of Holocaust stories, Nora Krug frames her work with a Leitz folder—a sturdy, German-made organizational binder. The visual devices they utilize show their awareness of the war's effect on their lives, but the appearance of the diary and folder also implies their exploration of their complicity/roles in those narratives. Kurzweil's and Krug's works self-consciously respond to the memory texts of the war and, in a sense, become supplemental memory texts for the future.

If Krug's memoir is an attempt to uncover and take responsibility for her family's involvement in the Nazi Party, the notebook on which her memoir is "written" testifies to her cognizance of, as well as her commitment to explore, her attachments to German objects and memory. The first images of *Belonging* attest to Krug's affective attachment to German objects and their links to the history of Nazi values and history. Like the use of the diary in Kurzweil's text, the binder suggests that Krug's exploration of her past is inextricably entangled with the stories she uncovers here; in effect, she creates her own archive within the German folder—an archive that places her text squarely within the story of her family's Nazi past (fig. 2.5).

The German three-ring Leitz binder within which Krug visually encloses her text is described as sturdy, durable, and utilitarian, and she writes that even now "in New York City, the Leitz binder is the German consulate's binder of choice" (chap. 4, "Things German No. 4"). The binder was designed "in an attempt to establish order during Germany's increasing bureaucratization" (chap. 4). The first page of the prologue shows an imprint of a brownish-yellow folder cover that faces graphed notebook paper, a detail that might be missed by the reader at first glance. The last page of the text ends with this same yellowed folder. Between these reproduced covers of the Leitz binder, Krug includes many lined or graphed notebook pages as the background for her investigation, as if to reiterate that the text she creates belongs within the aging, yellow German organizational system design. The sturdy, reliable, utilitarian Leitz binder is an organizational aid that Nora admits "provided reassurance in matters of utmost importance in [her] life" (chap. 4). In the description of the Leitz, Krug implicates herself as a third-generation German with family ties to the Nazi Party (see fig. 2.5). She writes that the binders are associated with German sayings such as "Ordnung muss sein" (order is essential), "Ordnung ist das halbe leben" (order is half your life's battle), and "Alles in ordnung" (everything is in order), which "meant that you have nothing in the world to worry about," suggesting a tongue-in-cheek reference to the Nazis' infamous organizational efficiency in the murder of millions of people (chap. 4). This aesthetic addition to *Belonging* emphasizes the project's connection to the efficient German approach to production and destruction. The folder and the organization and efficiency that it represents are a part of her memoir, encasing her graphic family story like an ambivalent love note to her German homeland.

The binder, among other objects, is used by Krug to critique her own orientation to Germany's role in twentieth-century genocide. The small, interspersed sections titled "Things German: Notes of a Homesick Émigré" (which include items like the German Leitz binder) punctuate Krug's unfolding

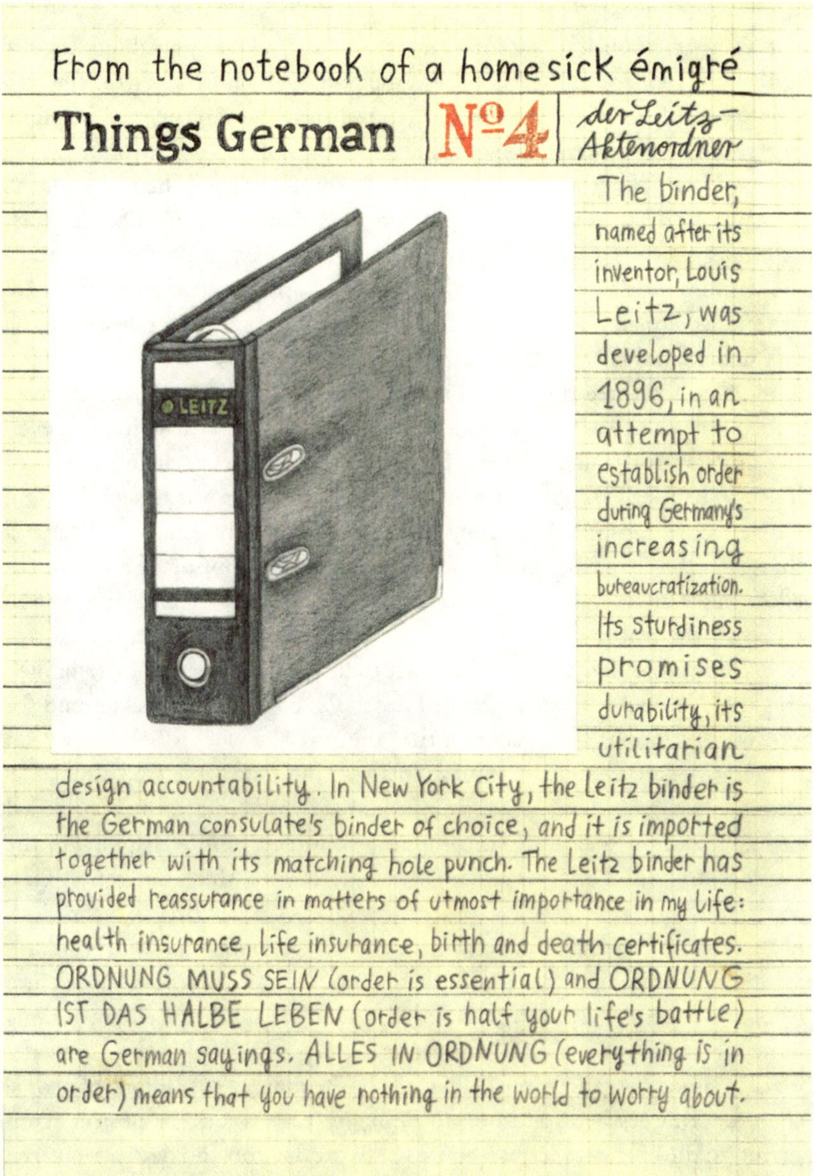

FIG. 2.5 Krug describes the Leitz binder and its object nationalism in a "Things German" interlude.

family story of Nazi involvement in the war. Each of the "Things German" sections introduces one German commodity. In addition to the Leitz notebook and the Hansaplast bandage, the objects in the "Things German" sections include the German forest, the red-and-white mushroom, the hot water bottle, and *Brut* or German bread. The descriptions of these items often reverberate with the language of the highly organized Nazi industrial complex, the organizational systems that facilitated the Nazis' efficient systems of human extermination in the Holocaust. While these "Things German" are ostensibly banal, Krug's descriptions resonate with the claims Hannah Arendt made about the Nazi industrial project and the banality of evil. To different degrees, Arendt, Zygmunt Bauman, Erving Goffman, Stuart Clegg, and others have theorized the idea that the process of evil (in this case mass murder) can be mundane and bureaucratic and therefore seem innocuous, when in fact it led to disaster and genocide in World War II. Krug positions German commodities cum national objects as material apparatus and as value apparatus (Clegg). The commodities that Krug includes in these sections are shown to be inseparable from the German use of industrial efficiency in the Holocaust.

Krug's descriptions and histories of the "Things German" illustrate the ways that her own third-generation attachments to Germany are complicit with the infamous German commodification and object nationalism. I suggest the term *object nationalism* to describe the ways that objects can support national feeling but also critique national attachments to a homeland that are uncritical and unwittingly a part of the Holocaust industrial complex. The President's Commission on the Holocaust report, written in 1979, states, "The Holocaust was not a throwback to medieval torture or archaic barbarism but a thoroughly modern expression of bureaucratic organization, industrial management, scientific achievement, and technological sophistication" (4). In essence, bodies became commodities that were used for slave labor and then the "parts" mined for value after death and invested back into the Nazi war economy (hair for mattresses, gold teeth, ashes for fertilizer, and so forth).[16] Through "Things German," Krug explores her attachments to Germany and the uneasy feelings she has about her desire for national belonging or *Heimat*. Setting her text within the visual representation of the Lietz folder positions *Belonging* as one more "Thing German," another material incarnation of the nationalism that Krug exposes—but with a difference. By enfolding her own creative object within the casings of the German product, she draws attention to both her creative agency and her artistic process: a personal, handmade, self-critical, and agentic approach that stands in stark contrast to the bureaucratic, efficient, or capitalist project of the "Things German" she describes.[17]

Kurzweil and Krug use creative graphic devices to question, challenge, and rewrite dominant cultural narratives of history and identity. While Kurzweil questions the repercussions of the weight of the Holocaust on Jewish identity,

Krug explores the place of responsibility for third-generation Germans. These questions are central for reimagining the ways that histories of war are taught and honored in the future, but they are also pertinent for thinking about the ways that the memory and memorialization of the Holocaust become subtexts and political tools in current geopolitical contexts. Both authors consider their positions in the history of the war and begin to challenge the very construction of boundaried narratives of war memory in the twenty-first century and, in doing so, create new configurations of identity, territorial, and nationalist prescriptions on their own terms. While Kurzweil reorients maps and uses graphic devices like the crack from the wall of the Warsaw Ghetto to create movement in her own story, Krug uncovers hidden family stories and boldly inserts herself into the narrative of responsibility, something her parents and grandparents before her were unwilling or unable to do.

Decolonizing Maps and Memory

Maps and boundaries are central to the narratives of memory and responsibility that Krug and Kurzweil struggle with and eventually challenge. Geographical location, for example, determines the positions their families inhabit as a result of the war, which for Kurzweil's family meant life or death. So, too, religious and ethnic affiliation determine the stories of their families in World War II. Krug was born and educated in Germany; her uncle and grandfather were Christians who chose to align with the German Aryan narrative that developed around the National Socialist rise to power. In contrast, Kurzweil was born in the United States to Jewish parents; members of her grandmother's family located in Poland were forced into ghettos, and many of them were killed because of their outsider status. Her family is constructed outside of the bounds of humanity by the Nazi Party during the same period. Unlike the visual elements in geographical and colonial mapping projects, Kurzweil's and Krug's works position bodies within affective geographical locations in order to give a sense of their proximity to physical, affective, and political influences.[18] Despite Kurzweil's and Krug's heavy identification with the past and the burdens they carry as a result, each artist finds a way to remap their inherited memories of World War II; through graphic text and lines, they redraw the boundaries of cultural memory.

In addition to the maps of domestic spaces, Kurzweil includes hand-drawn maps of the Warsaw Ghetto, Poland, Europe, New York City, and the world. While boundaries and walls determine her European family's existence and her bubbe's ability to survive the war, the maps in Amy's story are a way for her to locate affective narratives alongside (or on top of) sometimes limiting geographical maps. For example, in a series of maps of the Warsaw Ghetto, Bubbe (through her diary) tells Amy that she sneaked out of the ghetto through a crack in the wall to find water for her grandmother, but when Lily (Bubbe) returns to the ghetto, her grandmother has died. She writes, "Can you imagine? To come home . . ." (*Flying Couch* 68). This text directly precedes images of the ghetto map becoming smaller, going from a full page to a series of three 2½-inch-long frames in which the outline of the ghetto map is visible but the detail has disappeared (fig. 2.6). Within the three frames, Lily is shown first kneeling, then standing up, and finally throwing down her yellow Star of David armband in despair (see fig. 2.6). The text reads "and home is gone" (69). Lily's home is taken from her, she loses her grandmother (her affective home), and she decides to throw off her Jewish identity for the duration of the war as a means to survival. In the three frames, the maps of the ghetto are replaced first by outlines of the ghetto and then by a blank rectangle (third frame); she is now part of an unfamiliar blank space, which she needs to navigate and write for herself. Underneath the frames of Lily throwing off the star is the diary that Amy presumably inherits. The diary seems to stand in for the physical spaces of her home and community; Lily will fill its pages with her story—one that will eventually turn into the visual diary that we read in Kurzweil's work.

For Lily, boundaries on landscapes and maps determine the fate of her young life and her family's death. The Nazis used maps and boundaries to facilitate the occupation of countries like Poland and France; lines corresponded to militarized zones, occupied territories, ghettos, and even concentration camps. Lines on maps like these are not just boundaries, but they delineate physical, controlled spaces. By mapping her coming-of-age story in late-twentieth-century Massachusetts and California together with her grandmother's story of survival during World War II, Kurzweil subverts the formal conventions of the geographical war maps, focusing instead on the cracks and movements that facilitate Lily's survival. In the process of telling Lily's story through her own graphic devices, Amy realizes that Lily's movement outside of the ghetto, outside of her Jewish identity, outside of Jewish law, and outside of social conventions are what determine her survival and, as a result, Amy's family's survival.

The crack in the wall facilitates Lily's escape from the ghetto and becomes a symbol of storytelling and survival as she maneuvers wartime Poland. She takes on a new identity, gives herself a new name (Helene), and pretends to be "a nice Polish girl, an orphan" (Kurzweil, *Flying Couch* 94). The cracks in her story become tools with which she reinvents herself through new narratives of identity and gains the courage to protect herself. Throughout the war, Lily moves from farm to farm asking for food and work, fights off a Nazi who tries to molest her (97), and even goes to church—taking communion in order to hide her Jewish identity (98). As the memoir progresses, Amy begins to use tools from Bubbe's stories to tell her own life story; visually she inserts and

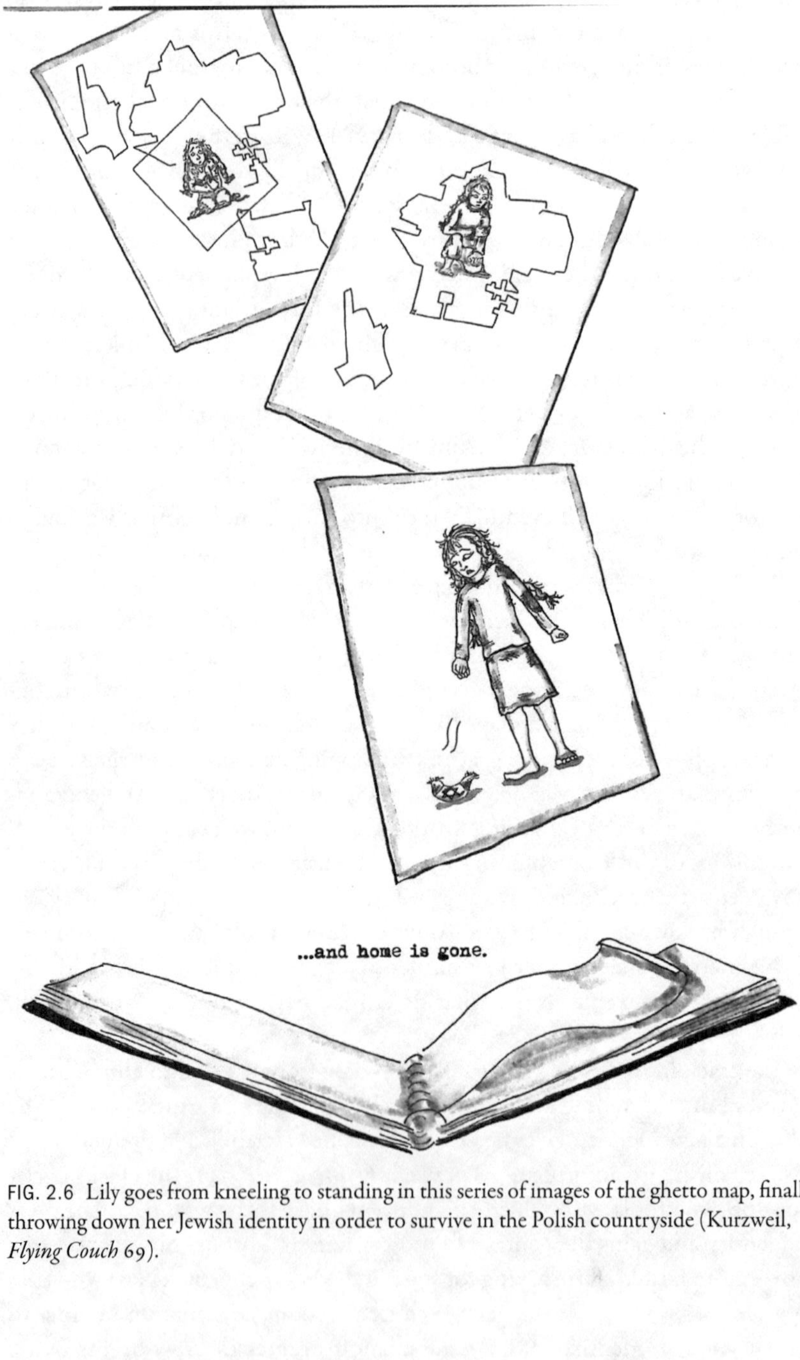

FIG. 2.6 Lily goes from kneeling to standing in this series of images of the ghetto map, finally throwing down her Jewish identity in order to survive in the Polish countryside (Kurzweil, *Flying Couch* 69).

explores openings and cracks in the narratives around her in order to discover her own voice outside of the boundaries of her family expectations and Holocaust memory.

Throughout her memoir, images of the cracks in the Warsaw Ghetto wall permeate Amy's young life: She sees them while she daydreams at home (Kurzweil, *Flying Couch* 22), when she goes to sleep at night (24–25), when she listens to her grandmother's taped testimony (23), and when she reads her bubbe's diary (66, 68). A full-page drawing of the ghetto wall implies the importance of the crack to Lily and by association to Amy (fig. 2.7). Lily narrates, "There was a wall around the ghetto, and one side was Jew, one side gentile. There was a hole. Maybe four bricks missing. Somebody had dug it out. I was skinny and I went out like that. I went back and out three times because I was afraid to leave my parents. How can you leave your parents?" (86; fig. 2.7).

Kurzweil's work depends on the use of maps to situate Amy in space. Her work presents several full-page maps of her home spaces along with several political and carceral maps that illustrate her grandmother's Holocaust stories. Kurzweil structures many of her chapters around maps of familiar geographic spaces; renderings of house floor plans, blueprints, and maps of her neighborhood and her college campus often dominate her story in full-page images. These maps seem to convey a sense of stability for Amy as she maneuvers through the unsettling representations of World War II that permeate her everyday life.

When read carefully, the maps are not just spaces of comfort for Amy but visual renderings of Amy's resistance to family boundaries and enclosures. For example, on the second-floor map of her house, she includes details like "Vent: good place for putting ear to wall to spy on mom and dad" (Kurzweil, *Flying Couch* 5), and on the first-floor house plan, "Big rug (good for practicing cartwheels when no one is looking)" (6). This information interrupts the image of a static, seemingly objective map—interjecting Amy's own mininarrative of agency onto the physical structure of her parents' house. Kurzweil superimposes round panels[19] on top of these maps to show her family's placement in the house as well as their idiosyncrasies. For example, a series of three round panels drawn over a map of Amy's house interior shows her mother wiping crumbs from a counter, then triple-locking the door, and finally closing the curtains. The series reveals some of her mother's compulsive behaviors (6), while in a round frame below Amy draws about her young life (6–7). The juxtaposition of Amy's mother's ostensibly compulsive behaviors and the image of Amy drawing quietly on the floor shows the family's varying coping mechanisms in the face of the intergenerational impact of the Holocaust. While Amy's mother appears to tightly control the world around her (perhaps an attempt to contain the out-of-control Holocaust narrative), Amy experiments

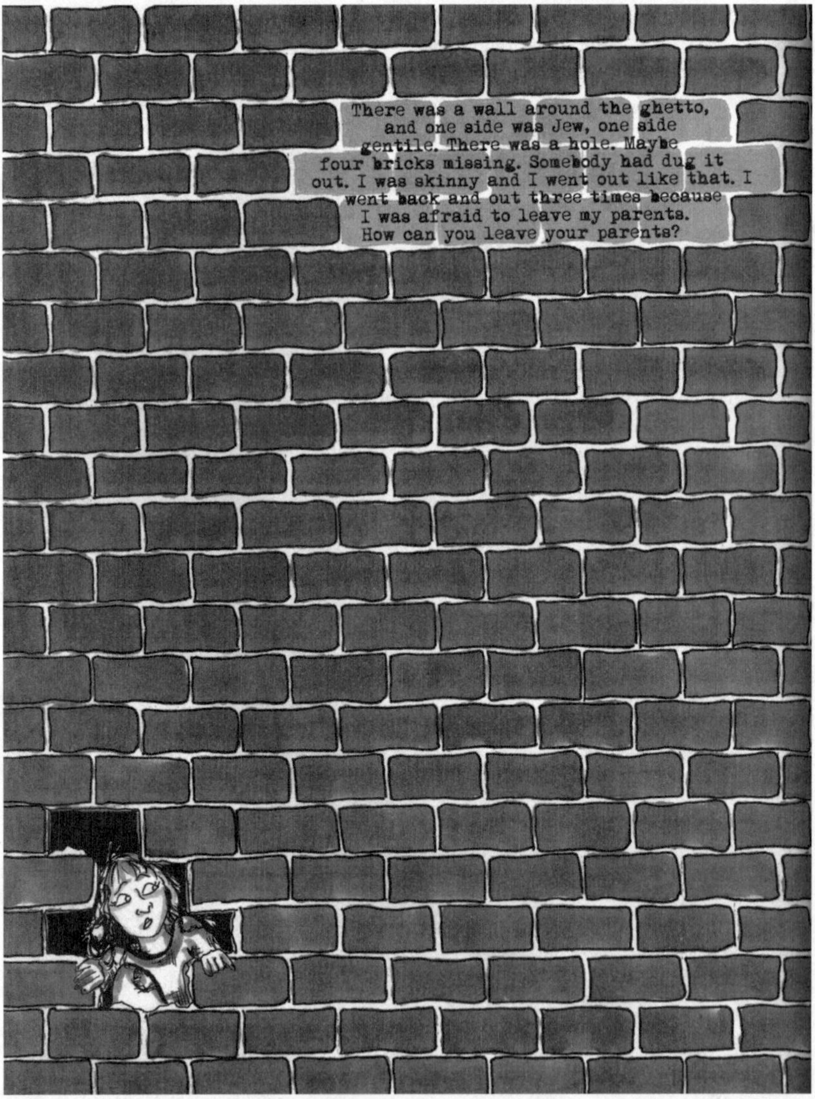

FIG. 2.7 Lily (Bubbe) peeks out of the crack in the Warsaw Ghetto wall.

with creative expression as an outlet. The cracks of her bubbe's story eventually become her tool for resisting the weight of memory and its control over her young life.

The cracks in the wall from Lily's story begin to show up in Amy's own narrative—in the stories she hears from teachers, tour leaders, and Israeli settlers. The cracks facilitate an escape from unquestioned cultural narratives that Amy encounters in her young life. Amy first sees cracks forming in the cultural narrative of Jewish history in her Sunday school classroom. During one lesson about anti-Semitism, the image of a scroll that represents Amy's understanding of Jewish history—including images of Theodor Herzl, the Israeli flag, Israeli pioneers, the infamous Auschwitz gates, and her bubbe's diary—hovers above her head (Kurzweil, *Flying Couch* 78). Amy listens intently to her Sunday school teacher talk about the Holocaust and the importance of the Israeli state until the teacher tells the class, "Israel has endured many wars because of persistent anti-Semitism in the Middle East. And many heroes have given their lives in service of PEACE" (81). As her teacher writes the name of Yitzhak Rabin on the board, Amy raises her hand and asks, "On the TV they said he was killed by another Israeli person . . . why would an Israeli want to kill its own leader?" When her teacher does not answer her question, cracks very similar to the ones she draws in the Warsaw Ghetto wall appear in a series of round panels that show Amy looking increasingly frustrated as the teacher ignores her question (83). Finally, the scroll above Amy's head cracks open, and the images depicting the birth of Israel (the Israeli pioneer, the flag, and Herzl) tumble off the scroll (83). The Sunday school narrative that was told in a linear form on the scroll is destabilized by Amy's frustration at not getting the information she seeks. The visual rendering of this crack or opening from Lily's escape becomes a visual symbol and a tool that Amy uses to question the uncomfortable cultural narratives she continues to encounter.

In mapping her coming-of-age story in late-twentieth-century Massachusetts and California along with her grandmother's story of survival during World War II, Kurzweil subverts the formal conventions of carceral maps of the war and focuses instead on the cracks, openings, and movements that facilitate Lily's survival. In the chapter titled (somewhat ironically) "Homeland," Amy visits Israel on a Birthright trip. On the trip, Amy identifies strongly with Israeli culture, wearing the same headscarf and facial expressions as her tour guide, Noam (Kurzweil, *Flying Couch* 130–131). She writes proudly, "When I wore my patterned headscarf, I could pass for an Israeli." On the next page, however, as Amy listens to a presentation about the Golan Heights given by a man wearing a Cleveland Indians baseball cap, narrative cracks begin to appear. Amy's exuberant identification with Israel dissolves as she connects the various narratives of oppression and displacement that she encounters. Kurzweil zooms in on the speaker and his Cleveland Indians hat (134–135) as one of the American Birthright students questions him about Palestinians who were displaced by Jewish immigrants in 1948 (135). The speaker replies, "What 'PALESTINIANS'?" and then as steam comes out of his ears, he shouts at the student in all capitals, "The PALESTINIANS DESERVE?? F-CK THEM! THEY ARE TRYING TO KILL ME—AND YOU! You are all so—" (136; emphasis in original). Following this event, Amy questions the settler's response and makes multidirectional connections between historical oppressions: A full-page collage shows a dream in which Amy redraws the narrative in an order that makes sense to her (fig. 2.8). She combines different images of displacement and oppression, remapping the cultural narratives she hears on her trip: Images of her Israeli tour guide Noam, the Cleveland Indians, the Star of David, the angry settler, a soldier firing a gun, and the Warsaw Ghetto wall with its crack mix together. Though there is no textual commentary on the settler's angry outburst or on the collage of images, the visual rendering of multidirectional memory shifts the ways Amy feels about her identification with Israel. In an image that roughly parallels her bubbe's throwing down of Jewish identity (see fig. 2.6), a full-page bleed shows Amy on the bus waving goodbye to the Golan Heights, her Israeli scarf discarded on the seat beside her; the idealized narrative of Israel and her place in it has been ruptured. Her identity experiment ends badly, and she abandons the Israeli scarf that she so proudly wore three pages earlier (137).

Dana Mihăilescu suggests that third-generation artists like Kurzweil use memory to reflect on the future of violence, arguing that they use the Holocaust experience to "address ethical concerns . . . including Israel's politics in the West Bank and Gaza, and the commodification of Holocaust memory in the United States" ("Mapping" 110). Kurzweil addresses these ethical concerns by visually assembling narratives of war and colonialism that overlap and inform one another through their formal affordances. The use of the Cleveland Indians icon suggests racist tropes of the untamed Indian within a longer history of Native peoples that are fetishized and marginalized in North American culture; these tropes resonate with longer cultural biblical narratives of the Promised Land and religious exceptionalism in Israel (Kavaloski 9).[20] Kurzweil reorients memory across geographic spaces within the boundaries of the page, creating a graphic assemblage that critiques geographical boundaries as well as nationalist and racist structures. Using boundary cracks, artistic collages, and the inky overlay of the Star of David (a symbol that represents Jewish life—but also the compulsory yellow star of the Holocaust) together with the firing soldier, Kurzweil recombines genocide and racism across time and space, thereby challenging the separate memory of violent colonialist histories (fig. 2.8; *Flying Couch* 138–139).

Kurzweil addresses the public memory of the genocide of Native peoples when she zooms in on the speaker's hat and the racist image becomes a part of her questions about occupation and injustice that arise in the group's visit to the Golan Heights. The double-page collage of images includes an Israeli soldier shooting, blood, and the image of the Cleveland Indian; these memories are not separate in Amy's consciousness (fig. 2.8; Kurzweil, *Flying Couch* 138–139). The racism of the Indian caricature resonates in a profound way with the answer the settler gives the group when he is asked "What about the Palestinians?" (134). The inadequate and explosive answer the students receive

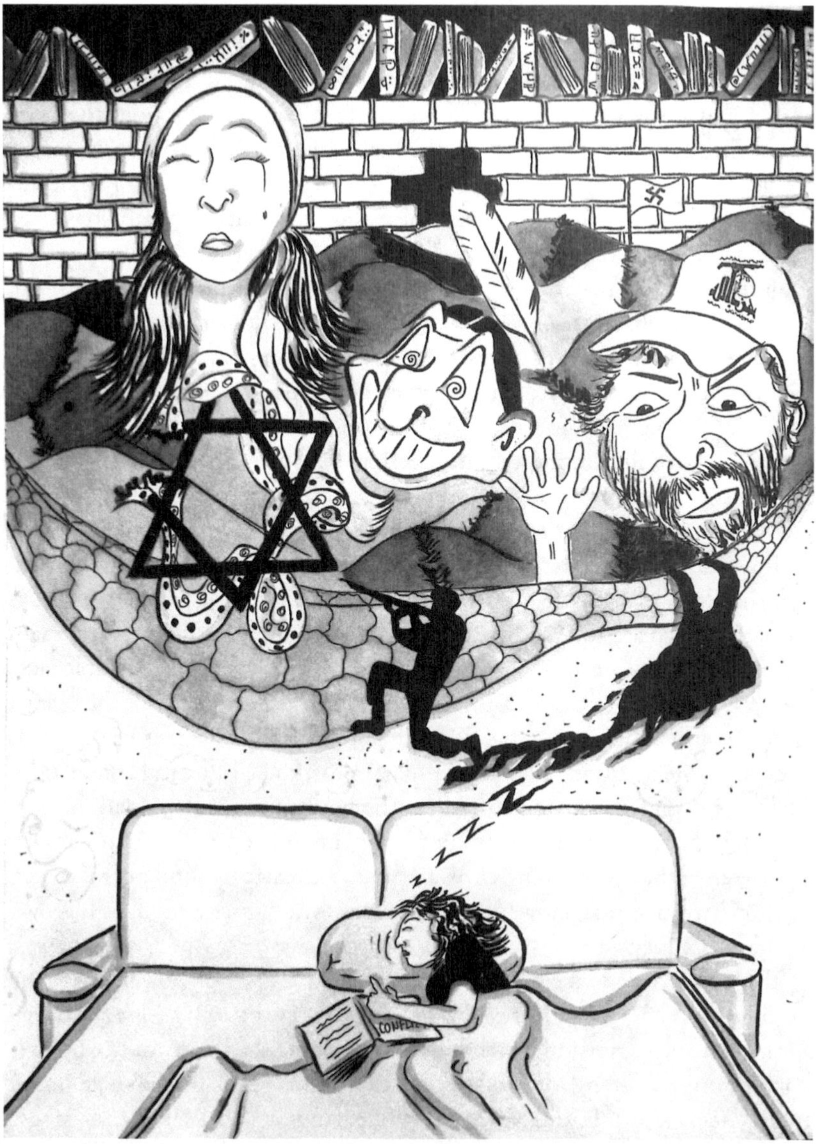

FIG. 2.8 Amy connects her inherited memories of the Holocaust to Israeli militarism, the Cleveland Indians (U.S. colonialism), and her own identification with Israel (Kurzweil, *Flying Couch* 137).

("The PALESTINIANS DESERVE?? F-CK THEM!") reminds Amy of other unresolved issues of race and oppression in her country of citizenship, the United States. As a result, Amy reorders the various elements from her encounters to create a different story of Israel on her own terms.

The discontinuities and cracks in the stories Amy hears become spaces within which she connects past to present in order to understand the complex contradictions of the stories of the Holocaust, the Israeli occupation, and the genocide and oppression of Native Americans (fig. 2.8). Rosi Braidotti calls assemblages of knowledge like these the constellations that allow us to think across previously segregated categories and domains, "because power is a multilayered and dynamic entity, and because as embedded and embodied, relational, and affective subjects, we are immanent (immersed/embedded in) to the very conditions we are trying to change." These assemblages, she suggests, make gestures toward a more equal and collective imagining or future ("Critical Posthuman" 90). The graphic form in *Flying Couch* creates assemblages of power, illustrating a multidirectional memory of war and oppression that allows Kurzweil to question dominant narratives of nationalism—in this case, Israeli and U.S. nationalisms and colonialisms.

The border walls in Kurzweil's graphic text represent the Warsaw Ghetto wall that haunts many of her young interactions but also provide openings for her to re-create the maps and walls that permeate her life. As she maps the past onto the present, she questions dominant narratives of Holocaust memory and their relation to Israel's position in Jewish identity. The fear of the Holocaust in her dream (fig. 2.8) coincides with the Israeli settler's anger as he answers the question about Palestinian rights; these historical connections finally give Amy permission to redraw the boundaries of these narratives in relation to her own life. Her memoir reconfigures memory: from a traumatizing narrative that positions her as an anxious, fearful young person to an agentic narrative that shows her as a woman who writes and maps her own story and identity.

Through a visual assemblage of multiple structures of power (German, Israeli, American), Amy creates new lines of inquiry through which she develops her artistic expression to tell her own story. As she listens to her bubbe's story after graduation from college, instead of images of Bubbe's tale dominating the page as they did earlier in her life, Amy sits on the floor and draws while she listens. Amy now takes control of the stories she creates (Kurzweil, *Flying Couch* 215), placing and reordering photographs of her family and her bubbe onto her own drawing pad (visible on several subsequent pages; 216–231). Amy (re)writes the stories now on her own terms, perhaps creating the pages of the memoir we are reading. She writes, "To order the objects of real life, the things I can feel and name, reminds me that my life is my own, and it has not . . . been pre-written" (283). Through the comic medium, Amy can question the dominant cultural narratives of Jewish identity, of history, and of politics that she encounters.

The cracks not only represent escape routes within cultural narratives but also stand in for the creative process of drawing lines in order to tell stories of her own. She writes that in childhood she found "relief in the drawing of lines" (Kurzweil, *Flying Couch* 168). After graduation from college, Amy moves to Brooklyn, in a sense following the path of her bubbe's immigration to New York. She notices the cracks in sidewalks and walls, using them as inspiration to create her own story—this time a story that resists static cultural and familial memories of the past. Amy's work is no longer dominated by the maps and lines of her house or neighborhood or by images of her bubbe's story; rather, she determines the spaces around her by ordering them herself, interjecting her own story on top of her grandmother's in a way that feels comfortable to her. As maps appear at this point in the text, Kurzweil makes the process of ordering and creating stories evident. For example, as her bubbe tells of immigrating to the United States and moving to Michigan, Amy's drawing pad and computer lay on top of the map. The fourth wall is broken here, and Amy's creation process becomes transparent. In the process of drawing her own life, the cracks in her bubbe's story become lines of inquiry through which Amy connects various stories of historical displacement.

Drawing lines and geographic spaces gives Amy a sense of control over her story and Jewish identity and at the same time connects her to an artistic tradition. As she forges new lines, borders, and attachments through her own artistic interpretations she builds on the legacy of other graphic novelists/memoirists, often directly referencing artists like Art Spiegelman, Alison Bechdel, Miriam Katin, and Miriam Libicki through visual allusion (Kurzweil, *Flying Couch* 168). Kurzweil writes, "I dream in comics. . . . Ever since I was a little girl I've had this problem, a meta-haunting, a too-awareness of the self, of my own impermanence, my malleability. . . . I need something tougher than myself, something with edges and corners, something with a beginning, a middle, and an end" (248–249). She finds these corners and stability in the comics she reads—and finally in her own graphic work.

The visual medium creates a limited physical environment in which Kurzweil shows the ways that female bodies, objects, and emotions interact. The relationships between the three women within the work (Bubbe, Amy's mom, and Amy) center the ways that generations of women experience, inherit, and reimagine war. Even the artistic community that Amy chooses to identify with is largely made up of women. Within the memoir, Amy flees the hypermasculine arena of scholars and artists that influence her (Freud, Harvey Pekar, Will Eisner, and Theodore Herzl; 114–115) and instead opts for a women-centered world populated by artists like Alison Bechdel, Miriam Katin, Ariel Schrag, and Leela Corman (284).

In Kurzweil's and Krug's texts, the graphic devices and material proximities to outside forces show self-awareness and agency that move beyond destructive memories of war and trauma. In *Belonging*, for example, Krug's sense of agency and control over memory is illustrated by her bodily proximity to German symbols and ephemera as represented and altered by her own warm watercolor paintings. Perhaps most obviously, the cover of *Belonging* is a photograph of a German landscape of rolling hills and red-roofed homes. A childlike watercolor of Nora looking out over the landscape is superimposed onto the photograph in a whimsical and weighty exploration of familial-historical responsibility.

The cover of Krug's *Belonging* is a montage of a German landscape and a hand-drawn watercolor image of Nora standing on a rock. Her red-and-white polka-dotted avatar looks out over the house, hills, and lakes beneath her. This telling image is superimposed onto yellow-lined paper; green-and-orange watercolor clouds hover above the photograph of the landscape. This blend of found images with a looser, ethereal style placed on notebook paper (presumably inside the Leitz binder) creates an affective dissonance for the reader. Rather than conceal, justify, or explain her proximity to the Holocaust, Krug allows the archival photographs—along with her struggles to discover her family's role in the watery pages—to stand as testimony for her responsibility and shame. As Ahmed suggests, shame impresses upon the skin, as an intense feeling of the subject "being against itself" (*Cultural* 103). The juxtaposition of artistic mediums on the cover creates a structure of witnessing by the reader, a visual interpretation of how Krug unearths and faces feelings of shame. While feelings of shame generally include the desire for concealment (Ahmed, *Cultural*) Krug makes transparent the atrocious acts of the Germans and her family's role in that history.

The red-and-white polka-dot jacket that Nora wears in this montage is the same pattern as the mythic German mushroom she discusses in the chapter titled "Poisonous Mushrooms." The mushroom is not just a mushroom, as Krug reminds us, but represents the "poisonous Jew" in the popular anti-Semitic German tale she finds reproduced in her uncle's old-school notebook. Later in the text, Krug reveals that the red-and-white poisonous mushroom is associated with a 1938 collection of anti-Semitic children's stories that were given out freely to the public by the National Socialist Party. Krug includes the story in chapter 3 as a handwritten version from her uncle's school notebook. In the story, a mother warns her son against Jews, "Just like the poisonous mushroom can kill a whole family, the Jew can kill a whole people" (chap. 3).[21] By framing the book with this image, Krug associates herself in visual terms with the poisonous mushroom and the German anti-Semitism of the story and at the same time reveals her self-conscious position as a German in proximity to her family's Nazi past.

Sections of *Belonging* directly implicate the intergenerational responsibility of her family, testifying to her uncle's and family's role in the anti-Semitism of 1930s Germany.[22] An archival photo of Nora's mother wearing the handmade red-and-white mushroom costume associated with the anti-Semitic story acts as visual testimony to the family involvement in these cultural narratives (Krug chap. 3; fig. 2.9). The red-and-white polka dots on the clothing they wear implicate Nora, her mother, and her grandmother and signify that their bodies too are tied up with the myth of the Fatherland and its dangerous xenophobic narratives. Ahmed reminds us that emotions are not psychological states but rather social and cultural practices (*Cultural* 9). The visibility of social forms as in the case of the mushroom can align bodies against other bodies. That is, the signifying mushroom divides Germans from those they condemn; in the case of the poisonous mushroom, it aligns the German body against the Jew's body. Krug's memoir toggles between scathing revelations about her family's history and her own self-awareness of deep connections to her German roots and culture. In this same chapter, Nora describes a memory of her family foraging for edible mushrooms. She writes, "By eating the mushrooms, I feel as if I've become part of the forest" (fig. 2.9). Throughout the text she shows the desire to unearth and take responsibility for the buried Nazi connections of her German family while also revealing her own affective connection to Germany. Through design and metaphor, her work maps her embedded position in her family memory machine. As *Belonging* illustrates, unearthing the silences and taking public responsibility for narratives that we may not have directly participated in but in which we are implicated as citizens is a move toward more productive models of memory and cultural belonging.

Germany of course is not the only nation that grapples with national responsibility for historical oppression and murder. Writing about national shame, Ahmed argues, "The projection of what is unjust onto the past allows shame to be represented (here) as a collective shame that does not affect individuals in the present as it surrounds and covers them like a cloak or skin" (*Cultural* 102). In other words, past atrocities permeate our present world—even or especially if we do not face them head-on. In the United States, the repercussions of slavery and the subsequent century and a half of the systematic oppression of people of color are still present in the twenty-first century showing up as countrywide protests and in a recent backlash of seismic shifts in national policies and laws.

Krug does not present solutions to feelings of shame or guilt but admits her own confusion and uncertainty about the project. Near the end of the memoir, upon her return to Brooklyn from Germany, she likens her work to her overgrown garden. She muses, "Creating order in my domestic chaos promises simple satisfaction. But while I tear down the weeds, cut back the boxwood, prune the roses, while I pick up the diseased leaves, my mind is

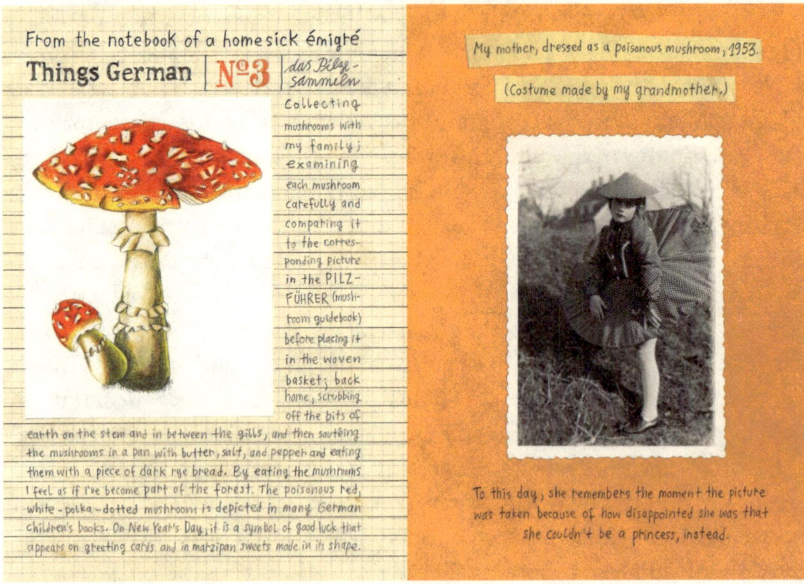

FIG. 2.9 "Things German No. 3" describes Nora's connection to the mushroom, while the facing page shows a photograph of Nora's mother wearing a poisonous mushroom costume (Krug 153).

preoccupied with Willi [grandfather], with my uncle Franz-Carl, and with the people I spoke to while I was away. I've excavated the shards of my relatives' existence, but I don't know yet how to piece them together" (chap. 13, "Peeling Wallpaper"). Indeed, as she implies, her fragmentary, mixed-media approach mirrors her unresolved and sometimes competing attachments.

In her investigation of her family's history, Krug exposes her family's National Socialist past and acknowledges her proximity to the narrative she uncovers. The German objects and archives that she includes suggest that German culture and memory are inseparable from her identity and sense of self. The juxtaposition of her desires for German comfort and for a transparent family history is not reconciled here. The meaning of home then for Krug must encompass the culpability of the past or as she says, the "inescapability of who we are" (chap. 14). There is no real "moving beyond" in *Belonging*; rather, Krug gestures toward one way to take responsibility for the past, toward one way to take the position of the implicated subject: She publicly recognizes her proximity to her German family's history and sits with the contradictions and shame it evokes. By doing so, she models a way to approach the often-paralyzing national shame of the past.

The graphic form in Krug's and Kurzweil's work mimics and subverts the bounded spaces of German and Jewish memory and their relation to identity:

the lines of home, affiliations with Israel and Germany, feelings of shame and fear, attachments to nationalist objects, and postwar cultural memory. In Judith Butler's terms, Krug's and Kurzweil's works reveal that as subjects, they "are acted upon" by social and discursive powers. The graphic form visually articulates Krug's and Kurzweil's *awareness* of the forces of memory and the cultural narratives that have shaped their identities; in this process of *sensing* the impact of outside forces, they illustrate their desire for agency within the process of memory transformation. As Butler argues, in sensing the cultural and political forces that shape us, we are already in the process of thinking and moving toward agency (*Senses* 15). Krug and Kurzweil make transparent the ways that memory and cultural narratives of war work to limit post–World War II Jewish and German identity. In doing so, they affirm *being acted upon* by these forces—but also create a "sense of the subject." The dual structure of sense is a cultivated sense of agency within which the "rupture with those formative relations" gives the subject a chance to respond in a more ethical way (Butler, *Senses* 10). For example, Kurzweil uses the wall cracks from Bubbe's Holocaust story to rearticulate a way forward, to create space for interpretation and new lines of inquiry for herself.

Reading across these two texts suggests at least three important conclusions for considering the future of Holocaust memory. First, the graphic devices in these works engage visually with the bordered territories on the space of the page, revealing the hegemonic structures of memory and their lasting repercussions on subsequent generations. The artistic devices like repurposed symbol, collage, and mixed medium in the context of war and memory allow for an affective rendering of World War II and its repercussions for new identities in the twenty-first century. Second, juxtaposing Kurzweil's and Krug's texts reveals a multidirectional memory that illustrates the destructive nature of repressed and unprocessed national violence; these two texts together connect not only German and Jewish experiences but also Native American genocide and racism in North America and the repercussions of national violence on contemporary renderings of memory, nationalism, and gender. Third, the voices of third-generation women here suggest more productive orientations of post-Holocaust memory and Jewish identity for the twenty-first century. By challenging the narratives of war that haunt their personal lives within the two-dimensional space of the page, they find new voices through which to tell these stories. In the graphic border poetics, Krug and Kurzweil recognize and *process* the burden of history on their lives, and by doing so, they create a dual structure of sense, a cultivated sense of agency within their overwhelming identification with family histories of World War II.

While Krug tries to uncover a family history that is steeped in silences and absences, Kurzweil reveals a desire to wrestle control of her own story from her bubbe's overwhelming narrative. Together these two texts explore the legacy of the Holocaust on third-generation Germans and Jews; we begin to see a multidirectional narrative that shows the implications of dominant narratives of Holocaust memory for younger generations across borders of nationalism.[23] Indeed, as Krug states in an interview, "I felt a growing urge to move beyond the abstract collective guilt I had come to feel. . . . I want my daughter to grow up with the same sense of responsibility, but without the paralyzing guilt" (Mouly). Through their family explorations, Kurzweil and Krug throw off secure stories and directly address previously unexamined attachments to burdens of war memory.

3

"The Drug of H"

Holocaust Addiction, Pulp Horror, and Jewish Identity

The cover of Bernice Eisenstein's *I Was a Child of Holocaust Survivors* shows a distorted figure of a young girl with oversized head and eyes in a pleated skirt and saddle shoes clutching a doll dressed in a suit, presumably a figure of her father. A bright light casts a shadow behind her, but the shadow is not in the shape of her own body as one might expect; instead, it casts two figures of her parents behind her (fig. 3.4b).[1] Above the young Bernice, the bold black-and-white text of the title, "I Was a Child of Holocaust Survivors," floats on a blood-red background, invoking the aesthetics of pulp horror novels and sensationalist B-movie posters.[2] The graphic choices of the cover image hint at the deep sense of responsibility that Bernice Eisenstein conveys for her parents' experiences as well as the dark shadow it casts on her own life. As Victoria Aarons writes, this image suggests "the indelible ways in which her parents' trauma has been grafted upon and subsumed by the author" (*Holocaust* 98). In this cover image, Bernice's family story is inserted into a genre of sensationalist fiction that exaggerates the trauma within the design of a kitsch aesthetic. The bright colors and distorted figures allude to expressionistic and pulp images that map her inherited trauma onto her family's narrative with dark, self-deprecating humor. Her graphic work plots visceral feelings and memories of the body onto contemporary spaces, showing the impact of Holocaust memory on twentieth-century Jewish culture and identity.

Eisenstein's graphic memoir *I Was a Child of Holocaust Survivors* (2006) is a coming-of-age story that follows a young Bernice as she navigates her family's Holocaust experiences. Eisenstein grew up in Toronto above her father's butcher shop just after World War II trying to make sense of the world of the adults around her, all survivors of the Holocaust. *I Was a Child of Holocaust Survivors* has been called a graphic memoir, an illustrated memoir, and a graphic novel, among other genres, and has been translated into ten languages.[3] Eisenstein has also illustrated an art book of poetry (written with Anne Michaels) that includes gouache portraits of important twentieth-century European intellectual figures from the period of the Holocaust (*Correspondences* 2013). Eisenstein's memoir is not a comic narrative by conventional standards. More text than image, she uses heavy prose and mostly unpaneled drawings to express childhood experiences with her family and her fantasies about them. Her stylistic drawings resonate with pulp-fiction illustrations as well as the artistic techniques and experimentations of the twentieth century.

Eisenstein recounts that while reading Primo Levi's *The Voice of Memory* as a girl, she was impacted by his answer to the question of how he was able to write about this time in Auschwitz: He says that writing worked "as a sort of 'prosthesis,' an external memory set up like a barrier between [his] life today and [his] life then" (95). While writing served as a sort of prosthesis for Levi, Eisenstein uses graphic images and objects to assist her in articulating her relationship to the absent or obscured family stories of the Holocaust. Eisenstein's work employs artistic style and objects as aids to a memory to which she has little or no access as a second-generation survivor. The objects are so integral to her body that she articulates them as artificial limbs—implying that she is missing a body part. Her body is a map for creating the narrative of her text; drawing objects and events in proximity to her own body creates affective narratives that assist her in moving through the text. Like an artificial limb or bionic body, she employs intellectual and artistic aids in her work. Objects and images such as clothing, dolls, rings, and books (her own memoir included) stand in for the voice she did not have as a young person, prosthetics for understanding the absent narrative of her family's experiences.

Eisenstein's first-person graphic narrative *I Was a Child of Holocaust Survivors* excavates the silences she experiences as a child through experimental form and structure. As Bernice travels through the fraught terrain of childhood as a second-generation survivor, she explores the ways that the memory of bodily violence is passed down in her family, suggesting that the experiences of insecurity, loss, and melancholy have a continued presence in bodies and landscapes. Eisenstein's stylistic form illustrates the ways that her fixation on the Holocaust narrative structured her young life and, in doing so, delivers a devastating critique of the addictive narrative of the Holocaust in contemporary Jewish identity. Through metaphors of drug addiction, references to pulp horror, and haunting stylistic form, Eisenstein's work asks how the devastating destruction of bodies affects Jewish cultural memory and, in turn, how the memory of destruction affects the living Jewish body.

Ingesting the Holocaust: Addictive Memory in Jewish Culture and Identity

As an eleven-year-old, Eisenstein has an epiphany while watching the Eichmann trial on TV (1961), an international event that her parents and their friends are drawn into deeply. This first televised trial of a Nazi war criminal took place in Israel. The evidence presented at the trial consisted primarily of survivors' testimony—thus giving a significant voice to those who had previously been discouraged from expressing their Holocaust experiences in the wider culture. As if her own parents were in the witness box, she writes, "Adolf Eichmann is on trial in Israel and in our rec room, with my parents and their friends seated in chairs" (19). Bernice views her parents and friends as witnesses and even as part of the jury in the trial she watches on television (24); like many survivors' testimonies at the center of the judicial and evidentiary process, her parents' stories are finally acknowledged and understood by Bernice.

The images of piles of emaciated bodies shown on television during the Eichmann trial changed Bernice's perception of her parents' experiences and, as a result, her perception of her own position in the Holocaust narrative. Framed as a drug habit, the addictive narrative of the Holocaust in the memoir becomes intricately intertwined with Bernice's identity and everyday life. Within Eisenstein's trope of addiction, the Eichmann trial is Bernice's gateway drug. Eisenstein writes, "I had always known my parents were survivors of the Holocaust. . . . Yet until today its relationship to me had remained invisible. . . . Pictures of skeletal bodies piled one on top of another are on the screen, and suddenly *I am injected with the white-heat rush of a new reality*" (19–20; emphasis mine). Bernice's visceral reaction to the screen events evokes a feeling in her body that coalesces her family's fear, loss, and pain into a single moment in time. At this moment Bernice's "addiction" begins: "The Holocaust is a drug and I have entered an opium den, having been given my first taste for free, innocently, by everyone here. I have only just glimpsed its power, scanning the trail of needle marks on the left forearms of each person in the room. This is when my addiction takes hold" (20). She describes the tattooed numbers of her parents and their friends as the "needle marks" of intravenous drug addicts, "an entry into a hallucinatory world of ghosts" (20). This obsession with Holocaust narratives becomes a self-proclaimed "addiction" that sustains her throughout her childhood.

As Bernice grows up, she realizes that her identification with the events in the Eichmann trial can be used as social capital in her everyday life. She explains that her addiction allows her to "socially trade" with other children to gain status or favors. Her parents' catastrophic experience becomes social currency from which she realizes she can benefit. She says to other children in the schoolyard, "Can I play with your shovel and pail? No? Well, my parents were in Auschwitz. . . . At recess: Stop pulling my pigtails because my parents were in Auschwitz" (21–22). Eisenstein's descriptions of these transactions contain a self-awareness that manifests as self-deprecating humor, a device that only partially breaks the tragedy of her circumstances. Bernice's use of her parents' Auschwitz experience as a means of gaining favors or sympathy from those around her reveals the depth of resonance and trauma that the Holocaust caused for Jews and the uncomfortable reactions of those around them. By employing a humorous parodic tone in the story about her younger self's obsession with the Holocaust, the retrospective voice of the more mature Eisenstein permeates the text to critique the child's position.

The Eichmann trial becomes a catalyst for Bernice's insatiable childhood search for "drugs" that create a "white-heat rush" in her body (20), a rush that she seeks in the form of stories, books, and information on the Holocaust. Bernice's expression of being addicted to Holocaust narratives is articulated as a visceral act: injecting information and feelings related to her family stories, which then pervade her behaviors, sense of self, and identity. A recreational drug is something taken into the body, a substance that is ingested to create a high or feeling of altered reality. Bernice imagines the Holocaust texts she gathers in cinemas and libraries as a powder she can ingest like cocaine: "Reels of film, along with printed pages from books, could all be chopped up into a fine powder, laid down, row upon row, and snorted" (20). The "den" of addiction that she describes is not singular to Bernice. The Eichmann trial gave voice to the hidden and previously shameful narratives of survivors with whom society was not ready to engage.

The uncontrollable desire or feeling of addiction that Eisenstein articulates in her work is a part of the larger cultural narrative that drove Jewish memory after the Eichmann trials. Jewish communities felt a weighty sense of responsibility to Holocaust memory. This sense of responsibility is apparent when Bernice's parents, who Bernice describes as "[Eichmann's] witnesses and jurors," whisper to her, "Never forget." Eisenstein writes, "Those words, mixed into a syringe's heady cocktail, not only overtook me in a dark room in our basement, *they were injected into the world: Attention must be paid*" (24; emphasis mine).[4] The phrase "Never forget" is a directive that commands Jewish communities to be vigilant about remembrance and to actively seek out ways to not forget or to remember. In this narrative, Bernice acknowledges that she is not the only addict to Holocaust memory but part of a much larger network of addicted survivors and their families. The phrase "Never forget" became synonymous with Jewish Holocaust memory and memorialization.

Affect—or in this case, a command and active desire to understand and identify with the Holocaust in Eisenstein's text—lies in the realm of aesthetics but at the same time is intimately intertwined with the ways the larger culture feels about and acts upon ideologies.

Dark humor again penetrates the serious tone of the narrative plot as Eisenstein imagines a Holocaust Anonymous program or a "Ten Commandment Step Program" for those addicted to the Holocaust. As she enters the room of addicts, she says, "Hello, everyone. I am addicted to the Holocaust. Today is my first day of being clean and I don't need the Holocaust anymore to feel like a worthy person" (25). In this statement, she realizes that basing her self-worth on a narrative of victimhood and genocide is ultimately destructive. Despite her self-awareness of the obsession with her parents' lives and trauma (and thus her own), she acknowledges that the Holocaust has become so much a part of her identity and her body that recovery would be an impossible task, an act that would damage her physically. She writes, "To rid myself of this habit, this calling, I would have to blind my eyes, cover my ears, seal my lips, and erase the truth that without the Holocaust I would not be who I am. It has seared and branded me with its stippled mark on my forearm and pulled me into its world, irrevocably, as its offspring" (25). Her sense of self is inextricably tied to her understanding and feeling about her parents' past and trauma; it is not a feeling or an identity that can be thrown off or stripped from her person. Continuing the dark addiction metaphor, Eisenstein recognizes the impossibility of "recovery" and, in doing so, acknowledges the heavy fallout of Holocaust memory on her life: "There is no Holocaust Anonymous to go to, no Ten Commandment Step Program, no audience to stand before" (25). While the book itself might be seen as evidence of an attempt at recovery, Eisenstein seems to suggest in its last pages that the Holocaust will always have a hold on her body and psyche. In this acknowledgment, Eisenstein reflects a fundamental conflict in postwar Jewish identity: While the Holocaust is a devastating and catastrophic event that must be remembered, the memory of the event also contains an element of danger in its enormity, the possibility of consuming both personal and collective Jewish history and identity.

Bernice's addiction is an extension of the way she views the Holocaust as overwhelming her world and her Jewish identity. Eisenstein's images illustrate the power of the Holocaust in the larger social fabric of her life and her sense of Judaism. In an image of Moses on Mount Sinai, Bernice imagines the Holocaust retroactively taking a place in the ancient biblical canon. A large drawing shows Moses standing on Mount Sinai holding a giant *H* in the place of the Ten Commandments (23). As he raises up the stone *H* for Holocaust, it emits flames or light beams (fig. 3.1).[5] An image of the young Bernice stands watching as Moses hands down Holocaust memory to the Jewish people.

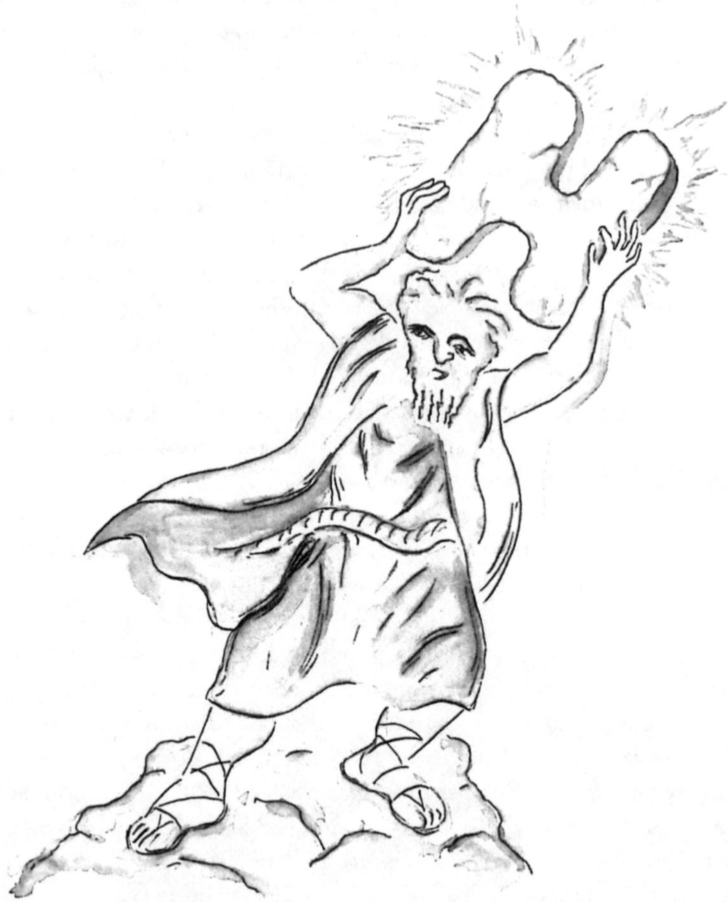

FIG. 3.1 Moses carries a large *H* for the Holocaust in place of the Ten Commandments.

In Bernice's consciousness, the stone tablet of *H* has replaced the set of laws handed to Moses by God.

While the humorous illustration shows young Bernice's confusion about the place of the Holocaust in her life, it also implies a darker shift. This image of Moses suggests the ways that an understanding of Judaism itself is dominated by the memory and history of the Holocaust. The tablet of the Ten Commandments, a set of imperatives that define Jewish law and culture, is replaced within the twentieth-century narrative of tragedy and genocide. Metaphorically, the centrality of the Torah and biblical stories that are foundational to Jewish thought and culture is replaced by the immensity of the Holocaust narrative. Instead of handing down God's laws, Moses is handing down the memory of the Holocaust, indicating a major shift in the defining space and time in Jewish history. Eisenstein suggests that the Holocaust has become a central narrative within Bernice's perception of Judaism and in her Jewish identity. As Miriam Harris argues, though some might see scenes like that of Moses holding up a giant *H* as blasphemy, they show some deeper truths: "The Holocaust has become a cornerstone of identity for many Jews, even those whose families were not in Europe during the war" (132). By equating Holocaust memory to biblical stories in the Torah, Eisenstein's work unveils the sacralized quality that the Holocaust and Jewish victimization have taken on in the postwar years.

Mapping an Artistic Lineage from the "Degenerates" to Pulp Horror

Eisenstein's memoir references artists and aesthetics that become an inextricable part of her visual *Künstlerroman*, or an artist's coming-of-age novel. By inserting visual references to works by post-Impressionist, Expressionist, and avant-garde artists, Eisenstein creates an extended artistic lineage for herself. In an interview, Eisenstein writes that she was influenced by Vincent van Gogh, Max Beckmann, George Grosz, and Saul Steinberg, along with Charlotte Salomon (Panofsky 135).[6] As the Nazi Party condemned the style of these modernist artists, many were forced to flee Europe, and many others were killed. Works by Beckmann, Chagall, Picasso, Matisse, and van Gogh, among others, were shown in the infamous *Degenerate Art* exhibit. Much of this work included collages and text/image combinations. Eisenstein's images resonate with the aesthetic works of twentieth-century artists like Matisse and Chagall and, in some cases, even mimic some of their iconic works. Eisenstein's unique style expresses the emotional and physical pain and loss experienced by her characters and at the same time illustrates the loss of Jewish art and culture in Poland (and in Europe more generally) during the war. Her representations of works by artists and writers who lived during the 1930s and '40s especially evoke a rich artistic tradition that was cut short in World War II.

Eisenstein's text acknowledges its roots in earlier Jewish artists and thinkers from its first pages. In an epigraph that precedes the title page, Charlotte Salomon, Bruno Schultz, Hannah Arendt, Elie Wiesel, and Primo Levi sit at a table around a game spinner discussing the challenges of expressing the Holocaust. The arrow of the spinner points between Salomon and Levi, perhaps giving the reader a clue as to Eisenstein's approach to her own memoir. A speech bubble containing advice about how to express one's story in the context of trauma and/or the Holocaust hovers above each character. Salomon's figure argues, "You must first go into yourself—into your childhood to be able to get out of yourself," while Levi's character says, "I fear that my language has become inadequate, that you need to speak a different language today." Eisenstein addresses these two approaches to memory expression in the content and structure of her graphic memoir. By using the child-author as a narrator who goes "into [her] childhood" as Salomon's character advises, along with experimental artistic techniques in answer to Levi ("a different language"), Eisenstein assigns agency to her younger self while illustrating the vulnerability of the childlike Bernice. Her book becomes the voice she did not have as a young person, a first-person retrospective narrative of the shadows of her parents' experiences. While Eisenstein uses stylized expressionistic and pulp images along with dark humor to fill the absences of the Holocaust, she also creates an extended artistic family lineage. In doing so, she draws her way out of the gaps and absences left by the Holocaust and into a position of agency as the artist-author of her own life story.

The thinkers and artists of prewar Europe help Eisenstein articulate the terror and silence of her parents' past. Her explicit visual references to specific artists and works, such as *La Danse* (or *Dance I*) by Henri Matisse,[7] are macabre, humorous, and self-reflective (fig. 3.2). In one image, Eisenstein replaces Matisse's dancers with her parents and aunt and uncle in the chapter titled "Two Brothers, Two Sisters" (130). She tells the story of how her father's brother marries her mother's sister, their stories of surviving the war, and their role in her childhood (132–137). Matisse's dancing figures, often associated with hedonism, take on a more somber, ironic dance in the context of the four young people's Holocaust experiences (fig. 3.2). Eisenstein's four naked figures look awkwardly at one another as they dance through a pool of water. In the accompanying prose text, Eisenstein suggests the river is symbolic of the Rivers Phlegethon, Cocytus, Styx, and Lethe, the mythical rivers of fire, wailing, the dead, and forgetfulness, respectively (132). Memory, too, she reminds the reader, is associated with water. In this image, her art celebrates the survival and love of her parents, aunt, and uncle but also acknowledges the dark past from which they emerge. Eisenstein's references to early twentieth-century European artists in part constitute a return to the site of prewar culture and artistry, a site of mourning and revival simultaneously. By shifting the artistic and historical context of earlier artworks like Matisse's *La Danse*, Eisenstein's illustrations assist her in expressing and processing her family's past.

Eisenstein incorporates these artists into her own world of artistic expression in part to fill the absence of understanding in her own family and, at the same time, to evoke the artists' importance in her own artistic development. Studying the works of artists like Matisse and Chagall

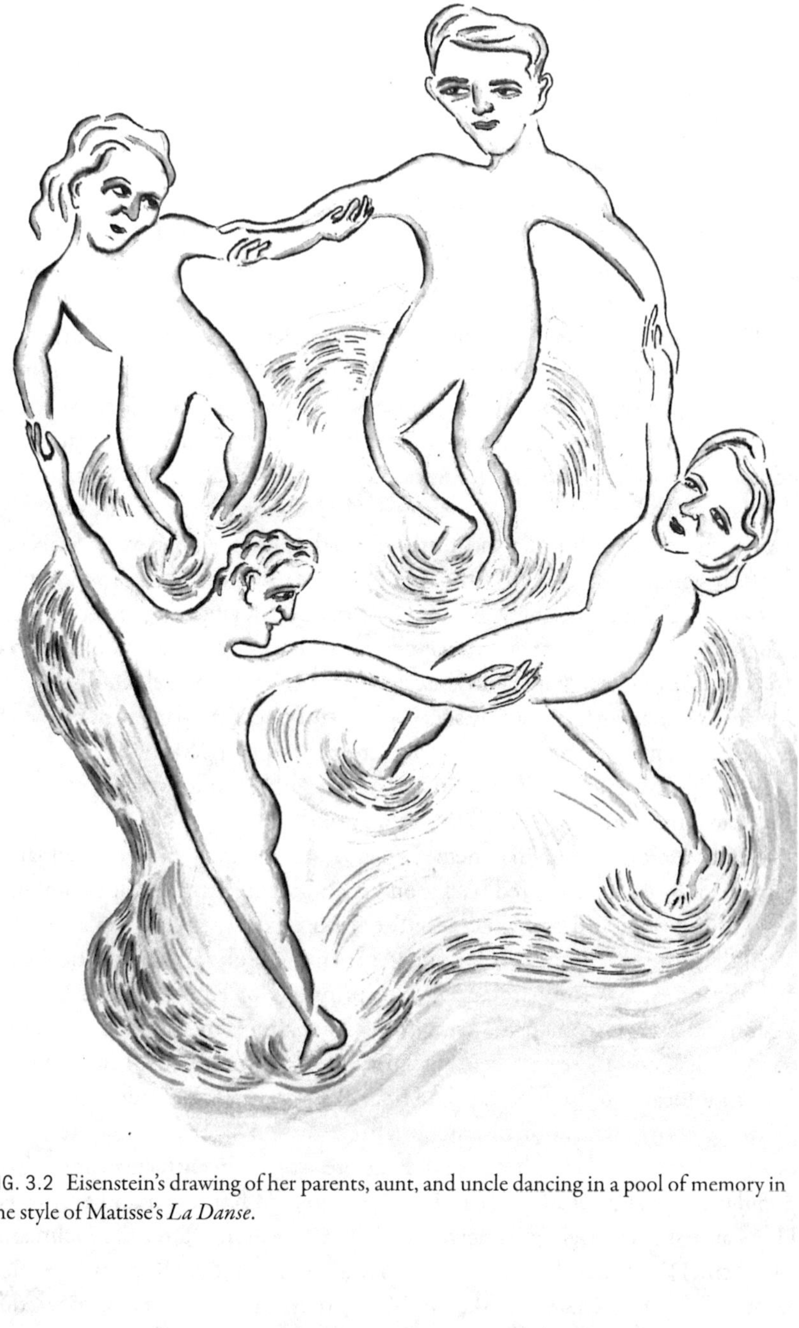

FIG. 3.2 Eisenstein's drawing of her parents, aunt, and uncle dancing in a pool of memory in the style of Matisse's *La Danse*.

becomes a way for her to reconnect to the lost world of European artists from her parents' generation—and, perhaps most importantly, to infuse the prewar art world into her work. In doing so, Eisenstein suggests the continuity and contemporary relevance of these artists: The paintings of Salomon, Cezanne, Chagall, and others illustrate a world that existed before the war and that represented a wide and rich artistic tradition and identity rather than a more narrow, circumscribed identity based in war and victimhood. In creating a graphic narrative that incorporates the legacy of these artists, Eisenstein closes an artistic gap or rupture caused by the war. Eisenstein's images resonate with the celebrated aesthetic works of European artists but also, more surprisingly, with the less-celebrated American pulp fiction of the 1930s and '40s.

While much has been written about the references to European artists in Eisenstein's work, scholars have not discussed her allusions to American pulp horror and Stalag fiction. Perhaps Eisenstein's pulp-fiction aesthetic is less obvious than her allusions to well-known European painters. American pulp-fiction novels were popular genre fiction printed as affordable paperbacks between 1890 and 1950. Pulp genres included horror, mystery, espionage, science fiction, and humor and featured bold aesthetics that were conveyed through sensationalist covers. The bright covers often used shadowed bubble font coupled with enticingly grotesque or risqué drawings (fig. 3.3) that were designed to sell the inexpensive paperbacks (hence the name "pulp" derived from the use of cheap paper). Eisenstein's use of the aesthetic elements of pulp fiction, together with her family's Holocaust story, acts as a parody of the genre as well as a metacritique of her approach to her parents' tragic past. Eisenstein's pulp aesthetic may be considered distasteful by some in the context of a Holocaust memoir, but perhaps this is her point.

The cover of Eisenstein's memoir features a bold, shadowed black-and-white font against a dark-red background, mimicking typical color combinations of the pulp and Stalag genres. The featured cover image of a small girl with a large head holding a doll resonates with the Holocaust pulp title *House of Dolls* (fig. 3.4a). The hardcover (sixth printing) of *House of Dolls* features a gaunt, ghostlike woman drawn with heavy shading, much like Eisenstein's cover image, and its style is reminiscent of the drawings within the memoir. Israeli Holocaust pulp fiction, called Stalag fiction, used the pulp-fiction aesthetic to convey sensationalist fictionalized accounts of the Holocaust and often included pornographic stories that were set in concentration camps. The popular cultural interest in narratives that depicted fetishized and eroticized Holocaust stories reached its height during the 1960s, just after the Eichmann trial. Yehiel De-Nur, otherwise known as Ka-Tzetnik 135633, the popular Holocaust pulp author, was even asked to be a witness in the Eichmann trial, adding credibility and weight to his sensationalized narratives of the Holocaust.[8]

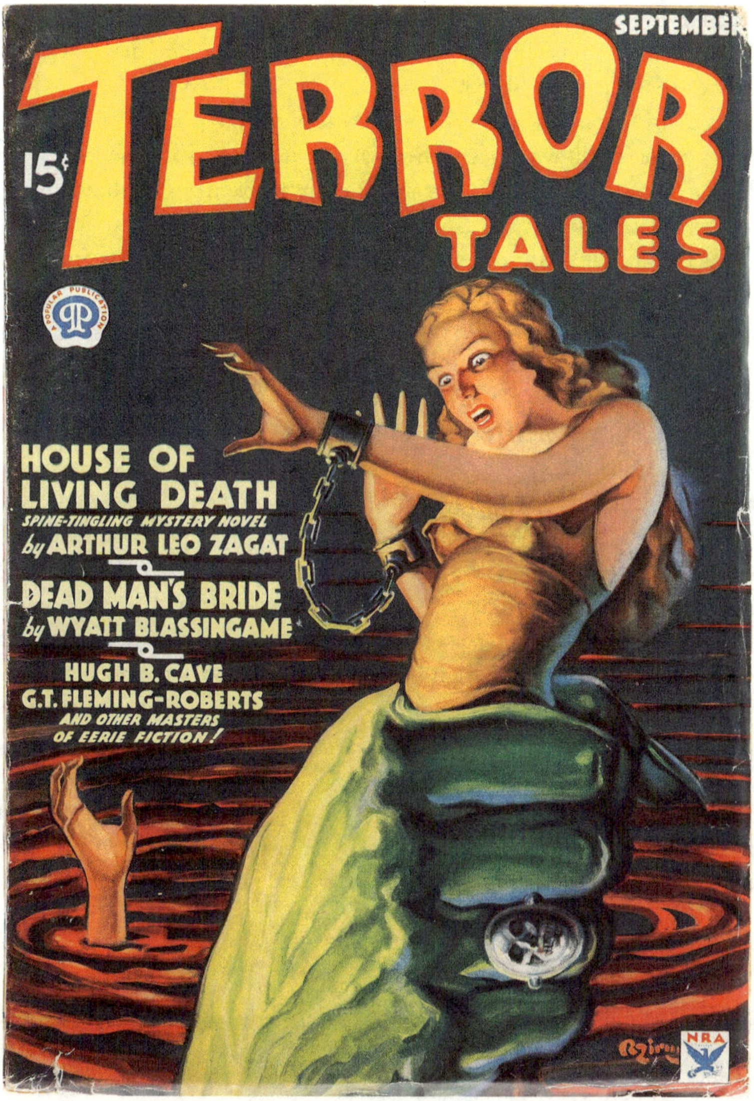

FIG. 3.3 American pulp-fiction comic with shaded and stylized font, published in 1940 (*Terror Tales*, edited by Harry Steeger, Popular Publications, vol. 12, no. 3).

Many of the so-called Stalags featured sadomasochistic plots—often involving female camp guards and Allied soldiers. Amit Pinchevski argues that these novels acted "as a text upon which the Israeli young generation negotiated issues of power and identity" (387). The survivors who arrived in Israel were encouraged to keep silent about the horrors of the past, and many were sent to the south to hospitals that would physically contain the carriers of the stories. The precursor to these Stalag authors was Ka-Tzetnik 135633, author of the first Holocaust memoirs and the famous *House of Dolls* (1953), a book that was taught in Israeli high schools and that was eventually translated into twelve languages (Mikics).[9]

Instead of a somber account of Holocaust memory, Eisenstein's memoir exudes a parodic self-awareness of her place in the genre. The flashy and kitschy pulp-fiction aesthetic reflects Eisenstein's awareness of the ways that Holocaust stories translate into cultural capital (a point she makes earlier in her text and one that has been made by other artists and scholars, including Art Spiegelman and Michael Rothberg). The cover shows a self-awareness of her own story as firmly placed within this genre, and at the same time—through the self-deprecating humor in her brash allusions to pulp horror—Eisenstein resists Stalag fiction's fetishization of the Holocaust (fig. 3.4). The metaphor of addiction and the visual references to pulp horror not only inject humor into her text but move the Holocaust out of a state of cultural reverence (often American culture's default) and into the more visceral and emotional realm of drug dens and soft-cover, dime-store horror novels. By desacralizing the narrative of the Holocaust, she allows the reader to grapple with the complexity and messiness of its legacy for survivor families and for Jewish culture more widely.

Eisenstein's allusions to Stalag and pulp-fiction aesthetics, such as dark shading and oversized heads, highlight the vulnerability of the body and at the same time pose a challenge to the reader. How *does* one represent the abject bodies of friends and family at the hands of the Nazi death machine? Her illustrations depict a struggle with the difficult reality of bodily decimation in the Holocaust as well as the absence of voices and bodies her family feels. In this sense, form mimics the cultural resonances of the Holocaust in Bernice's life of ghosts, dolls, and uncanny shadows, a way of expressing loss and vulnerability.

The Legacy of the Holocaust: Bodies Etched with Memory

I Was a Child of Holocaust Survivors is a particularly fertile text for understanding and depicting the body as vulnerable. Addiction itself is a position of extreme vulnerability. It suggests, humorously in this case, that Eisenstein is not in control of this narrative—rather, the narrative holds her body and emotions in its grip. Emotion is essential to our sense of fear and insecurity and to how we understand our bodies' position in the culture around us. Like other artists and scholars in this study, Eisenstein shows the ways that identities that are rooted in war, memory, trauma, and victimhood create a sense of insecurity—a sense of bodily vulnerability and fear that remains into the second and third generations. Exploring the ways that bodies are shaped by emotion is imperative to understanding the future of both individual and public feelings and rhetorics.

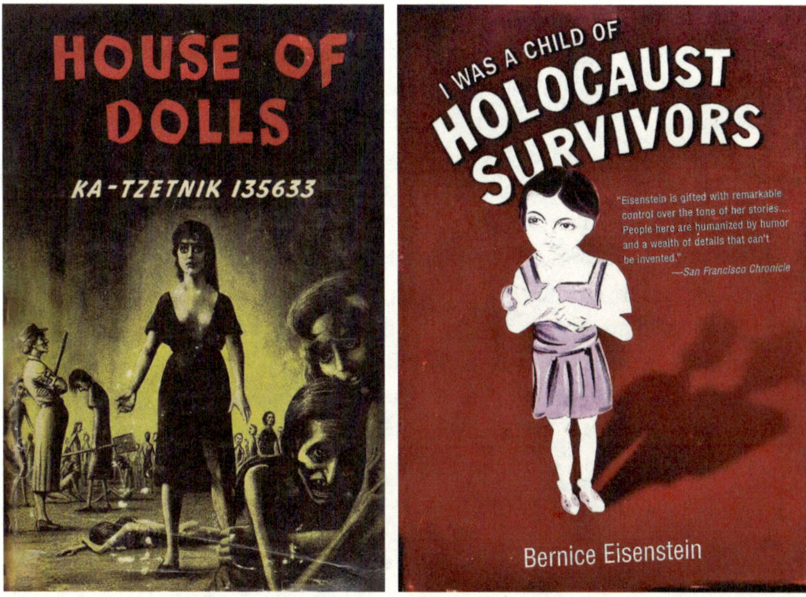

a b

FIG. 3.4 The cover of an English translation of Ka-Tzetnik's *House of Dolls* from 1956 (*a*) compared to Eisenstein's cover (*b*).

Discussions of fear and victimization in the Holocaust are often intertwined with shame; for example, the female body and the feminized body of the victimized Jew in World War II are often portrayed as "soft" or emotional. As Sara Ahmed writes, "'Being emotional' comes to be seen as a characteristic of some bodies and not others.... In order to discover how this process works, we need to discover how emotions operate to 'make' and 'shape' bodies as forms of action" (*Cultural* 4). In contrast to the "soft" affective depiction of the Jewish body, the narrative of the "new Jew" in Israel has been reinvented as a strong, militarized body, one that would ensure that the slogan "Never Again" would hold true.[10] In the context of Eisenstein's memoir, tropes of addiction, the pulp horror aesthetic, and the child's body (often shown unclothed) all show a deep vulnerability of the self in the shadow of such a monumental and terrifying history, a vulnerability that demands protection and vigilance.

The phrase "Never Again" becomes central to Bernice's life just after the Eichmann trials. Her work makes clear the detrimental weight of the vow that young Bernice takes upon herself. In the context of the memoir, the phrase encapsulates a sense that the weight of the memory of the Holocaust is an obligation on the living that is itself unbearable. Eisenstein likens her compulsion for Holocaust narratives to an addictive drug that is injected into the body, the needle marks of the drug visible as tattooed numbers or as the shadows of those numbers on survivor families. This weighty comparison acts not only as an affective description but also as a warning: Carrying the memory of the dead and the responsibility of the Holocaust as a promise into the future ("Never Again") ravages Bernice's life.

In the larger culture, the phrase "Never Again" takes on several meanings depending on the context, audience, speaker, and speaker's intention. The rhetorical power of the phrase in Eisenstein's work, one mirrored in the dominant Jewish culture in the form of Yom HaShoah and Holocaust literature, is tied to the human destruction and to the emotional toll these horrors took on the Jewish people and culture. At the same time, the phrase is an imperative or demand exacted from the survivors on behalf of the dead—"I/you/we will never forget!"—and implies a communal promise in the negative: "We the Jewish people" will never let this atrocity happen to us again (a protective stance based on creating security for the vulnerable or precarious body). Might a shift in the rhetorical speaker of "Never Again" have the potential to reshape Holocaust memory and its burden on survivors and Jews more generally? In the larger American culture and in more interfaith circles, the phrase takes on the connotation that "all of us, Jews and non-Jews" will not let this happen again; this meaning is a protective stance, but this time it includes a promise from a larger community to share the responsibility of security. This second meaning takes part of the obligation and weight off the Jewish community alone and creates a promise of security from Jews and non-Jews alike. A third meaning of "Never Again," and perhaps the least common understanding of the three, suggests that "we" ourselves will never commit or support genocide or violence against minoritized people; this third meaning is an active humanitarian stance that focuses on a promise of the speaker(s) to take responsibility for the ethical treatment of others.

Eisenstein's text shows the destructiveness of the weight of "Never Again" (the first meaning) as an internalized narrative in Bernice's life in various ways. The metaphor of addiction structures the young Bernice's compulsion toward—and proximity to—the Holocaust narrative in Eisenstein's work. Bernice's addiction takes several forms, including leveraging a Holocaust-based identity to get recognition, reimagining Holocaust narratives as part of the biblical canon, and wearing clothes or physical markings that make her feel connected to the Holocaust. The text is not simplistic in its depiction of Bernice's obsession, however. The homunculus, or child narrator, that Eisenstein describes is a combination of a naive child and an older, wiser voice. The stylized images and artistic choices that Eisenstein presents show the meta-analysis of Bernice's younger actions and feelings. Bernice's more mature retrospective voice seeks out a more productive way to express and perhaps live with the compulsion to express the Holocaust.

Eisenstein's experimentation with structure and style illustrates the struggle to represent her memory of her parents' past adequately. Within the various forms in her text, she finds a unique voice that is attuned to the intellectual and artistic struggles of Holocaust representation. Her self-reflective approach echoes the words of Charlotte Salomon in the epigraph, "You must first go into yourself—into your childhood to be able to get out of yourself" (7). Her representation of the body, and the child's body in particular, shows a meta-awareness of the visceral fallout of the Holocaust.

The Abject Body Speaks

Eisenstein's use of the horror aesthetic in representations of the body articulates her deep desire to understand and be part of the *present* of the Holocaust. Though Eisenstein makes it clear that her own body was never in *physical* danger (as she did not experience the Holocaust firsthand), she explores how the young Bernice internalizes the psychological and physical markers that were imposed by her parents. She clarifies for the reader, "My life was not cursed, theirs [her parents] was. They were born with an unfavorable star and forced to sew it onto their clothing. Yet here I am, some Jewish Sisyphus, pushing history and memory uphill" (53). Bernice suggests that though she herself is not in the same position as her parents, she is compelled to grapple with the abjectness of her parents' experience.

Within Eisenstein's style, it is difficult *not* to see a reflection of the grotesqueness of the abject and discarded body at the hands of the Nazi death machine. While the figure of the young Bernice struggles with the horrors of the past on the plot level, Eisenstein's stylized images reflect the reality of the decimation and abuse of the body in the Holocaust. The pulp horror aesthetic in Bernice's distorted body suggests a kind of monstrous identity that reflects an inherited sense of shame and burden, a burden that is affirmed by the larger culture around her and that in turn "rewards" her for taking on this identity. By taking on this unbearable weight, the young Bernice is consumed by an identity born out of the Holocaust years after its conclusion.

One of the ways Eisenstein illustrates this legacy of Holocaust trauma is through the poignant depiction of the child narrator. Eisenstein's first image, that of an unclothed young girl in a position of remembering and mourning, resonates with subsequent tropes that evoke the female body and its relation to vulnerability and memory. Early in her text, Eisenstein writes, "I am lost in memory. It is not a place that has been mapped, fixed by longitude and latitudes" (19). Though Eisenstein's work does not use traditional maps as in Kurzweil's work (chap. 2) or structures of experience as in Libicki's text (chap. 1), the body becomes a map for Eisenstein, a way to connect with the darkness of her parents' experiences and to process her parents' feelings.[11] In

Eisenstein's work, emotions are material rhetoric that has significant affective power. As Sara Ahmed suggests, the starting point of orientation is the position of the body: "the 'here' of the body and the 'where' of its dwelling" (*Queer Phenomenology* 8). Eisenstein's "here of the body" is the depiction of a child character, unclothed and unprotected, who dwells in the pervasive loss and memory of her parents' world; the young female body becomes a way to map the residue of emotion and trauma of her past in relation to the world around her.

In terms of location, most of Eisenstein's figures are set within a missing/absent backdrop or setting. The figures of Bernice and her family are often drawn within a dark opaque backdrop or just floating on the blank white paper of the page (see figs. 3.1, 3.2a, 3.4b, and 3.5). The absence of any context in these backgrounds seems to signal the missing memory and information for which Bernice is constantly looking. As Ahmed writes, we find our orientation by turning "this way and that . . . until we find our bearings" (*Queer Phenomenology* 1), but in the case of Eisenstein's images, the opaque and missing settings signal her lack of bearings as a second-generation survivor.

Bernice tries to "find her bearings" by rehearsing her parents' past experiences. One way she does this is by mimicking the physical markings that her parents were forced to wear during the Holocaust. She adorns herself with outward markings of "Jewishness" as defined by the Holocaust. Bernice rehearses her parents' experiences in moments of proximal devastation, creating a metanarrative that speaks to ways that residues of physical markings continue to impact subsequent generations. The young Bernice uses several affective objects to articulate her deep desire to be a part of the continued presence of the Holocaust. Eisenstein's depiction of the body in relation to objects gestures toward an orientation that moves closer to the Holocaust experience. The figure of Bernice, for example, is drawn in proximity not only to objects like a memorial stone but also to metal chicken tags and her father's wedding ring.

The Child Narrator and Prosthetic Objects

Through the character of the child, Eisenstein illustrates the visceral experiences of a second-generation survivor trying to understand her parents' loss. The book's title page shows a small, unclothed girl without clothes atop a pile of books. The child, in the position of Rodin's thinker, is a serious contemplative figure who is incongruous in time, at once showing a small Bernice with her already-finished book from 2006. The haunting childlike figure sits atop a book titled *I Was a Child of Holocaust Survivors*. The vulnerable position of a young girl unclothed and exposed to the world alongside the words "I was a child of Holocaust survivors" creates an uncomfortable juxtaposition of the unprotected female body and the memories of one of the most horrific, body-destroying events in the twentieth century. In an interview, Eisenstein explains that she created a visual persona that represents her eight-year-old self and her forty-year-old self at once. She calls this merging of past and present selves "ironic, playful, philosophical, confused and serious, angry and loving" (Panofsky 137). The image of the author-child allows Eisenstein to return to her early memories while interpreting them through a retrospective lens. On the one hand, the small, unclothed child atop these books reveals feelings of bodily insecurity in the face of Holocaust memory; on the other hand, the books she sits upon testify to her position as an intellectual and published author, the figure of a mature adult who can reflect on the feelings and actions of the small vulnerable child.

The various narrative tracks alongside the image deepen the theoretical power of the text. These tracks include the first-person retrospective prose, first-person simultaneous speech track, and the image track that "speaks" differently to (and apart from) the other voices. The whole of these three narrative tracks is greater than the sum of their parts: Each track engages with and changes the ways the reader interprets the other tracks. These simultaneous narratives provide room for one of these tracks to comment on or theorize another track, in effect processing events or feelings from a different perspective or in a different voice. The comic form—that is, an image of the young, vulnerable Bernice—along with the analysis of her position embodies subjectivity. The various tracks—image and text—make it possible to visualize something that may be impossible to articulate in prose alone: silences, bodily intensities, and familial or historical fractures. This method offers a way to express contradictory feelings or intersecting identities that thinks through the ideas it represents. In doing so, Eisenstein gestures toward a way to theorize larger structural issues of cultural loss, Jewish memory, and bodily vulnerability.

The image of the unclothed figure from the title page reappears in the first chapter of the book. This time Bernice sits on a memorial stone, a rock in a triangular shape that Eisenstein uses throughout the book to represent the rocks that are set on gravestones as a sign of respect and mourning in the Jewish tradition. Eisenstein maps Bernice's proximity to fear, vulnerability, and mourning more than sixty years after the war. Bernice's physical orientation on the page places her squarely on top of a marker of the past and a manifestation of her affective environment of mourning/loss. Bernice is shaped by what *she comes into contact with*; in this case, the emotions of Eisenstein's childhood are assigned to an object (the rock) that represents her experiences in the present. By situating the small figure of Bernice on the rock, Eisenstein opens a way to express her proximity and orientation to the Holocaust through her body's position. The memorial stone becomes a motif that represents her journey to understand her parents' lives and trauma. In the drawing of the vulnerable young Bernice, the too-large head, unclothed body, and gaunt features speak to the detrimental effects of the narrative she takes on, a narrative that has haunted and perhaps subsumed Bernice as a young person. The solidity of the rock and its status as a memorial symbol suggest an ossification of a devastating narrative of war and violence—one perhaps best represented in the horror genre.

Jewish life during the war years included visual and physical markers of otherness that symbolized the removal of Jewish bodies from state or legal protection. Symbols like the yellow star that many Jews were forced to wear marked bodies as outside of the law and thus "bare" and unprotected.[12] These markings made them recognizably "other" and helped create a rhetorical separateness that led to the death and destruction of the Jewish people. This suspension of legal status or state of exception created by the National Socialist Party deemed the Jewish body, for all intents and purposes, disposable. Markings like yellow stars sewn onto clothing and later the numbered tattoos etched onto the arms of people sent to concentration camps, haunt the cultural stories of the Holocaust.

Eisenstein uses objects like her father's wedding ring, his sweater, and greasy chicken tags to explore her relationship to emotional loss and precarity. In one image, a small Bernice wears a necklace and bracelet made from the small metal tags that were taken off the slaughtered chickens from her father's butcher shop (fig. 3.5). She tells the reader, "When I strung together the kosher chicken tags as jewelry, I discovered that 'kosher' spells 'Jew' sideways. . . . My neck and wrist are always greasy. I made gifts for my bubbe and aunt but they never wore them. They had their own tags" (see fig. 3.5). The greasy metal clips that marked the chicken carcasses as kosher become a stand-in for the physical signs that marked her parents' bodies as Jewish in the Holocaust. In place of the yellow star, Bernice uses oily chicken tags as jewelry to emulate her parents' and her grandparents' experiences. Bernice's recognition of the spelling of "Jew" in the tags becomes a way to understand and claim her own identity, one that is created *sideways* through a symbol intended to mark the processing of slaughtered poultry. The irony and humor of Bernice wearing these tags as adornments to mark her Jewish identity is not lost on the reader. The grease and smell associated with the dead poultry make young Bernice's attempt to understand her parents' bodily markings visceral, while at the same time, they underscore the impossibility of her replication of those experiences. Instead, this image illustrates *an absence of experience* as it is manifest in the humorous makeshift metal jewelry. As an inadequate stand-in for her parents' experiences in Auschwitz, the tags instead become a marker of her visceral desire to connect with that lost world.

The tags she puts on *herself* of course do not equate with markings forced upon her parents under the Nazis, as Eisenstein's humorous metanarrative

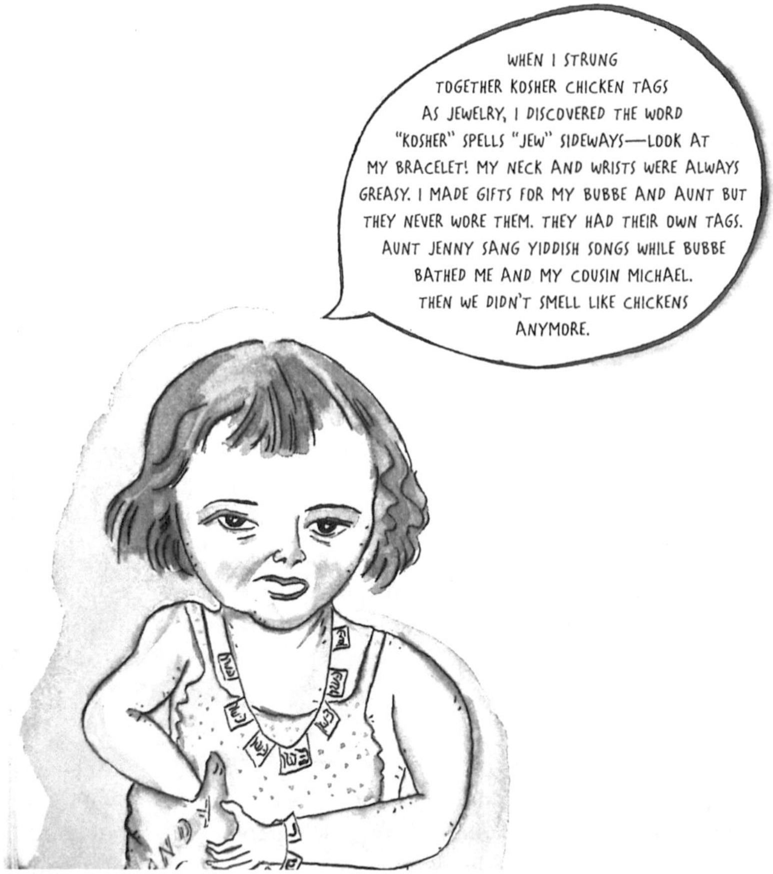

FIG. 3.5 Bernice makes jewelry for herself out of metal chicken tags. Each tag is marked "kosher" in Hebrew and, when turned sideways, reads "Jew" (52).

implies. The bodily markers that are forced upon her parents, first in the form of the yellow star and then later in the inked numbers that are etched permanently into their arms, mark experiences of precarity, loss of identity, and subjugation. Perhaps the most poignant image of bodily marking in the memoir is in a drawing of an old photograph of three women—her mother, grandmother, and aunt—sitting side by side, staring up at the camera, and holding up their arms to expose the tattooed numbers there: 54090, 54092, and 54091 (112). The sequential numbers on their arms mark the order in which they entered the camps, but more importantly, they show that the three women entered together and survived together. The tattoos are physical markers of the female lineage of Bernice's family, a collective experience that connects the women in her family—an experience that Bernice is not a part of despite her attempts to mark herself. The young Bernice comments on the image of the three women, "I briefly saw something I'd never seen in them or never recognized—a kind of innocence, a lightness, as if their arms don't even carry the mark of the past" (113). Despite the heavy burdens of Holocaust memory that Bernice takes on as a child, she realizes in this drawing of a photograph that the women in her family who experienced the horrors of the Holocaust are focusing on their present lives and relationships with one another, at least at this moment.

An image of the small Bernice stands near the photograph holding paint brushes, as if she has just created the image herself. She says in a retrospective voice: "When I found this photo recently, I couldn't believe it. My mother, grandmother, and aunt posed as I wanted to draw them—sitting close together wearing watches, their numbers in a row" (113). Though Bernice sits outside of this photograph, she is a part of its legacy, painting it and making it visible to herself and to others. As the artist of her family's story, she shows that she has the agency to shape the narrative of the past. The violence that was inflicted upon these three women in the Holocaust does not belong to Bernice but is a part of her experience as a child survivor. Instead of sitting on a stone of mourning, vulnerable and unclothed, the Bernice in this image is the artist/creator of the family story.

Conclusion

The end of the Eichmann trial cements Bernice's lifelong addiction to the Holocaust. Eichmann's sentence does not bring her relief or closure; rather, her life becomes framed by the trial and the outcome. When Eichmann is sentenced to death by the judge, she writes "I knew from that day on that I had been sentenced as well" (26).[13] Just below this text, a drawing of barracks wrapped in barbed wire illustrates Eisenstein's sense of proximity to the horrors her parents experienced in the camps. Ghostlike faces are crowded in the windows, looking out through the barbed wire and dark trees that cage them in. Through Bernice's relation to objects that move her closer to her parents' experiences, Eisenstein points toward a reorientation to the past. Her proximity to alienation, loss, and fear is painfully apparent and literally visible on the space of the page. Within the recognition of the addiction to pain and loss though is an opening, an opportunity to adjust direction. Eisenstein's art and creativity become a record of this responsibility but also afford her the choice of how to tell and paint her own story.

In an image of her parents' friends' annual memorial Yizkor gathering (remembrance of the dead), distorted figures are surrounded by the words of the Kaddish or Jewish prayer of mourning. Eisenstein writes that the importance of remembering the Holocaust dead is a sentiment she has heard all her life (168–169). Hebrew and English words swirl around the hunched bodies, some with heads in hands, ghostlike faces and bodies pushed out of shape, contorted by age but also disfigured by death and pain of loss.[14] Speaking in a first-person retrospective voice, Bernice continues her musings about memory and asks herself, "Can I be trusted to look into my heart and find theirs?" (19). As if to answer Eisenstein's question, the ghosts respond, "We have no room here for her. Dahlink, Go—dance, live. It's enough just wanting to speak our names" (18). The ghosts suggest that Bernice move out of a world steeped in the living dead and decimated bodies and into a life away from fear and nostalgia. Eisenstein's text becomes a way for her to speak the names of the survivors while at the same time moving into the world of the living herself. In contrast to the pulp-fiction genre that she references, Eisenstein's work is a careful and poetic account of her observations and feelings around the residues of her parents' Holocaust experiences and the long-term consequences and impact of the Holocaust on individual Jews and Jewish identity.

4

"Work for the Future, Not Only for Memory"

Agency, Activism, and Joy in the Works of Leela Corman and Julia Alekseyeva

> In the world of the living, I find that I have fallen in love with Poland, with Papa's mountains, with beautiful Krakow, a city of cafes and bookshops and layers of history, MY history, too, that calls me back. And with the work of the people I met there, which is, at its heart, profoundly anti-fascist. *It is work for the future, not only for memory.*
>
> —Leela Corman, "You Are Not a Guest"

Several scholars have argued that the Holocaust has had an outsized influence on Jewish American identity, as discussed in chapter 3. Historians Ewa Stanczyk and Peter Novick suggest that the Holocaust has become the central unifying event in American historical memory and Jewish American identity.[1] Instead of a focus on religious practice or the social consciousness that was once a hallmark of American Jewry, death and destruction are now common identifiers (Novick 10). Other scholars have claimed that a focus on the uniqueness of the Holocaust in some cases has prevented Jews from identifying with other victims of oppression due to the comparison of atrocities.[2] In other words, instead of focusing on human connection, shared values, and social justice issues across borders of identity, Jewish identity since the 1970s has shored up its borders to emphasize an identity of victimhood.

Instead of the dread and trauma that often constitute narratives of victimhood,[3] Leela Corman's and Julia Alekseyeva's graphic memoirs develop contemporary agentic identities based in rich cultures, family connections, and the strength of ancestors. Their works rehearse a liberatory aesthetic that models a socially conscious activist Jewish identity.[4] In the quotation that begins this chapter, Corman aligns herself with the activism of the Poles she meets while exploring her grandparents' past in Poland. She suggests that the antifascist work of her new friends and indeed her art and writing are essential to making changes in the world, or as she articulates it, "It is imperative work for the future, not only for memory" (Corman, "You Are Not"). While the memories of Soviet oppression, Polish anti-Semitism, and the Holocaust loom large in Jewish collective memory, Alekseyeva and Corman forge connections with their family's pasts in these locations and, in doing so, shift the persistent Jewish identification with oppression toward a narrative based in agency and political change.

Leela Corman is the author of several graphic narrative texts including *Unterzakhn* (2012), *We All Wish for Deadly Force* (2016), *You Are Not a Guest* (2023), and *Victory Parade* (2024). She publishes comics and illustrations in *The New York Times*, *Nautilus*, *The Nib*, *Tablet*, and *Bust*, among others. *Unterzakhn* was nominated for the *Los Angeles Times* Book Award and the Eisner Award. She teaches at the Rhode Island School of Design and the Sequential Artist Workshop. Corman's work uses unique graphic devices to give voice to women's narratives and to make women's bodies visible. The bold strokes and strong, angular lines in her work are often colored with bright water-based paints—a medium that allows for the mixing and blending of images and metaphors on the space of the page.

In several of her short autobiographical works, Leela Corman returns to sites of her family's former life in Poland, using visual rhetorics and artistic techniques to articulate how Leela's experiences in twenty-first-century Poland merge with Holocaust narratives.[5] While Leela sinks into the lyrical and familiar landscape of her grandparents' former lives in Poland, she is persistently haunted by the memories of the Holocaust that have been passed down to her. Her body is both drawn to and repelled by the landscapes and people she visits; she sees herself as abject (as a Jewish survivor in Poland) and at the same time as intimately connected to the people and land of Poland. On her journey she forges a profound connection to the living landscapes and people of her family's past. I look at four of Corman's interrelated short comics in this chapter: "You Are Not a Guest" (2021), "Drawing Strength from My Grandfather" (2013), "The Blood Road" (2018), and "The Irreducible Essence of Jewishness" (2015).

Like Corman, Julia Alekseyeva connects to the fraught war-torn landscape of her great-/grandparents' past. Author and illustrator Julia Alekseyeva published *Soviet Daughter* in 2017; has written and illustrated works for *The Nib*, *Jewish Currents*, *The Sixties*, *Paper Brigade*; and guest edited the *Jewish Currents* "Soviet Issue" in winter/spring 2022. She is an assistant professor at the University of Pennsylvania. She immigrated to the United States from the former Soviet Union in 1992. Alekseyeva's work introduces the often overlooked Soviet Jewish experience into this project's constellation of Jewish memories of war and violence. *Soviet Daughter: A Graphic Revolution* employs a unique structure that alternates between numbered chronological chapters of her great-grandmother Lola's life in the USSR and short "Interludes" that describe Julia's life in the United States. By illustrating and engaging with Lola's years in Ukraine and the Soviet Union, Julia gains inspiration and support for her own story as an immigrant from the former Soviet Union and as a young woman coming of age in the United States.[6] The stories of Lola's life in the Soviet Union, which Alekseyeva takes from Lola's diary, reveal experiences of anti-Semitism, pogroms, and famine but also joy, love, and a deep connection to Russian and Soviet politics and culture.[7]

The graphic border poetics in Corman's and Alekseyeva's works theorize a way through contemporary Jewish identity by weaving narratives of war and victimization with individual stories of agency and activism in the present. These texts articulate the importance of specific geopolitical locations, gendered experiences of war, and the memory of familial connections in forming contemporary Jewish identities. Alekseyeva's and Corman's unique rhetorical devices circulate between and through locations that tie their families' pasts to their present lives as a source of comfort and inspiration. Alekseyeva's spatial rhetoric moves between sections and locations, alternating Julia's life in the United States in the twenty-first century with numbered chapters about her great-grandmother Lola's life in the USSR; this structural shift in locations and historical periods narrates the ways that Julia's life is influenced and inspired by Lola's life in the Soviet Union.

While Alekseyeva uses structural strategies to weave together these women's positions and locations, Corman uses graphic devices to depict affect, ambivalence, and belonging together on the spaces of the page. For example, Corman's short online comic "You Are Not a Guest" tells how Leela creates new bonds from a severed past by mapping a "fractal beauty" or wholeness, a feeling that she acknowledges as a connection to the Holocaust dead and simultaneously to the contemporary Polish landscape and people. A focus on the geopolitical location in texts by women highlights the movement between personal and public locations that exist between "the interface between self and other" (Friedman, "Locational" 27). In these works, geography, style, and medium work together to create nuanced narratives of Jewish women's experiences of Soviet oppression, Holocaust memory, and personal identity.[8]

In the first part of this chapter, I examine two of Leela Corman's short, interrelated autobiographical comics, "You Are Not a Guest" and "Drawing Strength from My Grandfather," which explore Leela's relationship to her family's past in Poland. The second part of the chapter examines Julia Alekseyeva's double memoir *Soviet Daughter* and Julia's relationship to her Soviet past through the diary of her great-grandmother Lola. The last part of the chapter focuses on the ways that Corman[9] and Alekseyeva utilize their families' pasts to facilitate an empowered and activist stance. Through artistic renderings of history and place, Corman's and Alekseyeva's works explore the cost of carrying generational loss and the importance of incorporating those pasts into a future-facing narrative. Their works weave transnational identities based in landscapes, living culture, and people and in doing so, register a shift away from a persistent Jewish identification with twentieth-century oppression and toward a narrative of Jewishness based in agency and activism in the twenty-first century.

Fractal Wholeness in Leela Corman's Graphic Texts

In Leela Corman's short comic "You Are Not a Guest" (the title story in her collection *You Are Not a Guest*), Leela, the autobiographical protagonist, visits her grandparents' former home in Poland to explore her roots. In the first panel of the story, a bloody severed arm hovers above the Atlantic Ocean creating a spreading stain of red in the watery blue ocean below (fig. 4.1). Half of the arm overlays the map of America, and the other half overlays Europe. The words above the image read, "Where do I begin?" (1). As Corman starts the story of her visit to Poland, the severed limb illustrates the visceral pain of her family's experiences during the Holocaust and at the same time represents the ways that Leela is torn between the two places, not whole in her identities as an American granddaughter of Holocaust survivors *nor as* a young woman with a family history steeped in Polish culture and landscape. The arm not only implies the violent separation of her family members from one another and from their geographical home due to the war but also represents the affective absences and pain that still exist in Leela's life as a result. As she writes later in the story, "There are many beginnings to this story, but the only real one is the severing—of Jews from Poland, of the living from the dead, of us from our homes, and as it turns out Poles from us" ("You Are Not"). While the detached arm rests on the Americas, the remainder of the body rests on

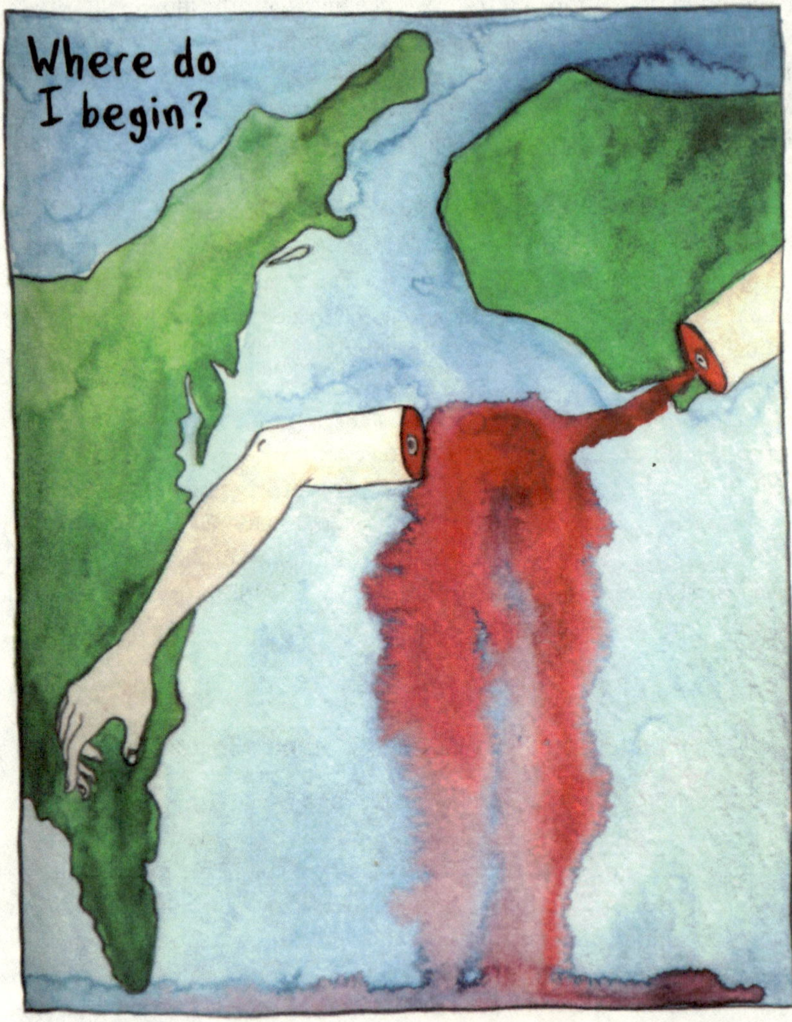

FIG. 4.1 A bleeding severed arm hovers above maps of the Americas and Europe.

the map of Europe outside of the confines of the panel; as a third-generation family member growing up in the United States, a major part of Corman's history has become inaccessible to her. The absence of the living archive is present in this image, much of the rich Jewish history and culture that was forged long before the stories of war and genocide that now dominate Jewish collective memory. Fragments of Jewish identity remain in what immigrants and children of immigrants in the United States often call the Old World, old because it is a past world that historically many would just as soon forget. Like several authors in this project, Corman explores the weight, power, and ethical implications of the fallout of the war on her and her family. She begins her inquiry in a liminal space, unsure where she should locate the story, where her roots reside, and where she stands locationally as a young Jewish woman in the twenty-first century.

Corman's use of watercolor in "You Are Not a Guest" conveys sedimented layers of history and identity that result from movement between locations (e.g., by overlaying the spaces of the Holocaust and the United States). By utilizing the medium's affordances such as varying hues and intensities, unclear edges, soft-edged panel borders, back runs (where a wet brush mark "runs back" into a cauliflower-shaped texture), gradations of color washes, and layering or glazing of watery spaces, the images in this story and in many of her other works indicate ambiguous and multilayered identities, affects, and spatial boundaries.

Corman's and Alekseyeva's proximities to Poland and the former USSR are layered and multiple due to the fraught histories and experiences of their families. Immigrant grandparents move through experiences and spaces, bringing geopolitical and affective memories with them to the United States and to their families there. The stories and emotions of these relatives shift the way Corman and Alekseyeva experience their own Jewishness. The comic images and devices often invoke the geographical borders and material conditions of past lives along with the protagonists' feelings of alienation, anger, and connection.

Initially, Leela feels ambivalent about visiting Poland due to her family's narratives of murder and anti-Semitism.[10] As Jews in Poland during World War II, Corman's family members were targeted for elimination, and several of those murdered were buried there. Her visceral reaction to visiting her grandparents' country is evident upon her arrival. Corman writes, "As soon as I arrived in Poland, I felt the multigenerational trauma. I felt it in my gut, in my soul, I felt it in the airport parking lot" ("You Are Not"). For Leela, the affective experience of the geopolitical location holds multiple layers of meaning for her. The landscape resonates with Leela because of her memory of family stories and because of the sense of familiarity she experiences in the countryside near her grandfather's village. When visiting the mountains near her grandfather's town, she writes, "From the freshly restored Jewish cemetery of Grybow, I look down into Papa's tiny town, and at the soft hills surrounding it, and breathe the air of the mountains he loved. The forest was his beloved hiking grounds, and then a place of trauma as much as refuge, for him and all who hid there with him. Its resemblance to the Catskills is impossible to miss" (Corman, "You Are Not"). Poignantly, she sees the town from the perspective of the graveyard, her feet firmly rooted in the reality of her family's tragic past, while at the same time, she notices that the rolling hills remind her of New York. She feels at once at home and a stranger in her family's former landscape.

The title of Corman's short story, "You Are Not a Guest," is a replication of the words that her Polish guide Przemek uses to welcome her to Poland: "As Przemek, who met me at the airport, said to me on the drive to Nowy Sacz, 'This is your culture, too. **You Are Not A Guest**'" ("You Are Not"; emphasis in original). With Przemek's words, Leela begins to think about her relation to her family's rich existence before the war. For Leela, this phrase is an acknowledgment of her right to belong in a landscape from which she has felt alienated. In part, it is also a recognition by the non-Jewish Poles of the horrors of their anti-Semitic past. While not quite an invitation to deepen into discussions of Polish collaboration or complicity in the war, this welcome phrase opens a space for further exploration and suggests a commitment to recognizing her family's tragic Polish past.

Leela's ambivalence toward her hosts and toward her own Polish identity is clear in the images that accompany the words of the title. As Corman begins her story about her trip to Poland, she recognizes the significance of her entry into a world littered with the graves and memories of family members. The images on this page reveal the ambivalence that Leela feels toward Poland. As Przemek invites Leela to reclaim her Polish culture and history, Leela's hair turns into rootlike strands, which intertwine with the dead who lay in a forest that grows up behind her and Przemek as they leave the airport (fig. 4.2). The boundaries of her body expand into the past to explore what remains for her here. Memory and affective history become extensions of Leela's body. Her hair becomes blood-red roots that explore and comfort the dead who lay beneath the forest floor (fig. 4.2). The blurred borders of the panel of her and Przemek at the airport merge with the image of the bodies of the dead to create one large panel instead of two separate images. Historical and chronological boundaries break down in this merged panel; Leela's visceral connection to the dead in the forest is not separate from her discussion with Przemek but integral to it. "You Are Not a Guest," written in blood-red, hovers above the image, suggesting that Leela's identity is intertwined with the murder of her family in Poland. The position of her body reveals her feelings of ambivalence toward Poland: She faces forward toward Przemek and Nowy Sacz, while part of her remains intertwined with the dead, not ready to embrace a country that is associated with genocide and her family's severed past.

Though Leela struggles to feel a sense of belonging at the start of the story, she quickly realizes that the fraught history of Poland during the Holocaust has created an absence for Jews and non-Jewish Poles: "It immediately became clear that my counterparts there feel [the multigenerational trauma], too. They fight the silence they were raised in about the past, and feel a deep sense of loss at our absence" ("You Are Not"). Her Polish friends ask Leela, "What did your grandparents tell you about Poland?" These questions belie a hesitancy to ask Leela directly about her family's experiences of genocides on those landscapes.

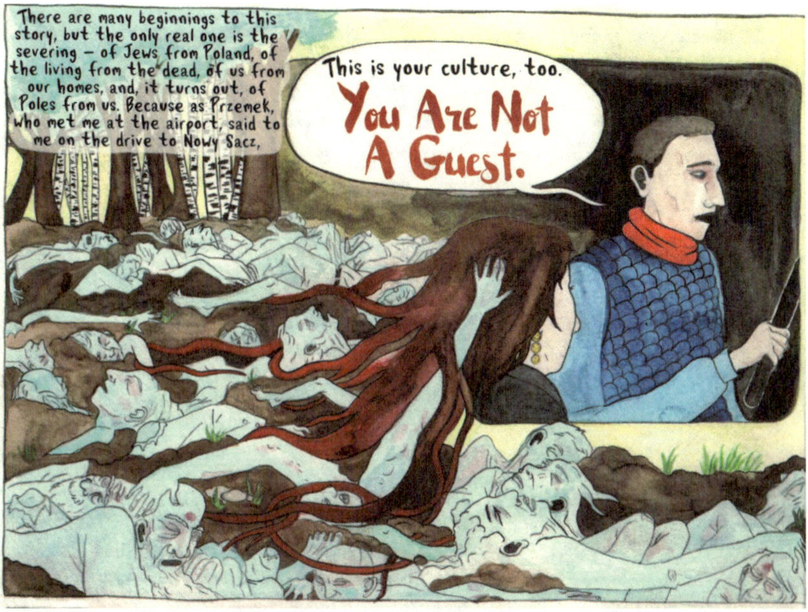

FIG. 4.2 Leela's hair becomes roots that intertwine with the dead as Przemek welcomes her to Poland.

Likewise, her friend Kamil asks why a tree is growing out of the roof of a ruined synagogue, and another friend inquires about the kind of pierogi Leela's grandmother makes. The side-by-side panels depicting this scene suggest Leela's ambivalence about what these questions do *not* ask (fig. 4.3).

On the left side of the page, a watery cotton-candy pink panel with images of plates of red borscht and pierogi exudes a light, saccharine tone, while in stark contrast the dark panel on the right side of the page shows sickly yellow corpses peeking out from behind black trees. The use of the bright, artificial pink seems to question the legitimacy of the Poles' interest in her family's past in the very color choice. The more somber panel, a dark forest in which arms, legs, and faces hide behind sinister-looking leafless trees, represents the murderous history that haunts Leela's memory and the Polish landscapes she visits (fig. 4.3). The darker panel includes weighty, unspoken questions that lurk behind the superficial questions from the Poles: "What did you absorb in their silences? That it was a place inaccessible to you? A place of betrayal? The graveyard of our culture?" The stark contrast between the color and content of these two panels suggests that the absent dialogue about the Polish past creates a fissure between the world of the Jews and the young non-Jewish Poles.

As the story develops, Leela builds relationships with her Polish guides and begins to feel more connected to the familiar landscapes, foods, faces, and cultures of Poland. She tours the countryside and is hosted by locals; her friend

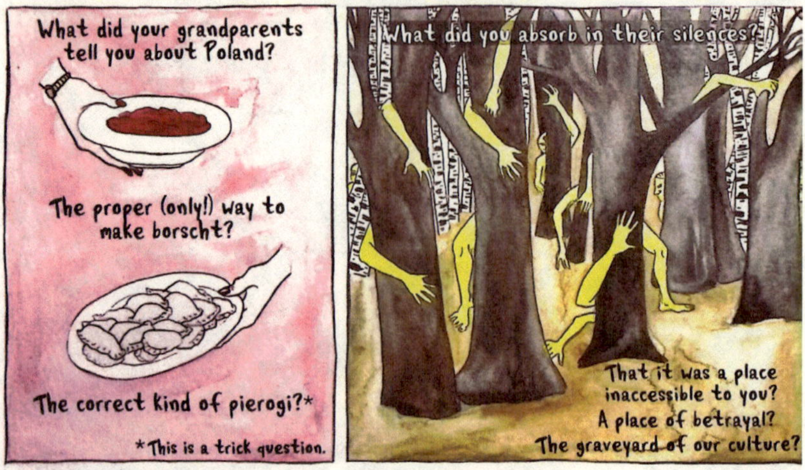

FIG. 4.3 Leela's friends ask her about her memory of her family's Polish food (*left*), while the contrasting image on the right asks darker questions.

Danuta prepares her an overflowing plate of pierogi as a welcome feast, and Kamil invites her to stay in his home. She writes, "I thought, before coming here, that I would feel so dark. But instead, something happened that I did not expect, at all: I recognized myself in this place" (fig. 4.5; "You Are Not").

As she draws the incongruous connections between the warmth and familiarity of the place and the horrors of the past, Leela experiences a feeling of uncomfortable belonging: "My body is a mass grave containing all the dead I never knew, whose names are on that black stone in the cemetery. But my body is lying beneath a feather quilt exactly like my grandmother's, in Kamil's parents' house" (fig. 4.4; "You Are Not"). The juxtaposition of the grave alongside the warm memory of her grandmother's quilt expresses feelings of belonging and alienation simultaneously. The panel of Leela lying in bed at Kamil's parents' house sits alongside a panel in which the dead speak to her as she visits their mass grave. Leela is welcomed by her dead relatives, a confirmation that she is connected to the landscape and people around her: "Welcome home," "You belong here," "It's nice to see you again, Leela," "Give my regards to your mother." In this panel, her legs seem to grow out of the earth, rooted in and growing from the landscape (fig. 4.4). The experiences of death, friendship, and familiar food and culture all help Leela connect to Poland and to her family's history.

Through an exploration of a living Poland, Corman probes the question, How does one move toward a future-facing narrative of agency and social change without betraying the dark reality of the Holocaust? Near the end of "You Are Not a Guest," Leela participates in the unveiling ceremony of a

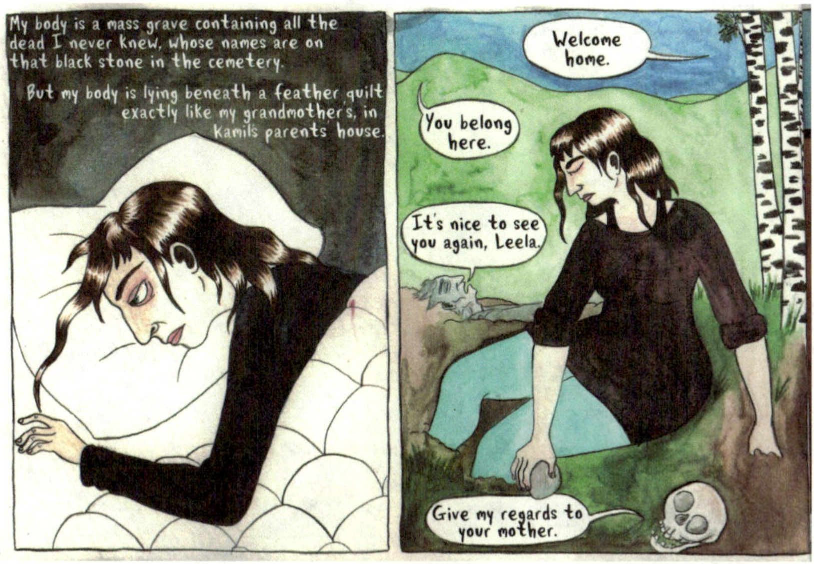

FIG. 4.4 Leela finds comfort in the memories of her grandmother's quilt (*left*) and in the warm welcome she receives from the dead (*right*).

memorial to the Jewish dead. Leela explains, "We Jewish descendants of Grybow stand with hundreds of Poles, as Jewish and Catholic prayers are spoken." Despite her strong connections to the dead, her connections to the living take precedence. She writes, "In the world of the living . . . I have fallen in love with Poland. . . . My history, too, that calls me back. And with the work of the people I met there, which is, at its heart, profoundly anti-fascist. It is work for the future, not only for memory." By traveling to places that are weighted by loss and death in her family's Holocaust story, Corman confronts and creatively narrates her relationship to the past and to Poland.

The visual medium reveals the position of Leela's body in relation to Poland. The severed limb that begins the story is replaced by images of Leela's whole body. In one panel Leela's full body poetically merges with the landscape of Poland (fig. 4.5). Leela lies upon the earth, the green of the forests and blue of the rivers create lyrical outlines of her body, while her hand rests on a skull. The watery washes of the paints allow the hills to merge seamlessly with Leela's body, but even as she merges with the beautiful land around her, she is firmly rooted in the memories of her family's past; the skull and the red landscape beneath her are an inextricable part of her feelings about the Poland she has come to love. She writes below the image, "I have never said, before this, 'I am Polish.' But these mountains, this food, the love and gravity I sense from the people I'm with here tell me that I am." The Catskill-like hills, clear rivers, and affective memory of death and genocide merge with her body,

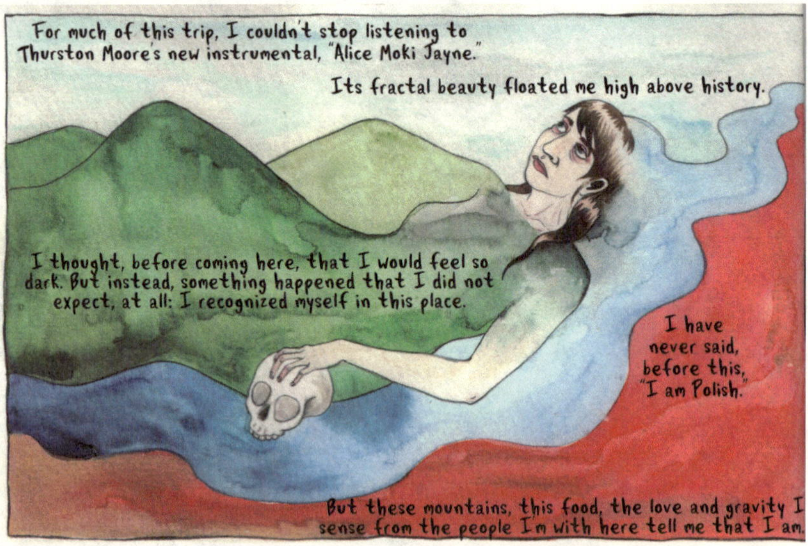

FIG. 4.5 Leela's body becomes part of the affective landscape of Poland.

suggesting a deep connection to the landscape she is severed from in the first panel of the story (fig. 4.1). She describes this as "fractal beauty." The beauty of the Polish countryside and her grandmother's food *along with* the murder of her grandfather and the destruction of his village and Jewish population create a complex and contradictory narrative of belonging and death at once. Her body takes on a kind of fractal wholeness—a sense of belonging that is still firmly connected to and aware of the horrors of her family's fate. There is no saccharine overlay of celebration or irony in this panel and no narrative of the erasure of war; rather, Leela's body is whole in its acknowledgment of the histories, people, and landscapes of her family—beautiful in its fractal wholeness.

Weaving a Double Narrative in Julia Alekseyeva's *Soviet Daughter*

Like Leela Corman in "You Are Not a Guest," Julia Alekseyeva struggles with a sense of belonging and Jewish identity in her graphic memoir *Soviet Daughter: A Graphic Revolution*. Alekseyeva alternates between chronologically numbered chapters that depict her great-grandmother's life and "Interludes" that tell of Julia's coming-of-age. The alternating structure illustrates the inspiration and solace Julia draws from her great-grandmother's life in the Soviet Union. In the prologue of the memoir, Alekseyeva describes the unique structure of the book: "This is the story held within her memoirs, growing up over the course of the 20th century. In between each chapter of Lola's life, you will find a short slice of my 21st century coming of age. It is a story of our two generations separated by 80 years—but somehow united in spite of everything" (6).[11] The narrative structure of these life stories functions in several ways: The alternating sections facilitate a transnational narrative that weaves women's lives and struggles across generations, Julia's life accumulates meaning and direction as she engages with Lola's world in the Soviet Union, and finally the intertwined stories create a third narrative in which the love and inspiration of two women sustain each other across time.

The structure and imagery of *Soviet Daughter* articulate the ways that specific geopolitical locations and gendered experiences of war, anti-Semitism, and trauma form the identities of several generations of Jewish women. Alekseyeva's pencil and watercolor images in *Soviet Daughter* are not reproduced in color like Corman's but rather in gray and black, borderless, watery washes. The images often appear without clear definitions of time or space, emphasizing the merging of Lola's and Julia's lives in the double memoir. Julia's and Lola's sections are narrated in the first person, lending a sense of immediacy and relevancy to each woman's narration. Though the reader discovers early in the memoir that Julia did not receive Lola's diary until she was a young adult, the structure of the text suggests that these two lives were interwoven even prior to Julia's knowledge of many of Lola's stories.[12]

The cover of *Soviet Daughter* immediately invokes the connection between the lives and idealism of Lola and Julia (fig. 4.6). A framed photo of a young Lola and Julia together at about the same age (despite being born over half a century apart) is set over a backdrop of major events from Lola's life in the Soviet Union. Julia's picture in this scene suggests that she is a part of Lola's experiences navigating the difficult terrain of the Soviet regime as a young woman. The bold white title splashed across the cover (*Soviet Daughter*) refers to Lola's journey in the Soviet Union and to Julia's immigrant journey from the Soviet Union to the United States: Both women are Soviet daughters. The visual rhetoric of the cover invokes geopolitical material conditions of war as well as the psychological, emotional, and cultural effects on these women and, in doing so, illustrates "borders that highlight the paradoxical processes of connection and separation" (Friedman, "Locational" 27). As Dana Mihăilescu suggests, "Jewish women's identities are always in process, the result of one's location in relation to others" ("Jewish Identity" 169). The geopolitical material conditions and their consequences are set within a collage that highlights the lives of Julia and Lola, who are connected by these places and events. The settings of the photograph depict two events that change their lives irrevocably. The top half of the cover shows a train moving across a bridge in 1941 that

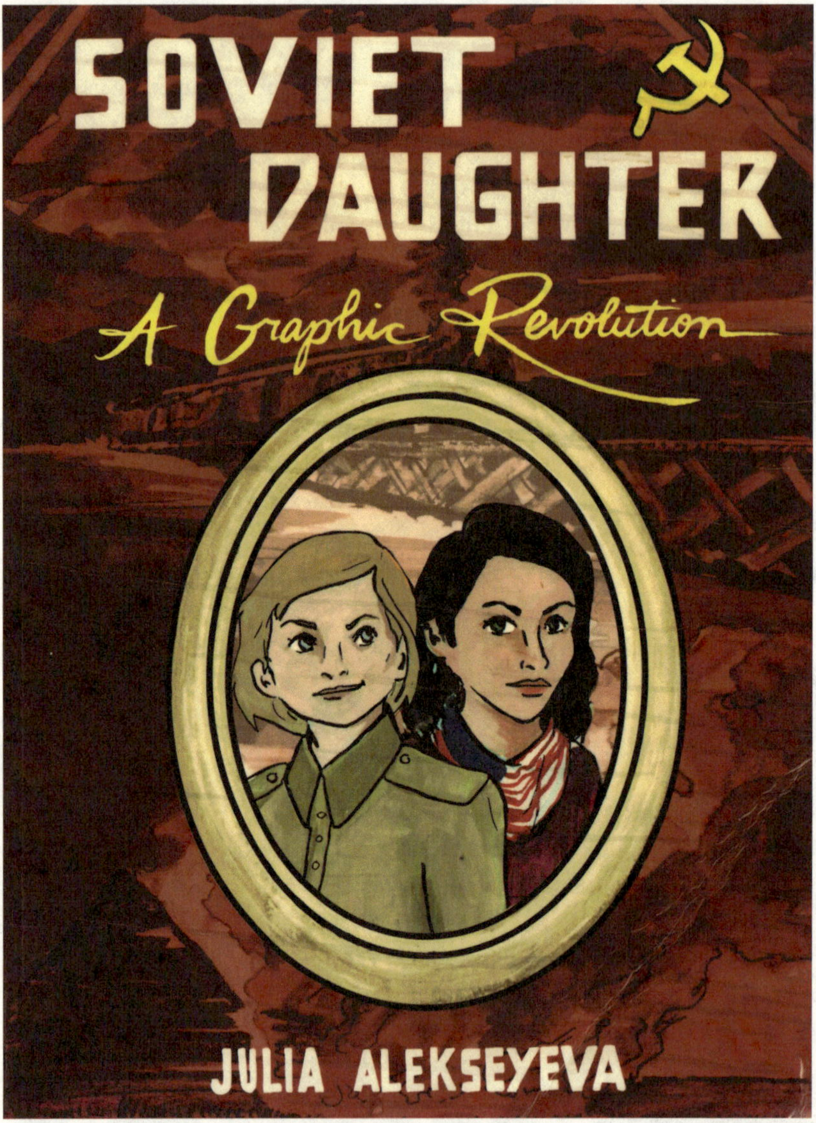

FIG. 4.6 A framed picture of a young Lola and Julia is set against the backdrop of war scenes from Lola's life in the Soviet Union.

carries Lola, her children, and other Ukrainians from Kyiv to Kazakhstan as they flee the Nazis (Alekseyeva 142); the bottom half shows the horror of the burning barn in which Lola's parents are murdered just after they were evacuated from Ukraine to North Caucus in 1942 (fig. 4.6; 156–157). In setting the picture of Lola and Julia together on top of these traumatic events, time collapses, and Julia is positioned as part of Lola's life. Though the photograph can be read as a metaphorical understanding between the two women, the structure of the double memoir suggests that Alekseyeva has incorporated Lola's life experiences into Julia's life story as a way to understand her own life trajectory. Visually and structurally, Julia's narrative becomes an extension of Lola's political life and legacy. Locationally, Julia is a young former Soviet, a young woman navigating multiple systems of patriarchy, an American, an ambivalent Jew (as portrayed in the memoir), an artist, and an activist.

Julia's family's movement across countries and identities shapes her sense of herself as a young woman and a Jew. The first "Interlude" in *Soviet Daughter* tells of Julia's immigration to the United States from the former Soviet Union at the age of four, unable to communicate with other children and often receiving negative messages about her Jewish and Ukrainian identity. When she arrives in Chicago with her family as a young girl, Julia is faced with the challenges of a new language, culture, and city—along with the loss of her former home. Julia suffers feelings of disconnection and loneliness in these early years in Chicago, writing, "We were refugees. I was 4 years old. My mother got a bookkeeping job and my grandparents were learning English at a community college, so I was left mostly by myself" (Alekseyeva 21). She describes the loneliness she feels even among her peers: "I didn't know English yet, and a lot of the kids on my block would tease me and purposefully only speak English . . . even if they were Russian themselves" (22).

The fear surrounding their Jewish status follows Julia's family from the USSR. Julia's mother's deep fear that Julia might be identified as a Jew in her new school impacts Julia's social interactions as well as her feelings about her Jewishness. Julia writes, "When I was a kid, I wasn't allowed to tell anyone I was Jewish. My mother thought that the entire world was antisemitic. I was told I wouldn't get into good schools or get jobs. After all that was what it was like in the Soviet Union" (Alekseyeva 35). When Julia is forbidden from going to her best friend's bat mitzvah in Chicago, she argues, "It makes NO sense. Everyone already knows SHE'S Jewish!" Her mother responds, "Yes, but then they'll find out *you* are!" (35). Her mother's fears are explained later in the text when Tanya (Julia's grandmother) is blocked from entering the University of Kyiv due to the Jewish marker on her identity card. Stalin's campaign against "rootless cosmopolitans," a euphemism for Jews, was played out in many institutions in the USSR where bans or strict quotas for Jews were implemented (183).

Unlike Julia's life in the United States, where she can choose to identify as a Jew with few consequences, in the USSR she and her family were forced to carry identity cards that officially marked them as ethnic Jews. Alekseyeva depicts this all-important identity card in a large panel in chapter 12, suggesting the weight of these cards in the lives of those forced to carry them. Perversely, while religious practice was illegal in the USSR, Jewishness as an ethnic identity was imposed upon those of Jewish ancestry. This identity marker not only restricted educational and job possibilities for Jews but also limited housing choices and access to food and travel; Jews were often suspected of colluding with the "enemy" and were prevented from traveling to other Soviet Bloc countries. Just before and during the fall of the Soviet Union, emigration policies loosened significantly under Mikhail Gorbachev, and over a million former Soviets fled to the West. This mass emigration is often referred to as the third wave.[13]

Julia and Lola's intertwining narratives create a transnational story of mutual love and inspiration, weaving together chapters that "speak to one another." Lola's chapter 5 is set between two of Julia's interludes, "Interlude: Summer 2008" and "Interlude: 2009." While the interludes depict Julia's difficult relationship break up ("Summer 2008") and her struggle with cancer ("2009"), Lola's "Chapter 5: 1930–1933" depicts her divorce from Mitia, a period of famine, and her daughter Tanya's illness (Alekseyeva 76, 81–83). Julia acknowledges that her great-grandmother's position almost a century ago influences her desire to change unequal circumstances in the twenty-first century. As a woman, Lola is expected to fulfill the Soviet ideal of working for the greater good, yet her gendered work at home is not supported by the system. Lola works full-time as required by the Soviet system (often pushed into undesirable jobs), raises children by herself, negotiates war and famine, and cares for a very sick daughter. She is not provided with childcare and is not allowed time off to care for her children. The last pages of chapter 5 describe Lola's daughter Tanya's brain tumor and scarlet fever. Lola's position as a woman in a larger patriarchal system that does not support women is evident here. She is a single parent to an ill child, a secretary for the NKVD among other organizations,[14] and a daughter trying to navigate parental ties. Lola's struggle to care for Tanya during her illness is the transition that leads to Julia's next section, "Interlude: 2009," which tells of Julia's own illness and struggle with thyroid cancer.[15]

The themes in Julia's section are informed and often shaped retrospectively by Lola's experiences. The first two pages of "Interlude: Summer 2008" silently depict Julia's difficult relationship breakup, the panels devoid of text or dialogue. Only when Julia visits Lola a few pages later do the dialogue or speech bubbles return, suggesting that in the safety of Lola's company, Julia is able to find her voice (Alekseyeva 63–67). After the breakup, Julia narrates her visits to Lola's house to help her clean twice a week. The hours that Julia spends with Lola are a time when they talk about life issues and exchange stories. As they drink tea together, Julia confides to Lola, "I don't think he loves me anymore. Something's wrong" (67). Lola reassures Julia by responding, "Oh honey! If only you knew the adventures, I'd get into when I was your age! . . . Let me tell you about my life as a 20-year old. How many adventures and terrible decisions!" (67). In chapter 5, Lola narrates her rocky marriage with her first husband, Mitia, alongside Alekseyeva's illustrations of their arguments in collage form: "Mitia and I did not have a smooth home life. . . . Whether it was just my character to crave independence, whether it was the way I was brought up . . . I just couldn't live under the same roof as him" (75). Using unpaneled illustrations, Alekseyeva imagines Lola's emotional pain and stress as she realizes that she can't stay in her marriage any longer. She tells of her divorce from Mitia (79) and her struggles to pay for rent and food as a young, single mother. In an interview with NPR, Alekseyeva says about this incident, "I was going through a breakup, so I thought everything was the most dramatic thing in the entire world. So [listening to her stories] gave me an interesting perspective" (Garcia-Navarro). Lola's and Julia's sections are connected not only by themes but also by the visual cues that signal their relation to one another, as the image on the cover suggests. The drawing on the title page of "Interlude Summer 2008" encapsulates their relationship (63): Lola stands behind Julia with her hands on her shoulders as Julia peers down at a photograph of Lola with her first husband. Chapter 5 (the following section) opens with a large image of the very same photograph of Lola and her husband, visually tying Lola's chapter to Julia's interlude (68). The connection of the images and the juxtaposition of these two sections create a dialogue in which Lola's story acts as a response to Julia's struggles with romance, Jewishness, illness, and gender disparity.

Agency and Activism in Jewish Identity

Corman and Alekseyeva turn to their (great-)grandparents' lives for comfort, emotional healing, a sense of belonging, and perhaps surprisingly, a model of how to make changes in the world around them. Rather than remain focused on narratives of war and victimhood, the connections of past and present within an affective environment allow them to imagine and move toward a different reality. In their respective stories, Alekseyeva and Corman explore the losses they experience from leaving their homelands, immigrating to the United States, losing family in the Holocaust, and for Corman, losing a child. Leela Corman connects to her grandfather's grief—but also to the rich Polish culture and her family's prewar life. The connections that she cultivates enable her to grow tendrils that reach out to empathize with the experiences of contemporary refugees and victims of war (Corman, "Irreducible"). Similarly, Alekseyeva's connections to her great-grandmother's life in the Soviet Union inspire her desire for freedom and passion for social justice. By weaving Lola's life story with her own, she connects her identity to a larger sense of purpose and change. Corman and Alekseyeva position agency and activism as central to their emerging Jewish identities, not as separate from their families' experiences of war and oppression but rather as extensions of them.

In an autobiographical comic first published in *Tablet*, "Drawing Strength from My Grandfather, Who Carried His Losses from the Holocaust" (2013), Corman tells of the tragic loss of her firstborn child. As Corman illustrates her feelings of grief, she imagines what her grandfather might have felt in the wake of the loss of his family in the war. She tells of her grandfather's experiences in the Polish army, the murder of his family, and his subsequent displacement.[16] In an imagined shared journey with her grandfather, Corman creates an affective solidarity and shared experience of grief in which she asks him how one carries the unbearable burden of loss across a lifetime.

Through graphic devices like merging images and visual symbols, Leela connects her own personal grief to the tragic family events in 1939 Poland. The borderless images in the story encourage a non-chronological reading that creates a simultaneity of time and events. The story begins with images of a dark tunnel that is located beneath tree roots (fig. 4.7). The image of a dark spiral—a representation of a time travel tunnel as well as a grave space—is a symbolic device through which Corman emphasizes her connection with her grandfather and deceased child across time and space. The word "YAHRZEIT" hovers above Leela's head as she imagines the grave-like space that leads her into a parallel world, a world where her child is still alive. A map of Poland lies just beneath Leela's tunnel of grief. Leela's face, eyes closed, merges into the map of World War II Poland (fig. 4.7). There are no borders or breaks between images, suggesting a sense of simultaneity with her current life. Merging their stories across a time-space continuum, Corman highlights the emotions and losses they share. As Gestapo boots march across the map, she writes, "The wind blows me *home*. We all know what happened in September of 1939" ("Drawing Strength"; emphasis mine). Leaves blow across the page, seamlessly connecting Leela's present life to the world of her grandfather in Poland in 1939 (fig. 4.7). Poland—and perhaps the war—is represented as "home" in this series of overlapping images. She locates herself then in the spaces of her grandfather's war experiences and affective memories as a way to understand her own painful loss.

Graphic devices allow Corman to merge the stories of her personal loss with the tragic family events in Poland in 1939. By drawing and remembering the losses that her grandfather endured, she feels a solidarity with the terrible burden she imagines he lived with after the war. In this graphic collapsing of time and space, her own story is visually interwoven with her family's longer European history. As the story toggles between her grandfather's World War II story and Leela's present life in the twenty-first century, Leela and her grandfather are positioned together, holding hands as if to comfort each

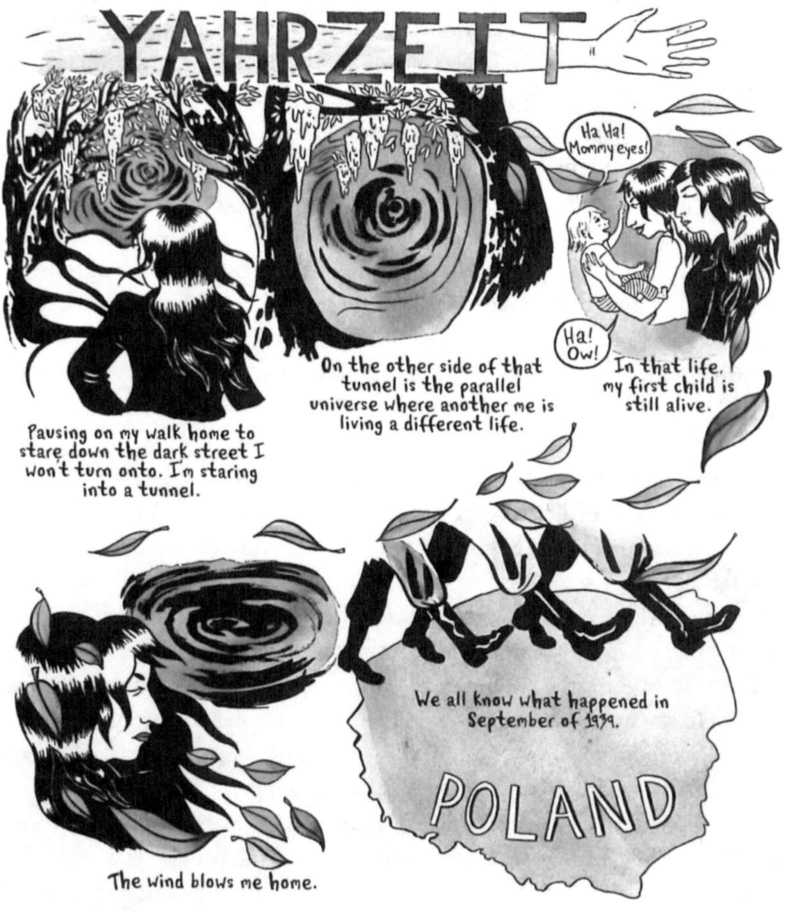

FIG. 4.7 An image of Leela's experience of grief positioned in relation to Poland in 1939. In the bottom images, her head merges with the map of World War II Poland, collapsing time and space between the two stories of grief ("Drawing Strength").

other in the grief they each carry. In this exchange, she links her tragedy directly to the grief she imagines that her grandfather must have carried after the loss of his family.

There is no neat, happy ending to this story: Leela does not unburden her grief or suddenly awaken from the darkness in her life; rather, she learns to carry the burden of loss *differently*. She writes, "There is really no safe place to be when you have experienced a grave trauma. The hole does not close." In one of the final images of the story, Leela walks beside her grandfather as both carry faceless human figures on their shoulders, representations of their dead who are clearly too large to be carried comfortably. In a series of figures, Leela walks along a black path that emanates from the dark tunnel. In each figure, a child sits on her shoulders, and in each successive drawing the child is larger and heavier, finally causing Leela's knees to buckle. Next to the images, she writes, "I have thought of [my grandfather] often over the years. How he didn't have time to be afraid or to mourn. How he carried his losses. I draw strength from him." Connecting his burdens to her own grief, Leela asks unanswerable questions as she plods along the dark path carrying her own unbearable burden. She asks about his deep losses during the war, "Did the weight of his dead ever make him ask 'Why am I still alive?'" As she is pushed to the ground by the weight of her child's memory, she wonders, "Did he sometimes get sick of talking to people who've never held the corpse of a loved one in their arms?" The prose suddenly shifts to plural pronouns, suggesting solidarity between them: "We trudge forward, carrying the weight of our dead. Dragging our phantom limbs behind us because they can't be buried."

In their imagined shared journey, Corman creates a graphic and affective solidarity that allows her to ease her way through the hole of grief she occupies. In the last image, a large faceless figure sits in a hole cradling Leela and her grandfather in its arms as it whispers "Shhh. . . ." A visual representation shows how, as the title suggests, she draws strength from her grandfather's difficult history during the Holocaust.[17] Like several of the texts in this project, Corman's work explores the weight, power, and ethical implications of her connections to the war, in this case, to glean strength for her own grief.

Instead of the fear and desecration of bodies that dominate Holocaust memory, Corman honors and empowers the female body to take action in spaces of death. In the story "The Blood Road" (2018), Leela visits the infamous Buchenwald camp in Germany. The defiance she feels during her visit is expressed via a superhero-like avatar of Leela. The defiant body is positioned as part of her movement toward activism and her commitment to human rights (fig. 4.8). Leela finds strength in feeling alive and defiant in a museum about death.

While inside the exhibit at Buchenwald, Leela is surprised at her feelings of hunger, saying, "Instead of being upset at my body for its mundane demands, I felt a surge of delight at having a body that can make those demands" ("Blood Road" 3). The image of Leela is a bright-red body covered in veins and energy (fig. 4.8). Yellow superhero-like rays emanate from her eyes as she stands over the museum building, one large boot crashing through the roof. She writes, "I felt fifty feet tall. I felt so strong. You assholes tried to kill all of us, but some survived" (fig. 4.8). Leela's giant red body and laser eyes defy narratives of victimization and passivity. Leela crashes through the buildings of Buchenwald as she sings a song from her favorite band. In this act, she changes the museum narrative and becomes the hero that might have saved her relatives during the Holocaust. She takes on their memory as action, activism, and agency. Stepping through the roof of Buchenwald, she explains about her family, "They

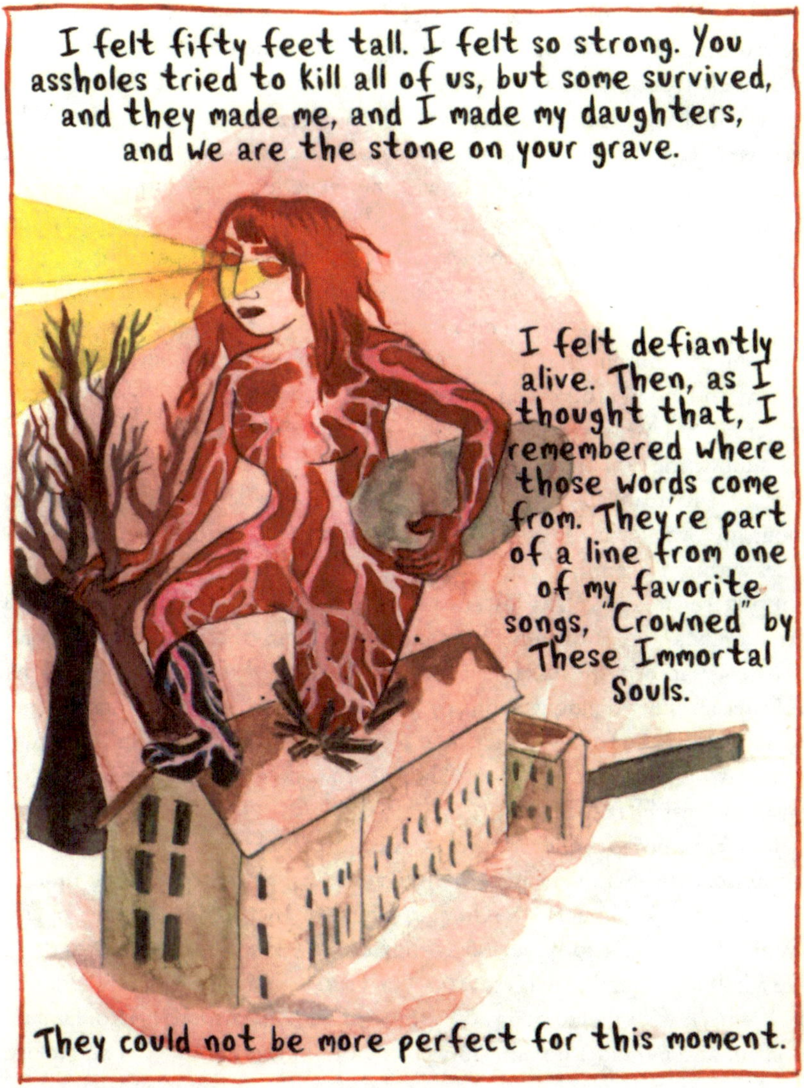

FIG. 4.8 Leela as strong, defiant, and fifty feet tall stomps on the roof of a building at Buchenwald camp.

made me, and I made my daughters, and we are the stone on your grave. . . . I put the biggest f-cking stone on that place." Her and her daughters' bodies act as the living memorial—not as passive victims but as agentic, powerful women with the strength to change the narrative of the past through creative work and activism. Her actions and feelings in the space of the death camp shape a narrative of defiance, power, and control over the stories of war and memories of genocide.

While Corman uses borderless pages and overlapping images to create an intertwining of past and present, Alekseyeva uses the juxtaposition of Lola's and Julia's lives to show the ways that Lola's Jewishness of the Soviet Union impacts Julia's Jewishness of the present. In Alekseyeva's *Soviet Daughter*, Julia expresses deep ambivalence about her Jewishness due to her family's stories of anti-Semitism in the USSR along with her experiences of anti-Semitism in the United States. Within the structure of the memoir's alternating sections, Julia's feelings about her Jewish identity are juxtaposed with Lola's experiences of anti-Semitism many years earlier. For example, Alekseyeva positions Lola's description of the pogroms and murders of Jews ("Chapter 2: 1917–1920") between the interludes that depict Julia's loneliness as a Jewish immigrant ("1992" and "1996–2002").[18] Lola's experience of a violent anti-Semitic attack on her father (Alekseyeva 28) sits uneasily next to images of Julia rejecting her Jewishness. She explains, "I felt haunted by something I had never even experienced. I still dream about it often. This of course was tied up with my feelings about my own Jewish identity" (106–107). By contextualizing Julia's experiences within the family's earlier terrifying experiences, a longer and more violent pattern emerges.[19] The historical perspective as told by Lola is positioned structurally as a part of Julia's contemporary narrative, suggesting that Lola's experiences inform the fear Julia experiences as a child while also allowing her to foster an inner dialogue about what it means to be Jewish. In high school Julia describes the feelings of fear and terror that she absorbs from the grandparents who helped raise her, which leads to a period when she insists that she is not Jewish (134–135).

Julia continues to question her connection to her Jewish heritage as she encounters anti-Semitism in the United States. She is bullied and endures anti-Semitic jokes in her new school in Chicago. These events lead her to ask, "What did it mean to be Jewish? I didn't know. It felt more than anything like a ball and chain" (Alekseyeva 37). In a full-page image, a young Julia lies on her back with matzo ball soup, wine, gefilte fish, challah, matzo, hamantaschen, and a dreidel floating above her head as she muses, "I'm an atheist. Why should it matter? But of course it did" (36).[20] The common Jewish symbols in this image suggest a simplistic view of Jewish identity. Julia identifies with atheism (like Lola) and remains detached from the symbols of Jewish culture and religion that float above her head (36).

In contrast to Julia's initial negativity about her Jewishness, Alekseyeva illustrates the sense of joy and freedom that Julia learns from Lola in several of her interludes. She writes, "While everyone was discussing my Jewishness, it was only around Lola where it seemed natural beyond discussion—something free from judgement, but not ignored completely" (38). Alekseyeva depicts the ways that Julia learns to cultivate a sense of freedom literally under Lola's watch. Just below the panel where Julia discusses her desire for freedom is an image that shows Julia learning to race across a grassy field under Lola's window. Julia says the field was a place where she could "run as hard and as fast as [she] could" (38). Running becomes a way for Julia to *practice* her desire to escape the constraints and confusion of her life and to cultivate the sense of freedom and joy that she sees in Lola's life. Despite Lola's experiences of anti-Semitic pogroms, revolutionary terror, and the genocide of World War II, she maintains a positive connection to her Jewish identity in a visceral way that Julia can absorb. In a telling image, a small Julia sits in Lola's lap reading a book; they are surrounded by dark, menacing shadows. The text on the top of the page reads, "Thankfully, there was Lola—my only refuge in a land of monsters" (26). To escape the fraught sense of Jewish identity that she absorbs from the Soviet Union and from her family, Julia finds solace in Lola's company. Julia learns joy that is practiced in the safety of her relationship with Lola.

As Julia matures, she connects to the love of culture and fun that she perceives in Lola's generation (Alekseyeva 107). Even during difficult periods, Lola's diary describes the various love interests, parties, and music and literature that sustain her. After a devastating series of events in 1933 that include famine, a divorce from Mitia, a serious case of colitis, and her daughter Tanya's nearly fatal illness (71–84), Lola moves into a period of excitement and joy ("Chapter 6: 1933–1937"). Her diary describes how she attends dance halls with her friends after work and holds parties at her apartment. She writes, "We danced, drank, listened to music until 2 or 3 in the morning. I felt revived, like I was truly living for the first time in my life" (95). While working as a secretary for the Komsomol's Raicom (the district young communist committee) in 1934, Lola has access to literary readings, music performances, and theater; she says about the performances, "I went more than anyone. I couldn't tear myself way" (99). Her love of literature is nurtured when she dates a man who introduces her to *War and Peace* and *Anna Karenina* and who tells her, "Lola, you have not lived until you read Tolstoy" (100). Alekseyeva sets this chapter ("Chapter 6: 1933–1937") alongside Julia's short section that describes her love of the arts and parties ("Interlude: 2008–2014").

As a young adult, Julia describes a penchant for culture and joy that mirrors Lola's: "How could I explain my desire for something other than what there was? Music, art, film, politics, books—these things restored a sense of wonder in the world that I thought my parents lacked" (Alekseyeva 106). Instead of an identity based on pain and war memories, Julia begins to associate with Lola's sense of joie de vivre. In chapter 6 and the subsequent "Interlude: 2008–2014," Julia describes the connection she sees between her generation and Lola's generation: "It is said that Lola's generation—called the 'G.I. generation'—is closest to Generation Y ('millennialism') in sentiment and personality" (107). Conversely, Julia sees caution, "rule following," and conservatism in her mother's and grandmother's lives and romantic relationships that she does not identify with (106). In an interview, Alekseyeva explains her identification with Lola's generation: "The early idealism of the Soviet period to me felt almost American; it was dissenting and critical, in contrast to the fearful reaction to the world of the middle generations, probably a reaction to the trauma of the Stalinist period. I don't remember my great-grandmother ever being afraid of anything. . . . She was a badass" (Mironova). In "Interlude: 2008–2014," Julia identifies her own love for the arts and parties with her great-grandmother's passion for literature, music, and dancing (106–107).

The structure of the memoir suggests that Julia's Jewish identity is inseparable from Lola's life in the Soviet Union, whether in relation to the pogroms and anti-Semitic policies or to idealist socialist values. Lola summarizes her activism and commitment to the ideals of the Communist Party (until she discovers some of the atrocities committed years later): "I had been a communist as long as I remembered! I marched in the parades, I tried to help fellow citizens, I volunteered. . . . It took a great deal of courage to retain my love for the idea" (Alekseyeva 184).[21] In an interview, Alekseyeva connects this political commitment to Jewish identity: "My Jewish identity is pretty much the same as my great-grandmother's—as a communist, she considered herself an atheist, and I've been an atheist for as long as I could remember. But for us, as for many Soviet families, Judaism was less of a religion and more of an ethnic identity" (Mironova).

Using Lola's stories as inspiration, Julia begins to identify as a staunch supporter of human rights and a political activist. Julia positions her involvement in social issues as a direct legacy of Lola's experiences under the Soviet regime described in chapter 7. Julia's sense of victimization as seen in earlier dreams (Alekseyeva 24) turns to agency as she attends protests, marches in Pride parades, and participates in union organizing. Within the structure of the narrative, Julia discovers her passion for changing the world around her against the backdrop of Lola's memory of the murder of her parents in Chechnya (155–157), the Babi Yar massacre (147), Stalin's political purges, her forced work with the NKVD (124), and the arrests of many of her friends. Though Lola's life and political activism were severely restricted under Stalin, her diary describes her resistance and idealism. In chapter 7, Lola details the 1937 Stalinist purges[22] that occur while she works for Raicom and then NKVD. One full-page panel shows her in front of prison bars holding her head in terror while arrests go on all around her (109). She says, "I couldn't handle going through a day not knowing whether I would be allowed to leave. 'Would this be the day,' I would think, 'that they'd arrest me? Will it be tomorrow? The day after tomorrow?' So I left" (109). Lola acts according to her conscience despite the possible consequences of leaving the secret police. Alekseyeva stages these experiences of political oppression in "Chapter 7:

1937–1938" as the backdrop for Julia's emerging activism in the section that follows, "Interlude: 2001–2006."

Julia's interest in political issues and continental philosophy is peppered throughout "Interlude: 2001–2006" (Alekseyeva 118–121). Julia connects this impulse directly to Lola's story to explain her commitment to social justice, explaining that in high school she "had a sense of civic duty that bordered on complete mania" (120) and admitting that she wrote "terrible politically themed opinion pieces for the school paper" (119). When she applies to colleges, Julia applies to "extremely political schools, with a strong history of student protest—places like Berkeley and Columbia" (121). She writes, "I imagined a place where students would read poetry in black turtlenecks, pin anarchy stickers on their bags, discuss Marx and Nietzsche at odd hours of the night" (121). Though Julia only discovers the history of Lola's activism in her diary after her death, *Soviet Daughter* retrospectively frames her own idealism as inextricably connected to Lola's experiences under Stalin in the Soviet Union.

In the memoir's conclusion, Alekseyeva positions her book *Soviet Daughter* as a part of the legacy of her relationship with Lola. In her will, Lola leaves Julia her life savings, $5,000, which Julia writes she "decided to spend on the production of this book" (Alekseyeva 189). The book (*Soviet Daughter*) connects Julia's sense of freedom, learned joy, and political passion to Lola's influence. Julia writes, "Since she died, my personality has unconsciously shifted to become more like hers" (189). Illustrations on these pages show Julia attending feminist gatherings, reading Marxist theory (189), and protesting at Occupy Wall Street while shouting "We are the 99%!" and "This is what democracy looks like!" (fig. 4.9; 190). Julia's idealism is narrated as an extension of Lola's early idealism and activism in the Soviet Union (Mironova). In the last lines of the text, Alekseyeva explains her idealism by quoting Lola: "After all—governments might change, the historical period might shift, generations might differ. But nothing, not all the guns and pepper spray and police batons in the world, not even time can kill a true idea" (191). In the final page of the memoir, Julia enters a workshop for union organizers, suggesting that her activism and social justice are the beginning of a new chapter or interlude of her life.

Like Alekseyeva, Corman explores components that make up her Jewishness in the twenty-first century. In her short comic "The Irreducible Essence of Jewishness" (2015), Corman and her coworkers discuss characteristics of their Jewishness, deciding finally on a "cocktail of darkness and slapstick." Though Corman's humorous approach to Jewish cultural identity rehearses the tropes of the comedic, self-deprecating American Jew found commonly in popular media, it takes a swift turn to weightier subjects. While the first part of the

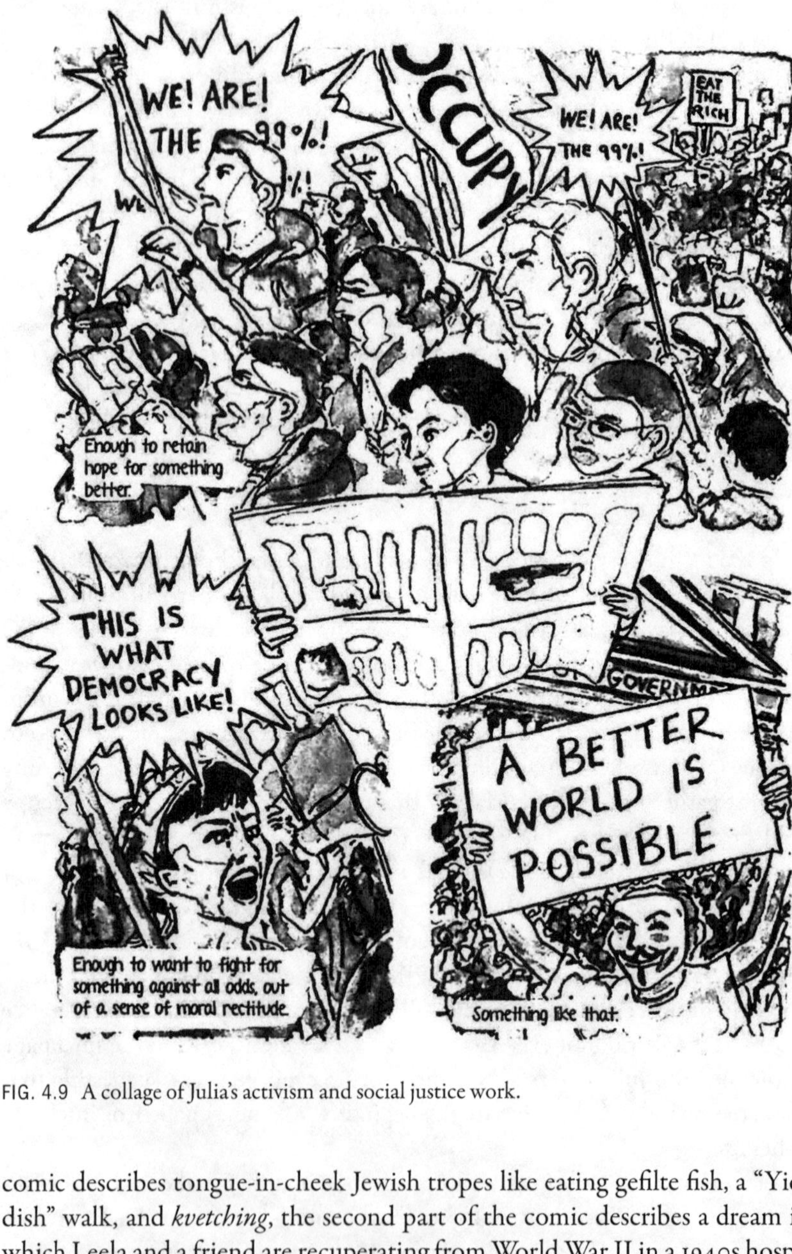

FIG. 4.9 A collage of Julia's activism and social justice work.

comic describes tongue-in-cheek Jewish tropes like eating gefilte fish, a "Yiddish" walk, and *kvetching*, the second part of the comic describes a dream in which Leela and a friend are recuperating from World War II in a 1940s hospital. She writes, "In the dream we both understood implicitly that 'this' meant being a Jew and all that goes with it. And what goes with it? What is there once all else has burned away? DOOM. It follows me everywhere I go in this world" (emphasis in original). The sense of doom and trauma that follows Corman also allows her to connect her Jewishness to the trauma of others. Corman does not refute the pain of Jewish history in her works; rather, she harnesses it to imagine ways to improve the world around her.

Corman often weaves together images of the past and present to imagine a more sustainable, socially just future. In several stories, Corman uses her body and especially her hair to illustrate her visceral connection to people affected by war and violence. For example, in "You Are Not a Guest," Leela's body merges with the landscapes of the dead several times. Corman uses the figure of the body to express pain and connection in the context of violence, displacement, and exile. Wars are waged not only over the terrain of geographies but also over the terrain of the body. Corman's connection to the dead and to the landscapes of the Holocaust signals a feeling of vulnerability, a sense that despite her being a third-generation family member, she feels the depth of the pain and precarity of war in her bones. Leela uses this same technique to envelop contemporary refugees in her own body in "The Irreducible Essence of Jewishness."

In a visual gesture of empathy, Leela's dark, ropelike hair reaches out toward people in small boats fleeing war in the Middle East. The larger panel of Leela's limblike hair extends to the edges of the half-page panel, the three smaller images of displaced people inset on top of her hair and hands. In the smaller panels, Leela's hair is reflected in the water around the precarious boats that hold the refugees (fig. 4.10). Leela's hair is of course an extension of her body, which is framed as still in recovery from generational trauma. Corman suggests it is precisely her family experience of war that allows her to reach out to others. She writes, "History wraps around us and won't let go. If letting go means forgetting that others suffer now as we once did not long ago, then let us be wrapped in it, let us hold on tightly and let that force try to pull people out" (fig. 4.10; "Irreducible"). Leela's hair is a metaphor for the history that envelopes her, but it also suggests that we have a choice to use the pain of historical trauma and experience in ways that change the future. She explains, "This looks so familiar. No one gets on these boats unless they have to. My feelings of empathy for refugees are irreducible" (fig. 4.10). "Irreducible" in this sentence and in the title of the text connects Corman's humanitarian empathy with the "irreducible essence of Jewishness." This set of panels is one of Corman's more serious attempts to define what Jewishness means to her.

In the short comic "The Blood Road" (2018), Corman continues to explore the ways her family's history shifts her awareness of exploited people. While visiting concentration camps in Germany, Corman expresses her discomfort about traveling on a road built by Buchenwald prisoners; this awareness leads her to question the history of oppression in the United States. As Leela sits on a bus going to Buchenwald, a sign catches her attention. The road, "Blood Road," is named for the fate of the camp prisoners who built it. Leela identifies

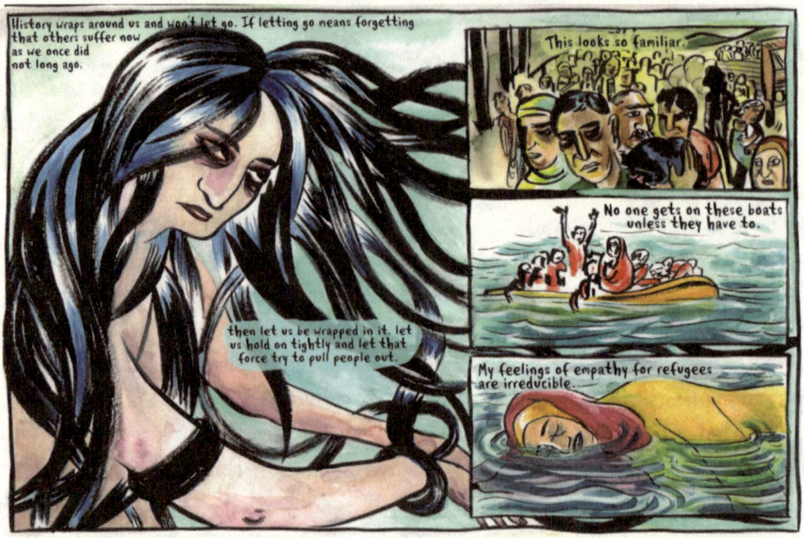

FIG. 4.10 Corman links her own memory to the experiences of refugees and oppressed peoples ("Irreducible").

her discomfort with the everyday use of this road built by exploited people, asking herself, "Why did we speed down it like it's an ordinary road?" Leela quickly connects the history of the Blood Road in Germany with the history of forced labor in the United States: "Who built America? How much did they suffer? Are all roads blood roads? This thought haunted me the whole time I was there" (Corman, "Blood Road" 3). As she passes over the Blood Road, Corman connects the horrors of the Holocaust to the experiences of exploited peoples in the United States; her knowledge of Jewish persecution leads her to question the oppressive practices of her home country and the infrastructure built by oppressed and enslaved people. The empathy Leela learns from family experiences of war is integral to her sense of responsibility toward others as a part of how she understands her Jewishness.

Conclusion

Corman's watercolor of the severed arm in "You Are Not a Guest" (fig. 4.1) that is discussed at the start of this chapter is a symbol for the ways that Corman and Alekseyeva position their families' European pasts, not just as macabre reminders of the losses due to war and anti-Semitism, but also as symbols of the narratives and connections that are lost as a result of trauma. While the severed arm rests on America, the remainder of the body is out of sight beyond the borders of the panel, suggesting the legacy of war that still resides in Europe. Alekseyeva's and Corman's texts explore the body that lies outside the frame of the panel, a symbol of the absent terrain of the past. In their respective works, they connect their lives in the United States to the rich Jewish lives of their families in the USSR and in Poland. Corman creates strong ties to the landscape, people, culture, and antifascist activism that she finds in Poland, ties that eventually define her future. Alekseyeva weaves lives together through the structure of *Soviet Daughter*, creating a narrative in which Julia claims the legacy of Lola's light and joyful spirit, love of culture, and commitment to political ideals and social justice in the former Soviet Union (106–107).

In these graphic works, the sedimented layers of meaning register on the level of the diegetic plot and are also articulated in visual images and devices located in spatial terms on the page. As a body moves through space it accumulates "sedimented and palimpsestic layers" that reflect the various locations and histories that then exert "influence on the other layers and on identity as a whole" (Friedman, "Locational" 28–29). Corman's illustrations reflect her geographical and gendered positions as well as the accumulated memory and inherited emotions from her family. As Corman travels between her life in the United States and Poland, her identity acquires meanings that reflect a rich familial past, connections with living Poles, and inspiration taken from the lives of the dead; the overlapping of time, emotion, and geopolitical landscapes in Corman's texts reflect a rhetoric that ultimately enables "spatial modes of thinking about identity."[23] Near the end of "You Are Not a Guest," Corman suggests that bodily memory is tied to these family geographies. Instead of feeling bodily precarity/insecurity in Poland, she suggests that Poland is a safe space for her memories: "My feet remember the sensation of my great-grandparents' bones beneath them. My eyes went to my boots, still dusted with dirt from their mass grave. . . . I floated above her history, along the river of my own blood, back to Poland, to where my living memories are safe" (unnumbered page 7). Corman feels a sense of belonging in this fraught landscape as she knits her family history to those who become a part of her living journey in Poland. Rather than just a landscape of war, Poland becomes another home, a safe space to keep her memories.

Similarly, in Alekseyeva's *Soviet Daughter*, the stories of Lola and Julia gather and accumulate meaning as they move between the alternating histories and geographies of the text: The sedimented layers of anti-Semitism, violence, and state oppression that Lola experiences as a Jew, a woman, and a mother in the USSR shape Julia's life as a young person growing up in Chicago.[24] Julia's acknowledgment of Lola's precarious position influences Julia's desire to improve the political environment around her in the twenty-first century. The movements back and forth between the two women's sections in the USSR and the United States constitute a *process* of meaning-making that knits the two lives into one larger transnational Jewish memoir. In the space of the memoir, and often on the space of a single page, Julia's contemporary narrative accumulates residues from Lola's diary, just as Lola's diary resonates and intertwines with Julia's narrative, shifting the ways that Julia represents her coming-of-age narrative.

These unique graphic memoirs advocate for a focus beyond war, violence, and mourning, one that gathers the pieces of the past to forge connections to prewar Jewish Europe and to the activist legacies of their *families for a better, more just future*. These women's bodies merge with landscapes, with painful life experiences, and with the strength of their ancestors. As hair becomes tendrils that reach out to heal the broken world around them, Corman and Alekseyeva take a decidedly agentic and activist stance that pays homage to the legacies of their families in Poland and in the Soviet Union, not through mourning but through joy, connection, and activism—a way of changing the world in the names of those they love.

Conclusion

Transforming Political Structures and Futures

In her short comic "The Art of War" (2017), Sarah Glidden makes the following observations after viewing Goya's *Third of May* and Picasso's *Guernica*, two paintings that depict the fear and horrors of war:

> What matters is that we have set
> aside this space:
>
> a space to feel something we
> may usually hide from,
>
> to think about war and the
> suffering humans inflict on
> one another,
>
> or maybe even just about history
> and the role of the artist in it.
>
> We don't have many spaces left where
> we can do that together. (Glidden, "Art of War")

She reminds us that art provides a space where we can think about violence, express suffering, and engage together with the long-term consequences of war. The comics in this study provide a space for us to dialogue with the artists' representations of war and generational trauma from different perspectives and locations, illustrating that *Jewishness* includes how one identifies—but also how one feels about national belonging, family histories of displacement and genocide, and the immediate (in)security of one's body.

After leaving Israel, the bodily pressures I felt during the years of the Second Intifada and other conflicts began to lighten. While the residues of those fears still live with me, I find that I now think from a different position; I live in a basically safe environment where sirens, bus bombings, and missile attacks are absent from my immediate surroundings. I am not in survival mode constantly.[1] My experiences of violence, though, continue to affect the ways I relate to my children, my Israeli citizenship, my American Jewishness, and my religious practice.

We often underestimate the ways that feelings of security and insecurity affect our bodies as well as our minds. As the works in *Graphic War* suggest, intractable war becomes embedded not only in real spaces but in our bodies and memories. What stories live inside us as we move through fraught spaces, as we travel to school and work, and as we raise families? How do those narratives and the accompanying feelings of threat change the ways we perceive political and national structures, and how do they shape the ways that we see others who are positioned as perpetrators or victims in those narratives?

The graphic texts in the preceding chapters remind us of the long-term consequences of war on bodies, on communities, and on subsequent generations. In these works, sedimented layers of meaning register on the level of the diegetic plot as well as the extradiegetic plot as articulated in visual devices located in spatial terms on the page. As bodies move through space, they accumulate palimpsestic layers that reflect locations and histories that then exert "influence on the other layers and on identity as a whole" (Friedman, "Locational" 28–29). The visual and spatial approach that I offer in the term *graphic border poetics* argues for methods of thinking through graphic landscapes that are animated by political, cultural, personal, and historical memory—as well as the very real consequences of violent conflict on our bodies and collective futures.[2] The ways we feel about the space around us and about the status of security for our tribes or communities affect political actions in the present.

Graphic border poetics in this project takes a neoformalist approach to geographical borders and wars, highlighting the ways that comic devices and graphic modes of resistance are positioned as directly representational of bordered spaces in the larger worlds they represent. The visual affordances of graphic narratives then provide a rich palette through which to study borders and develop an emerging vocabulary of graphic representations of geopolitics. Unlike strictly topological representations, comics allow for the integration of narratives of affect, resistance, and residues of war into the discourse around conflict and the nation-state. Border discourse in graphic narratives works differently than in prose texts. Instead of the single plane constituted by combinations of letters and numbers that prose occupies (left to right in English), the graphic form uses the two-dimensional plane to represent cultures, religions, and of course power relations in spatial terms. Images in graphic narratives work to represent the event or social construction in terms that allow for spatial articulation. By paying attention to the artistic devices that illustrate the relation of bodies to objects and cultural narratives, the graphic border poetics in these texts create a way of knowing, a method of understanding or making visible the narratives that are central to our collective futures.

In the current moment of heightened war in the Middle East, Ukraine, and elsewhere, Miriam Libicki's work illustrates the position of the female body in relation to the nation-state. Libicki's complex graphic renderings of her ambivalence toward Israeli power in spatial terms create a second story of identity that suggests a connection between her own gendered identity position in the Israel Defense Forces (IDF) and the larger systems of violence and territorial divisions she sees around her. Libicki's work illustrates the ways that patriarchal systems and institutions use the female body, while the metanarrative of their location in relation to patriotism, Israeli nationhood, and Jewish identity reveals a female agency that gestures toward a more sustainable model of memory.

Amy Kurzweil and Nora Krug consider and challenge boundaried or culturally defined Holocaust memory in the twentieth century by creating possibilities for new configurations of cultural and territorial identities on their own terms in the twenty-first century. Reading Amy Kurzweil's and Nora Krug's works side by side in chapter 2 highlights the importance of putting women's memory of the Holocaust at the center of understanding the long-term consequences of war that crosses boundaries of religion and geographical location. The experimental artistic devices in these texts serve as models for reorienting the overdetermined memories of past atrocities within a more productive ethics of comparison using Michael Rothberg's concept of the implicated subject in order to move beyond a damaging hierarchy of suffering.

In Bernice Eisenstein's work, the young vulnerable Bernice speaks with the voice of her adult self, revealing an intimate, embodied portrayal of her family story that reflects the postwar reverberations of the Holocaust and the impact of affective environments of memory on her life and identity in Canada. Much of Eisenstein's work illustrates Lauren Berlant's suggestion that the task of our present is first to recognize the "halting, stuttering, aching" feelings that often accompany the waning fantasy of the militarized homeland as security and then to produce some better ways of mediating "a historical moment that is affectively felt but undefined in the social world . . . so that it would be possible to imagine a present that does not reproduce all of the conventional collateral damage" (263).

Leela Corman's and Julia Alekseyeva's graphic narratives in chapter 4 advocate for a focus beyond war, violence, and mourning, one that gathers the pieces of the past to forge connections to prewar Jewish Europe and to the activist legacy of their families *for a more just future*. These women's bodies merge with landscapes, with painful life experiences, and with the strength of their ancestors. As hair becomes tendrils that reach out to heal the broken world around them, as in Corman's work, these artists take a decidedly activist stance that pays homage to the legacy of their families in Poland and in the Soviet Union, not through mourning but through joy, connection, and social justice.

My work in *Graphic War* seeks to accomplish at least three central tasks: first, to explore the theoretical outcomes of graphic spatial poetics for thinking through the consequences of war and violence on women's bodies and futures; second, to examine the consequences of the ways that embedded narratives of trauma and violence intertwine with and shape contemporary identities and politics; and finally, and more optimistically, to learn from the ways these artistic narratives create openings for agentic and joyous futures. In a time of heightened war and conflict in Israel, Palestine, Iran, Lebanon, Syria, Ukraine, and other places, I hope to provide a method or framework for thinking about the damage produced by boundaries and borders of conflict along with our place and responsibility in contemporary injustice and violence. The visuality of spatial border poetics in graphic narratives centers feminist frameworks and critical geographies to excavate seemingly static geographical or Cartesian space. Theoretical frames like these have a sizable impact on the ways we perceive and move through space and have a direct bearing on the practices and policies of warfare and on those caught in those spaces. These structures are not only architectural but contain deep emotional and psychic strata that illustrate the flows or pathways in which war and oppression are often enacted, solidified, dissipated, or transformed.

Notes

Introduction

1 George Steiner, for example, claims that Jewish diaspora is more about the Jewish people's relationship to text than it is to a geographical homeland: "In post-exilic Judaism, active reading, answerability to the text on both meditative–interpretive and behavioral levels, is the central notion of personal and national homecoming" ("Our Homeland" 5).

2 Experiences and narratives of diaspora, statelessness, immigration, and war have been central in Jewish history and identity. The destruction of the two Temples, Jewish diaspora from the Promised Land, subsequent forced mass exile from adopted homelands like Spain, and the abject body all contribute to this narrative.

3 All of the authors in this study live and/or publish in North America, though several have lived in various national spaces.

4 I previously argued for the affordances of feminist geographies in comic spaces in the article "Contested Spaces." (Kavaloski, "Contested Spaces").

5 Note: Due to discussions that weigh down the term *Jewish identity*, I prefer the more informal and open term *Jewishness*. For discussions of contemporary Jewish identity, see Jonathan and Daniel Boyarin, George Steiner, Nira Yuval-Davis, Michael Bernard-Donals, Yael Zerubavel, Emanuel Levinas, Jacquelyn Rose, Amnon Raz-Krakotzkin, Judith Butler, Caryn Aviv, and David Shneer, among others.

6 Adrienne Rich introduces the term *politics of location* in her famous essay "Notes Toward a Politics of Location (1984)" to refer to the way individual women are located / locate themselves according to their body, religion, citizenship, region, ethnicity, and so forth. Apropos for this study, she writes, "A place on a map is also a place in history within which as a woman, a Jew, a lesbian, and a feminist I am created and trying to create" (Rich 212).

7 Of course, the geographies in these works are representational in the literary sense; they show the artists' perceptions and interpretations of space, which allow the reader to see the imagined spaces of location and territory in relation to the bodies of women.

8 As Matthew Hart has argued, art and literature have neglected the role of the state in the production of political spaces in part due to the fetishization of territorial authority that is "both broadly cultural and more narrowly political" (6–7).

9 Though geographers Henri Lefebvre, Doreen Massey, Patricia McDowell, and Yi-Fu Tuan, among others, have challenged this understanding of space, perceptions of Israel and Palestine are imbued with these older, static notions of historical belonging and geographical origins. Questions such as who has been there the longest, to whom does the land really belong, and who has authority over which territory still shape political discussions of the land.

10 This study builds on Benjamin Schreier's claim that contemporary Jewish American identity has been shored up by a ghettoized version of Jewish studies and Jewish American literature that needs reconstructing (*Impossible Jew*).

11 I first wrote about ways locational feminism functions in the comic form in 2010 as a result of conversations with my dissertation director, Susan Stanford Friedman. I solidified these ideas of feminist locationality in comics in my dissertation (Kavaloski, *Fragmentary*) and in the published essay "Contested Spaces in Graphic Narrative."

12 Zillah Eisenstein argues that war unsettles previously gendered life, and thus "space itself is reconstructed. The language of war—home front, battle zone, combatant, civilian—challenges established notions of home, safety, and privacy" (33).

13 This personal reflection constituted part of my dissertation project conclusion (Kavaloski, *Fragmentary*).

14 Hilary Chute, Scott McCloud, Tahneer Oksman, and Victoria Aarons, among others, discuss the spatial form of comics, particularly the text-image configuration.

15 Tahneer Oksman discusses locational feminism in relation to comics in *How Come Boys* (2016); see endnote 4 in chapter 1.

16 Several other comic scholars use the spatial term *orientation* in their analyses, including Ramzi Farwaz, "Introduction: Queer About Comics" (2018); Oksman, *How Come Boys*; and Katherine Kelp-Stebbens, "Comics as Orientation Devices," in *Comic Studies Here and Now* (2018). I use the term to clarify the position or relation of the body and objects to one another in the images through Sara Ahmed's definition, which relates to how we find our bearings in the world, an idea important to affect theory.

17 See studies by Philip Hollander and Ranen Omer-Sherman on Jewish masculinity.

18 Limbs on a more literal level mark the death and terror of the Holocaust.

19 Early responses condemned Glazer for "refuting his Jewishness"; Glazer later clarified that what he meant was that he condemns the way his Jewishness and the Holocaust were hijacked by the media to justify an unethical war.

20 In January, March, and May 2024 the International Court ruled that under the Convention on the Prevention and Punishment of the Crime of Genocide, Israel should "immediately halt military offensive." This ruling adds to the fraught reputation of Israel in the United States and on the global stage ("Question of Palestine"). In November 2024, the International Criminal Court issued arrest warrants for Benjamin Netanyahu and for Hamas leadership ("UN News").

21 Scholars like Michael Bernard-Donals have suggested that the story of the United States as a rescuing nation, especially in contrast to the atrocities of the Nazis, make the Holocaust an especially productive narrative for the United States' own sense of national pride and patriotism (*Figures of Memory*).

22 Jewish diaspora and oppression are persistent realities in Jewish history and in biblical texts.

23 The first intifada began in 1987 and lasted for about three years. The Second Intifada, or the Al-Aqṣā Intifada, began in September 2000 and lasted until about 2005.

24 See scholars on trauma and Holocaust memory such as Marianne Hirsch, Shoshana Felman, Dori Laub, Cathy Caruth, and Dominick LaCapra.

25 The 3GNY website says, "Our generation is the last living link to survivors." 3GNY was founded in 2005 and now has over six thousand members in New York alone. There are also branches in New Jersey, Philadelphia, Detroit, San Francisco, Boston, Miami, Canada, and Washington, D.C.

26 This story is covered in Judy Rudoren, "Proudly Bearing Elders Scars: Their Skin Says Never Forget." *The New York Times*, 30 Sept. 2021; and also in Allice Bloch, "How Memory Survives: Descendants and the Progenic Tattoo." *Thesis Eleven*, 7 Sept. 2021.

27 Horn's argument rests on the premise that anti-Semitism accounts for the contemporary fascination with the Holocaust and tortured Jews by non-Jews, which is not an issue I take up here. In her argument, she usefully points to a myriad of case studies that focus on terror against the Jewish people while also arguing that the focus on death obscures the long, rich history of Jewish culture and religion.

28 Though there is a thriving culture of Yiddish theater, music, and language in places like New York City as well as a focus on diverse representations of Jewish culture and prewar Jewish life, stories and images of war still dominate the landscape of Jewish American culture. This book probes the question, What are the consequences of that limited Jewish story on contemporary Jewish culture?

29 In her insightful book *Third Generation Holocaust Representation*, Victoria Aarons examines how the third generation transmits memories that are removed from direct experience and how their tellings change the ways the Holocaust is remembered after the death of the first generation. She poses the question, Living in a time when Holocaust survivors are now few, how do we preserve their memories and respect their stories? My project extends this question to ask, How do we transform these stories so that they are not simply narratives of fear and trauma that are passed down to future generations?

30 I presented a paper on Libicki and Glidden (part of chapter 1 of this book) at the *Graphic Details* art exhibition and conference in London in 2014.

31 As Ewa Stanczyk points out, Holocaust comics and narratives are written not just by Jews but by non-Jewish Poles, Italians, Germans, and others (4).

32 A line on a colonizing map has a corresponding militarized border, wall, or fence—a concrete consequence of the seemingly innocuous line on paper. Practices of colonization and war depend upon the delineation and exclusion of the other in order to establish hierarchies of difference.

33 Spatialized stories in graphic narratives have an extraordinary ability to make use of the spatiality of the page and the panel to engage fraught geopolitical spaces. Comics such as Amir and Kahlil's *Zahra's Paradise* (2011), Toufic El Rassi's *Arab in America* (2008), J. P. Srasse's *Deogratias* (2000), Jeremy Love's *Bayou* series (2009), Craig Thompson's *Habibi* (2011), Jay Cantor and James Romberger's *Aaron and Ahmed* (2011), and perhaps most famously Art Spiegelman's *Maus* series illuminate the spatiality of politically contested landscapes, imperialism, and colonialist projects. These texts facilitate a recognition of the ways that we imagine and produce

bounded territory and, in doing so, challenge us to perceive and narrate borders differently.

34 Hunt and Stevenson suggest that because countermappings often use the same cartographic tools they are attempting to resist, they are subject to the same limitations of those tools (373). As an artistic practice, graphic narratives are not limited in the same sense as cartographic tools but can be limited by the dimensions, space, and panels of the page/screen.

35 Israeli architect Eyal Weizman's work on architectures of containment brings attention to the ways that humanistic traditions have been harnessed for purposes of occupation, perhaps most notably illuminating the ways the Israel Defense Forces (IDF) use critical theories from the works of Guy Debord, Gilles Deleuze, and Félix Guattari to fight guerrilla warfare in closed village spaces. The Operational Theory Research Institute (OTRI), the preeminent training ground for tactical warfare theory in Israel, claims that poststructuralist theory completely restructured their approach to warfare. Using concepts such as "swarming," "infestation," and rhizomic warfare, the walls and floors of villages became spaces that the IDF could now move through (Weizman 187–200).

36 Agamben makes the distinction between *zoē*, the purely biological factors of life (or "bare life"), and *bios*, which includes cultural, social, and political expression. This distinction allows him to critique modern political life and the ways that some bodies are deemed worthy of protection and others are not.

37 The field of border studies and the related area of border aesthetics combine the approaches of cultural geography and cultural studies in order to connect topographical spaces such as "local, urban, intimate, subjective spaces" in the studies of geopolitical boundaries (Rosello and Wolfe 2).

38 The field of border aesthetics examines works such as political and prose literary works. Comics and graphic memoirs have not to my knowledge been a part of the discourse of border poetics until now.

39 A version of chapter 1 was published in *Studies in Comics*, vol. 6, no. 2, 2015.

Chapter 1 Militarized Bodies and Contested Homelands in the Works of Miriam Libicki and Sarah Glidden

Portions of this chapter were previously published in *Studies in Comics*, vol. 6, no. 2, 2015.

1 The VanCAF board subsequently apologized for their rash claims about Libicki's work, stating that she was not a threat to the security of the community as they had originally claimed ("VanCAF Formal Apology").

2 Scholars who have explored these questions include Robin Cohen, Benedict Anderson, Salman Rushdie, Avtar Brah, Nikos Papastergiadis, Jonathan Boyarin, Edward Said, and William Safran, among others, though few have explored the ways that pictorial narratives represent the intersections of the homeland of the imaginary with the homeland of lived experience.

3 "Homeland" here refers to the historical idea of Israel as the homeland of the Jews, the cultural memory that links Israel to the Jewish people, and individual memories that shape patriotic loyalty and the desire for a homeland, as well as the sense of loss in the idealization of Israel as a homeland

4 Oksman published her book *How Come Boys Get to Keep Their Noses?* (2016) after the first version of this chapter was published. Oksman argues that Miriam's

disorientation in the comic medium mirrors a disorientation of location and homeland.

5 "The space of the human being is the most critical site to watch the production and reproduction of power," suggests Edward Soja in *Third Space* (114). Soja thus reminds his readers of the intimate relationship between the body and imagined homeland.

6 Works by Art Spiegelman, Phillipe Marion, Hilary Chute, Stephen Tabachnick, and Sarah Lightman, among others, directly address geography and/or spatiality in graphic narrative.

7 The labels "Israeli" and "Palestinian" are of course a simplification of the more complex layers and religious identifications in Israel-Palestine. Israeli citizens can be Jewish, Muslim, Christian, and Druze. Palestinians may be those who identify as the people/families that were present in Palestine before Israeli statehood, those who live in the occupied territories, or those who refuse to identify with the Israeli state. Religious and cultural identities of Palestinians might include Muslim, Bedouin, Druze, and Christian.

8 My use of the term *home* refers to an imaginary conception of a place of origin that is part of both individual and communal identity making. The result of the strong rhetorical position that Israel occupies as home within the Jewish psyche makes taking a position of "ethical deterritorialization" extremely difficult (Bernard-Donals).

9 Miriam's sense of doubleness resonates with W. E. B. Du Bois's concept of double consciousness in African American life. See *The Souls of Black Folk* (3).

10 The Holocaust holds a central place in the formation of the Israeli state. Too, it marks a point of anxiety in Jewish American connections to Israel. Birthright tours and fundraising campaigns regularly include references to the atrocities of World War II and the vulnerable position of the Jews in the world.

11 Sharon Rotbard details the *Homa Umigdal* project in his essay "Wall and Tower" in *A Civilian Occupation*, edited by Eyal Weizman and Rafi Segal (2003).

12 Making women visible in this process of nationalization and militarization is imperative because Jewish women have been not only members but also objects of the nationalist imagination. They have lived in some sense both inside and outside of the boundaries and borders of homelands—literal and imaginary.

13 The scholarship on Birthright trips includes Shaul Kelner's *Tours That Bind: Diaspora, Pilgrimage, and Israeli Birthright Tourism*; and Yehonaton Abramson's "Making a Homeland, Constructing a Diaspora: The Case of Taglit-Birthright Israel."

14 The construction of the wall began in 2002 by the Israeli government to try to prevent Palestinian suicide bombing and attacks, but it also had many personal and geographical consequences for Palestinians living near the wall.

15 Dallas Hunt and Shaun A. Stevenson discuss the ways that official cartographic practices colonize spaces and people and the countermapping practices that may resist these histories and practices.

Chapter 2 The Implicated Subject and World War II Identity in the Twenty-First Century

1 Joan Ringelheim writes that when she was doing research in the 1980s on death and survival rates of women in the Holocaust, there was no research at all available from the viewpoint of gender (349).

2 Sara Horowitz argues that Holocaust narratives often depict women as deficient and peripheral to the central story (368). Even graphic texts by second-generation survivors like Art Spiegelman's *Maus* series show women as fragile or smothering; Horowitz suggests that Anja's missing diaries "exemplify the marginality of women's experiences in constructing a master narrative of Nazi genocide." It is worth noting that Anja's only surviving stories of the Holocaust, her diaries, are burned by her husband Vladek—an action that results in Anja's story being subsumed by his narrative.

3 In "German Postmemory and Ambivalent Home Desires," Marinja Grujić and Ina Schaum suggest that Krug's book is an aesthetic representation of Marianne Hirsch's concept of postmemory, and that Krug's search for Heimat/Belonging results in her recognition that the Holocaust is a "part of the German family histories and . . . there is no way to overcome this discomfort" (Grujić and Schaum 207).

4 Historian Robert Frie argues that while Germans should not stay entrenched in the horrors of the past, it is imperative for them to confront personal German family histories in order to develop "a meaningful personal and political awareness of the future" (14).

5 As discussed in the introduction, the distance or sometimes lack of distance between bodies, objects, memories, and borders in graphic texts depicts the repercussion of these relations. This approach puts positionality and locationality at the center of comic studies and visual studies. Susan Friedman argues that in such an approach, "space . . . is not a static essence, but rather a location of historical overdetermination. . . . Spatial rhetoric suggests fluid and flexible ways of being that posit identity as relational, situational, and interactive—the result of an ongoing process of becoming" ("Locational" 20). Within graphic narratives, the creative organization of space such as collage, the use of lines and borders, maps, spatial metaphors, and the juxtaposition of different media make *visible* transnational trauma, intersectional identities, and multidirectional memories. I expand on Sara Ahmed's definition of orientation, which includes the proximity of bodies to objects and geographical places to include the *visual* and *spatial* orientation of images, objects, histories, and events.

6 Kurzweil also draws cartoons for *The New Yorker* and is the author of *Artificial: A Love Story* (2023).

7 Kurzweil invokes Art Spiegelman's iconic chimney smoke in his *Maus* series here, acknowledging the influence of other graphic novelists on her work while at the same time she expands the metaphor of the smoke of the gas chamber ovens from a male artist's work to the domestic space (the house) of a female artist's work.

8 These sorts of all-encompassing fears are not unusual in second- and third-generation survivors; indeed, they are quite common in narratives about Jewish identity. Amy's fears merge time and place, making her bubbe's stories so visceral for Amy that her own present and future are superimposed onto that of her grandmother's past; that is, the past becomes part of Amy's present, but Amy's present is also projected back into her bubbe's past.

9 The large, affective, watery images that loom in the shadows of Amy's life seem out of place and perhaps unfounded in the backdrop of her safe, upper-middle class life often creating a comedic effect. Instead of a direct reflection on Amy's position of relative safety and privilege, Kurzweil instead implies a disjunction between memory and reality as she toggles back and forth between Amy's fear of the Holocaust and her life in a wealthy suburb in the twenty-first century. For example, one

chapter is titled "Bed Bath and Beyond," alluding to the once-popular home decor franchise that was part of the 1990s suburban landscape.

10 This contemporary desire to return to a "before" is in part a result of a sociocultural structure that Lauren Berlant describes as an enabling optimism or attrition of fantasy: a fantasy that involves a collective investment in a narrative that sustains a particular meaning or promise.

11 Nora Krug's *Belonging* does not include numbered pages, so I use chapter numbers for in-text citations. The refusal to use page numbers may be the result of a hesitancy to comply with the German order and efficiency she equates with the death machine.

12 See the section "Object Nationalism and the Body's Proximity to National Shame" in this chapter for a discussion of the Hansaplast bandage.

13 Tammy Clewell writes that "following Allied initiatives, including the public recognition of war crimes at the 1945 Nuremberg trials and the process of denazification . . . the German struggle to acknowledge and overcome the negative consequences of the past . . . has taken place through official programs of commemoration and, perhaps primarily, through formal education in the schools, where children, starting around the fifth grade, learn about Nazism and typically visit a concentration camp museum" (460).

14 Michael Rothberg's implicated subject, like Krug and Kurzweil, is a figure of responsibility who is entangled in histories of violence and long traditions of nationalist pride ("Response" 514).

15 When Nora marries a Jewish man in New York, she carries the internalized shame of the past into her wedding and into her relationship with her in-laws. In a double-page spread, a drawing of a large white wedding cake decorated with pink flowers dominates the page, the cake split in half by the layout of the book and divided down the center. The groom remains on one side of the center fold, the bride on the other. The bride and groom dolls atop the cake are not holding hands or even standing together; rather, the uncomfortable-looking groom stands on one-half of the cake as a stiff, unhappy-looking bride stands on the other half. The cake is decorated with the words "Not even marrying a Jewish man has lessened my German shame" (chap. 2). Instead of an image of celebration and love, Krug depicts her marriage as infused with and tainted by shame and guilt of the past. (In a darkly humorous note, Krug adds that despite her own anxious feelings about the marriage, her father admits that his daughter's marriage to a Jewish man does alleviate *his* sense of guilt somewhat.)

16 The President's Commission goes on to say that the "operation of the camps [was] based on calculations of accessibility and cost-effectiveness, the trademarks of modern business practice. . . . Adjacent to the extermination camp at Auschwitz was a privately owned, corporately sponsored concentration camp called I.G. Auschwitz, a division of I.G. Farben. This multi-dimensional, petro-chemical complex brought human slavery to its ultimate perfection by reducing human beings to consumable raw materials, from which all mineral life was systematically drained before the bodies were recycled into the Nazi war economy: gold teeth for the treasury, hair for mattresses, ashes for fertilizer. In their relentless search for the least expensive and most efficient means of extermination, German scientists experimented with a variety of gases until they discovered the insecticide Zyklon B, which could kill 2,000 persons in less than 30 minutes at a cost of one-half-cent per body" (President's Commission 4).

17 As suggested in note 11, the absence of page numbers in Krug's narrative suggests a resistance or a refusal to follow the claimed purpose of the Leitz: a calculated, measured, or linear approach to her story's organization.
18 Matt Reingold suggests that these maps in part document Kurzweil's "move beyond childhood naivete and simplistic associations with people and places" ("Mapping Transformative Spaces" 1).
19 Alison Bechdel, whom Amy references more than once in her memoir, makes use of round panels in *Fun Home* using similar dark lines to show isolation and artistic endeavors in her family dynamics. Kurzweil often uses artistic devices found in graphic works by artists like Bechdel, Miriam Katin, Miriam Libicki, Will Eisner, Art Spiegelman, and others as a way to allude to their place in her chosen graphic family lineage.
20 For example, early discourses of Palestine as a land without a people along with the Jews' ability to "make the desert bloom" suggest that Jewish engagement with the land is, by definition, productive and also blessed. See Yael Zerubavel, "The Desert and the Settlement as Symbolic Landscapes in Modern Israeli Culture"; and *Desert in the Promised Land: Memory, Space, and the Counterplace in Israeli Culture*; along with Ranen Omer-Sherman, *Israel in Exile: Jewish Writing and the Desert*.
21 In *Belonging*, Krug outlines the story, which was published in *Der Giftpilz*, an anti-Semitic children's book by Julius Streicher, the publisher of *Der Stürmer*.
22 Matt Reingold argues that Krug absolves her Uncle Willi (who Krug discovers was a member of the Nazi Party) of responsibility by the end of the text ("Heimat" 563).
23 As Robert Frie suggests about the process of exploring his family's Nazi past with his Jewish wife, "the shared process of negotiating this traumatic history made me appreciate how readily the past can appear in the present: that we are situated in dimensions of history and trauma that shape our lives in ways that are often beyond our awareness" (10).

Chapter 3 "The Drug of H"

1 The shadows behind the young Bernice on the cover match up with the images of her parents standing arm in arm on page 17 of the memoir: Her father wears a fedora and her mother's hair is piled high on her head.
2 With names like *Satan's Shackles* and *Dolls of Doom*, these novels were published from the 1940s through the 1980s.
3 While Miriam Harris calls it an "illustrated memoir" and a "graphic novel" (129), Drewniak prefers "graphic memoir" (43), and Ruth Panofsky calls it "a graphic work" and "graphic memoir" (133). Eisenstein herself says "I never thought of it as an autobiography; it is a memoir of sensibility" (Panofsky 137). Eisenstein's work is difficult to categorize precisely because it uses an experimental form that mixes illustration, paneled comic form, and literary prose. The experimentation of form is the point here—not categorizing Eisenstein's text into one particular genre but rather witnessing the various ways she maps her own voice and territory of memory.
4 The heightened awareness of survivor stories and the depth of loss that occurred in the Holocaust became more prevalent after the trial in 1961.
5 In an image on the facing page, a young Bernice stands on a small rock and shouts to Moses, "Hey, wait! Which is it? Thou shalt not take its name in vain OR not take

it into a vein? Help me out" (Eisenstein, *I Was a Child* 22). The humor in the Moses scene is not lost on the reader. The comedic tone comes from both the illustration of the young Bernice asking humorous questions to Moses and the self-reflective first-person retrospective position of the writing.

6 In part as an homage to Charlotte Salomon, Eisenstein creates an artistic lineage that she alludes to and re-creates for herself several decades later in *I Was a Child of Holocaust Survivors*. During Salomon's upbringing in a well-to-do family in Berlin, she mingled with several famous thinkers and artists that became present in her work. Luminaries like Albert Einstein, Erich Mendelsohn, and Albert Schweitzer frequented her home and eventually influenced her life's work *Life? or Theatre?* (Ricci). In her poignant coming-of-age story that includes abuse, family suicides, and escape from the Nazis (and her eventual unwritten death), Salomon uses allusions to well-known artists. Salomon creates an artistic line that connects her to a larger lived community of artists and writers prior to the start of World War II.

7 Matisse's work appeared in Hitler's Degenerate Art Exhibition in 1937. Fortunately, Matisse did survive the war unlike many of the other artists in that exhibit.

8 David Roskies in "What Is Holocaust Literature?" divides the approaches to Holocaust memory into three periods: the first centers on communal memory (1945–1960), the second focuses on displaced memory (1961 and 1978), and the third centers personalized memory (1978–1991).

9 According to journalist Tom Segev, De-Nur influenced an entire generation of Israelis' view of the Holocaust. He writes that "Israelis internalized the descriptions of the horrors provided them by K. Zetnik, including sadistic torture, cannibalism and sexual abuse of children" (Segev, "Who Were You").

10 See studies by Philip Hollander and Omer-Sherman on Jewish masculinity.

11 Or perhaps, as Victoria Aarons suggests, the young Bernice is "infantilized by the enormity of her parents' history" (*Holocaust* 89).

12 Giorgio Agamben discusses the politicization of life in *Homo Sacer: Sovereign Power and Bare Life* (1998), in *Remnants of Auschwitz* (1999), and later in *The Kingdom and the Glory* (2011).

13 At the end of the trial the judge announces, "In order to punish the accused and deter others, the maximum penalty laid down in the law must be imposed on him" (26).

14 The page points toward a haunting that is a double loss: first, the loss of family in the Holocaust, which is mourned together with friends who consoled one another and created a new family in Canada (known as "the Group"). The second loss here is the death of members of the replacement family—which inevitably echoes with the first loss.

Chapter 4 "Work for the Future, Not Only for Memory"

1 Stanczyk claims that the popularization of Spiegelman's *Maus* and TV series like *The Story of the Family Weiss* (1978) both contributed to the Americanization of the Shoah (1).

2 Debates about which identity group has suffered the most or about how the word *holocaust/Holocaust* circulates are indicative of these divisions. For scholarly discussions see Judith Butler, Michael Rothberg, and Peter Novick, among others.

3 Carrying one's losses is a motif in several of the comic texts in this project. Amy Kurzweil contends with her grandmother's frightening Holocaust stories in the

form of a haunted home that is permeated by feelings of the terror of war despite living far from the world of the Holocaust (California). Bernice Eisenstein articulates the burden of memory she inherits from her parents as a deadly addiction and as a physical amputation that prevents her from feeling whole.

4 Peter Novick suggests that a focus on the Holocaust in the world of American Jewry comes at the cost of a larger social consciousness that was once at the center of American Jewry (10).

5 Though the works I discuss are largely autobiographical, I differentiate between the authors and the main characters. I refer to authors by last name (Corman and Alekseyeva) and the characters in the narrative by first name (Leela and Julia). The genres of autobiography and fiction can overlap as suggested by the term *autofiction*.

6 According to the text, Julia only discovers many of the stories she includes in *Soviet Daughter* after Lola dies, thus *Soviet Daughter* is a sort of retrospective narrative of intersecting lives. Though Julia and Lola have a strong bond during Julia's young years, many of the stories of Lola's life in the USSR are only woven into Julia's narrative after Lola's death, as Lola's diary is given to Julia after this event (5–6).

7 Julia says about her political activism, "I had no idea that Lola was as political as I was" (12). Alekseyeva's *Soviet Daughter* is a retrospective merging of the two women based on emotional and spiritual inspiration of the two.

8 I connect spatial theory and Friedman's theories of feminist geopolitical rhetoric to the comic form in *Fragmentary Returns* (2015) and in "Contested Spaces in Graphic Narrative" (2015).

9 In the third section, I incorporate two additional short works by Corman, "The Blood Road" (2018) and "The Irreducible Essence of Jewishness" (2015), which illustrate Corman's shifting sense of Jewish identity in relation to her grandparents' stories.

10 The Holocaust shapes a collective Jewish American identity, in part, as one of victimhood, as Peter Novick points out (7).

11 Dana Mihăilescu suggests that the unique format of the text "allows Alekseyeva to foreground anti-essentialist notions of the Jewish self" by ghostwriting Lola's story ("Jewish Identity" 149).

12 In an interview, Alekseyeva said that her memoir is an homage to her great-grandmother and that "eighty percent of this book is straight from [her] great-grandmother's memoirs" (Chute)

13 According to many statistics, between the years 1989 and 2006, approximately 1.6 million Jews left the former Soviet Union, largely immigrating to Israel, the United States, and Germany (Maltz)

14 NKVD stands for Narodny Komissariat Vnutrennikh Del, the Soviet secret police agency that predated the KGB (Komitet Gosudarstvennoy Bezopasnosti).

15 Although Julia's mother and grandmother prevent Julia from telling Lola about her illness, Alekseyeva chooses to narrate the past by depicting the connections between her and Lola in a retroactive reimagining of this period. When the news of Julia's illness is eventually leaked to Lola later in the year, she says to Julia, "Yulichka, I know about the operation—and I just wanted to say, don't worry. Everything's going to be fine. You're going to be ok. You're going to be ok" (90). By ending the section with Lola's support for Julia, Alekseyeva focuses on the narrative of mutual love rather than silence.

16 When her grandfather returns home after fighting in the Polish army, he finds that his family has been killed and his home has been stolen by neighbors.
17 The tunnel that leads to a parallel universe is connected to tree roots and trees. The tunnels and holes Corman depicts in this story are often created by the roots of trees and forests, perhaps due to the murder of her relatives in forests in Poland; at the same time, the roots are a metaphor for her feeling of connection to her family. This motif allows her to invoke various personal and historical positions/locations simultaneously.
18 Chapter 2, which describes several anti-Semitic pogroms and massacres, follows Julia's description of her struggles with Jewish identity and integration into American culture ("Interlude: 1992").
19 Living with her mother and grandmother, both of whom she has a difficult relationship with, adds to Julia's sense of isolation. In one full-page collage, Alekseyeva depicts the effects of the negative messages she receives from her mother. Phrases like "No one will ever love you," "You're wasting your life," and "Why don't you play with dolls like all the normal girls?" (23) swirl around the page and surround figures of Julia at various ages (23). In each of the three figures of Julia growing from childhood into young adulthood, she is sitting and doing a solitary task: reading, writing, and drawing. The image shows how her childhood challenges lead to creative endeavors like drawing and writing as a means of expression.
20 These stereotypical symbols of American Jewish life also appear in Corman's discussions of her Jewish identity (See "Irreducible").
21 Alekseyeva explains how she perceives her own idealism as connected to the early USSR: "If you look at what many individual people were striving for in the early days in the Soviet Union, it was inclusion and liberation, which is of course not what Russia stands for now" (Mironova).
22 Alekseyeva describes these events as "massive campaigns of political repression in the USSR which involved a large-scale purge of government officials and Communist Party members, caused by Stalin's paranoia of political sabotage and the desire to cement his own authority" (109).
23 This phrase is used by Friedman to discuss feminist theory and prose texts, though it applies beautifully to visual texts.
24 Under the Soviet system Lola's gender is seen as fit for equal work, while her body is burdened by the double standards and oppressive environments that did not support these women and the children they cared for.

Conclusion

1 The point of my personal observations is not to compare or equate my experiences of violence with others in Israel and Palestine but rather simply to describe the ways that violence and war have impacted my own body and my interest in this project.
2 This book highlights activism in art and comics, but I also want to be cognizant of the ways that women do activist work on geographical borders. Real borders confine and sometimes protect. Checkpoints, walls between drawn territories, and refugee camps often create insecurity for those on both sides; locked gates and armed guards at cafés create an environment of safety for some and fear for others. There are several groups of women that do activist work in Israel, in Palestine, and in the United States. These groups include *Machsom* Watch, Israeli women who

document soldier conduct at West Bank checkpoints and observe in military courts and detention centers; Women in Black, who protest the occupation weekly; *Bat Shalom* (Daughter of Peace) and *Profil Hadash* (New Profile), who work against compulsory enlistment in the military; and *Emahot Neged HaKibush*, or Mothers Against Violence, an Israeli network of activists who wear yellow vests while "opposing the occupation and Israeli militarism from a feminist maternal perspective" (*Mothers Against Violence Israel*).

Works Cited

Aarons, Victoria. "The Burden of the Third Generation in Germany." *The Holocaust Across Borders*, edited by Hilene S. Flanzbaum, Lexington Books, 2021, pp. 89–112.

Aarons, Victoria. *Holocaust Graphic Narratives: Generation, Trauma, and Memory*. Rutgers University Press, 2019.

Aarons, Victoria. *Third Generation Holocaust Representation*. Northwestern University Press, 2017.

Abramson, Yehonatan. "Making a Homeland, Constructing a Diaspora: The Case of Taglit-Birthright Israel." *Political Geography*, vol. 58, 2017, pp. 14–23.

Agamben, Giorgio. *Homo Sacer: Sovereign Power and Bare Life*. Translated by Daniel Heller-Roazen. Stanford University Press, 1998.

Agamben, Giorgio. *The Kingdom and the Glory: For a Theological Genealogy of Economy and Government*. Translated by Lorenzo Chiesa. Stanford University Press, 2011.

Agamben, Giorgio. *Remnants of Auschwitz: The Witness and the Archive*. Translated by Daniel Heller-Roazen. Zone Books, 1999.

Ahmed, Sara. *The Cultural Politics of Emotion*. Routledge, 2004.

Ahmed, Sara. *Queer Phenomenology: Orientations, Objects, Others*. Duke University Press, 2006.

Alekseyeva, Julia. *Soviet Daughter: A Graphic Revolution*. Microcosm Publishing, 2017.

Amatenstein, Sherry. "The Next Generation." *Tablet*, 27 Apr. 2022, https://www.tabletmag.com/sections/community/articles/next-generation-grandchildren-of-holocaust-survivors.

Anderson, Benedict. *Imagined Communities: Reflections of the Origin and Spread of Nationalism*. Verso, 1983.

Arendt, Hannah. *The Human Condition*. 1958. Harcourt, 1976.

Arendt, Hannah. *The Origins of Totalitarianism*. 1951. Harcourt, 1973.

Arendt, Hannah. *Responsibility and Judgement*. Schocken Books, 2005.

Bauer, Heike, Andrea Greenbaum, and Sarah Lightman, editors. *Jewish Women in Comics: Bodies and Borders*. Syracuse University Press, 2023.

Bechdel, Alison. *Fun Home: A Family Tragicomedy*. Mariner Books, 2007.

Benjamin, Walter. *The Arcades Project*. 1940. Translated by Howard Eiland. Belknap Press, 1999.

Berlant, Lauren. *Cruel Optimism*. Duke University Press, 2011.
Bernard-Donals, Michael. "'By the Rivers of Babylon': Deterritorialization and the Jewish Rhetorical Stance." *College English*, vol. 72, no. 6, 2010, pp. 608–620.
Bernard-Donals, Michael. *Figures of Memory: The Rhetoric of Displacement at the United States Holocaust Memorial Museum*. State University of New York Press, 2016.
"Border Poetics / Border Culture." *Arctic University of Norway (UiT)*, https://en.uit.no/forskning/forskningsgrupper/gruppe?p_document_id=344750.
Boyarin, Daniel, and Jonathan Boyarin, "Diaspora: Generation and the Ground of Jewish Identity." *Critical Inquiry*, vol. 19, no. 4, 1993, pp. 693–725.
Boyarin, Jonathan. "A Response from New York: Return of the Repressed?" *Grasping Land: Space and Place in Contemporary Israeli Discourse and Experience*, edited by Eyal Ben-Ari and Yoram Bilu, State University of New York Press, 1997, pp. 217–230.
Brah, Avtar. *Cartographies of Diaspora: Contested Identities*. Routledge, 1996.
Braidotti, Rosi. "Affirming the Affirmative: On Nomadic Affectivity." *Rhizomes*, nos. 11/12, fall 2005 / spring 2006, http://www.rhizomes.net/issue11/braidotti.html.
Braidotti, Rosi. "Critical Posthuman Knowledges." *South Atlantic Quarterly*, vol. 116, no. 1, January 2017, pp. 83–96.
Braidotti, Rosi. *The Posthuman*. Polity Press, 2013.
Braidotti, Rosi. "A Theoretical Framework for the Critical Posthumanities." *Theory, Culture, and Society*, vol. 36, no. 6, 2019, pp. 31–61.
Butler, Judith. *Parting Ways: Jewishness and the Critique of Zionism*. Columbia University Press, 2012.
Butler, Judith. *Senses of the Subject*. Fordham University Press, 2015.
Caruth, Cathy. *Trauma*. Johns Hopkins University Press, 1995.
Chase, Alisia. "Draws like a Girl: The Necessity of Old-School Feminist Interventions in the World of Comics and Graphic Novels." *Feminism Reframed: Reflections on Art and Difference*, edited by Alexandra M. Kokoli, Cambridge Scholars, 2008, pp. 61–85.
Chute, Hilary. "Comics as Literature? Reading Graphic Narrative." *PMLA*, vol. 123, no. 2, 2008, pp. 452–465.
Chute, Hilary. *Disaster Drawn: Visual Witness, Comics, and Documentary Form*. Belknap Press, 2016.
Chute, Hilary. "Interview with Julia Alekseyeva. Live talk at Harvard U," *Facebook* (video), uploaded by Davis Center for Russian and Eurasian Studies at Harvard University, 26 Apr. 2017, https://www.facebook.com/DCRES/videos/watch-a-selection-from-soviet-daughter-a-graphic-revolution-with-julia-alekseyev/10154321097031035/.
Clewell, Tammy. "Beyond Graphic Memoir: Visualizing Third-Generation German Cultural Identity in Nora Krug's *Belonging*." *American Imago*, vol. 77, no. 3, 2020, pp. 459–496.
Cohen, Robin. *Global Diasporas: An Introduction*. University of Washington Press, 1997.
Coole, Diana, and Samantha Frost. *New Materialisms: Ontology, Agency, and Politics*. Duke University Press, 2010.
Corman, Leela. "The Blood Road." *Tablet*, 11 Apr. 2018, https://www.tabletmag.com/sections/community/articles/the-blood-road.
Corman, Leela. "Drawing Strength from My Grandfather, Who Carries His Losses from the Holocaust." *Tablet*, 30 Dec. 2013, https://www.tabletmag.com/sections/community/articles/grandfather-carried-losses.
Corman, Leela. "The Irreducible Essence of Jewishness." *Tablet*, 19 Nov. 2015, https://www.tabletmag.com/sections/community/articles/the-irreducibles.
Corman, Leela. *We All Wish for Deadly Force*. Retrofit 52, 2016.
Corman, Leela. *You Are Not a Guest*. Fieldmouse Press, 2023.

Corman, Leela. "You Are Not a Guest." *Tablet*, 28 Apr. 2021, https://www.tabletmag.com/sections/community/articles/you-are-not-a-guest-leela-corman.
"Court Backs Claim That Al-Dura Was Staged." *Haaretz*, 22 May 2008.
Crenshaw, Kimberlé. "Demarginalizing the Intersection of Race and Sex: A Black Feminist Critique of Antidiscrimination Doctrine, Feminist Theory, and Antiracist Politics." *University of Chicago Legal Forum*, vol. 1989, no. 1, art. 8, 1989, pp. 139–167.
Deleuze, Gilles, and Félix Guattari. *On the Line*. Semiotext(e), 1983.
Deleuze, Gilles, and Félix Guattari. *A Thousand Plateaus*. University of Minnesota Press, 1987.
De-Nur, Yehiel [Ka-Tzetnik 135633]. *House of Dolls*. 1953. Simon and Schuster, 1955.
Drewniak, Dagmara. "Addicted to the Holocaust—Bernice Eisenstein's Ways of Coping with Troublesome Memories in *I Was a Child of Holocaust Survivors*." *Studia Anglica Posnaniensia*, vol. 50, nos. 2–3, 11 Jan. 2016, pp. 39–50.
Du Bois, W. E. B., *The Souls of Black Folk*. 1909. Dover Thrift, 2003.
Eisenstein, Bernice. *I Was a Child of Holocaust Survivors*. Riverhead Press, 2006.
Eisenstein, Bernice, and Anne Michaels. *Correspondences*. Knopf, 2013.
Eisenstein, Zillah. "Resexing Militarism for the Globe." *Feminism and War: Confronting US Imperialism*, edited by Robin L. Riley, Chandra Talpade Mohanty, and Minnie Bruce Pratt, Zed Books, 2008, pp. 27–46.
Ezrachi, Sidra. *Booking Passage: Exile and Homecoming in the Modern Jewish Imagination*. University of California Press, 2000.
Farwaz, Ramzi, and D. Scott, editors. "Introduction: Queer About Comics." *American Literature*, vol. 90, no. 2, 2018, pp. 197–219.
Fischer, Nina. "Facing the Arab 'Other'?: Jerusalem in Jewish Women's Comics." *Studies in Comics* vol. 6, no. 2, 2015, pp. 291–311.
Frie, Robert. *Not in My Family: German Memory and Responsibility After the Holocaust*. Oxford University Press, 2017.
Friedman, Susan Stanford. "Bodies on the Move: A Poetics of Home and Diaspora." *Tulsa Studies in Women's Literature*, vol. 23, no. 2, 2004, pp. 189–212.
Friedman, Susan Stanford. "Locational Feminism: Gender, Cultural Geographies, Geopolitical Literacy." *Feminist Locations Global and Local, Theory and Practice*, edited by Marianne DeKoven, Rutgers University Press, 2001, pp. 13–36.
Folman, Ari. *Waltz with Bashir*. Metropolitan Books, 2009.
Garcia-Navarro, Lulu. "'Soviet Daughter': How a Great-Grandmother's Diary Became a Graphic Novel." *NPR*, 22 Jan. 2017, https://www.npr.org/2017/01/22/509158334/soviet-daughter-how-a-great-grandmothers-diary-became-a-graphic-novel.
Glidden, Sarah. "The Art of War." *The Nib*. 2018.
Glidden, Sarah. "Drawing a Line: 40 Years of Angoulême." *Jewish Quarterly Magazine*, vol. 60, no. 1, Apr. 2013, pp. 16–17.
Glidden, Sarah. *How to Understand Israel in 60 Days or Less*. DC Comics, 2010.
Glidden, Sarah. "Monuments." *SarahGlidden.com*, 15 Aug. 2017, http://sarahglidden.com/monuments/.
Grosz, Elizabeth. *Volatile Bodies: Toward a Corporeal Feminism*. Indiana University Press, 1994.
Grujić, Marija, and Ina Schaum. "German Postmemory and Ambivalent Home Desires: A Critical Reading of Nora Krug's (2018) Graphic Novel *Heimat: A German Family Album*." *Ethnoscripts*, vol. 21, no. 1, 2019, pp. 196–212.
Hall, Stuart. "Cultural Identity and the Diaspora." *Undoing Place? A Geographical Reader*, edited by Linda McDowell, Routledge, 1997, pp. 231–242.

Haraway, Donna. "Situated Knowledges: The Science Question in Feminism as a Site of Discourse on the Privilege of Partial Perspective." *Feminist Studies*, vol. 14, no. 3, 1988, pp. 575–599.

Harde, Roxanne. "'Give 'Em Another Circumcision': Jewish Masculinities in the Golem's Mighty Swing." *The Jewish Graphic Novel*, edited by Samantha Baskind and Ranen Omer-Sherman, Rutgers University Press, 2010, pp. 64–84.

Harding, Sandra. *The Science Question in Feminism*. Cornell University Press, 1986.

Harris, Cecily. "German Memory of the Holocaust: The Emergence of Counter-Memorials." *Penn History Review*, vol. 17, no. 2, 2010, pp. 34–57.

Harris, Miriam. "Releasing the Grip of the Ghostly: Bernice Eisenstein's *I Was a Child of Holocaust Survivors*." *The Jewish Graphic Novel: Critical Approaches*, edited by Samantha Baskind and Ranen Omer-Sherman, Rutgers University Press, 2008, pp. 129–143.

Hart, Matthew. *Extraterritoriality: A Political Geography of Contemporary Fiction*. Columbia University Press, 2020.

Hirsch, Marianne. *The Generation of Postmemory: Writing and Visual Culture After the Holocaust*. Columbia University Press, 2012.

Hirsch, Marianne. Introduction. *Women Mobilizing Memory*, edited by Ayşe Gül Altınay et al., Columbia University Press, 2019, pp. 1–23.

Horowitz, Sara. "Women in Holocaust Literature: Engendered Trauma Memory." *Women in the Holocaust*, edited by Dalia Ofer and Lenore Weitzman, Yale University Press, 1998, pp. 364–378.

Hunt, Dallas, and Shaun A. Stevenson. "Decolonizing Geographies of Power: Indigenous Digital Counter-Mapping Practices on Turtle Island." *Settler Colonial Studies*, vol. 7, no. 3, 2017, pp. 372–392.

Kavaloski, Laini. "Contested Spaces in Graphic Narrative: Exploring Miriam Libicki's *jobnik! An American Girl's Adventures in the Israeli Army*." *Studies in Comics*, vol. 6, no. 2, 2015, pp. 231–251.

Kavaloski, Laini. *Fragmentary Returns: Revisioning Contemporary Militarized Homelands in Israel and the United States*. 2015. University of Wisconsin–Madison, PhD dissertation.

Kelner, Shaul. *Tours That Bind: Diaspora, Pilgrimage, and Israeli Birthright Tourism*. New York University Press, 2012.

Kelp-Stebbins, Katherine. "Comics as Orientation Devices." *Comic Studies Here and Now*, edited by Frederick Luis Aldama, Routledge, 2018, pp. 211–225.

Krasuska, Karolina. *Soviet-Born: The Afterlives of Migration in Jewish American Fiction*. Rutgers University Press, 2024.

Krug, Nora. *Belonging: A German Reckons with History and Home*. Simon and Schuster, 2018.

Kurzweil, Amy. *Flying Couch: A Graphic Memoir*. Black Balloon Press, 2016.

Kurzweil, Amy. "From the Notebook of a Fellow Graphic Memoirist: An Illustrated Review of Nora Krug's *Belonging*." *momentmag.com*, 13 Nov. 2018, https://momentmag.com/illustrated-book-review-belonging-by-nora-krug/?srsltid=AfmBOop8Gy5mUlLeyMR8238x-7NV_V7zgnX26KKoNYvlmXoas2Iocarn.

Lefebvre, Henri. *The Production of Space*. 1974. Blackwell Publishers, 2000.

Leitner, Helga. "The Politics of Scale and Networks of Spatial Connectivity." *Scale and Geographic Inquiry: Nature, Society, Method*, edited by Eric Sheppard and Robert McMaster, Blackwell Publishers, 2004, pp. 236–255.

Levi, Primo. *The Voice of Memory: Interviews 1961–1987*. Polity Press, 2001.

Libicki, Miriam. "How the Soviet Jews Changed the World: A Graphic Tale of Tragedy and Triumph." *The Conversationalist*, 2021.

Libicki, Miriam. "I Was Banned from the Comic-Con!!" *Canadian Jewish News*, September 2024, pp. 87–89.
Libicki, Miriam. "Jewish Memoir Goes Pow! Zap! Oy!" *The Jewish Graphic Novel*, edited by Samantha Baskind and Ranen Omer-Sherman, Rutgers University Press, 2010, pp. 253–275.
Libicki, Miriam. *jobnik! An American Girl's Adventures in the Israeli Army*. Real Gone Girl, 2008.
Libicki, Miriam. "A Kind of Resistance." *But I Live: Three Stories of Child Survivors of the Holocaust*, edited by Charlotte Shaille, New Jewish Press, 2022.
Libicki, Miriam. *Toward a Hot Jew*. Fantagraphics Books, 2016.
Lightman, Sarah. *Graphic Details: Jewish Women's Confessional Comics in Essays and Interviews*, edited by Sarah Lightman, McFarland, 2014, pp. 1–15.
Maltz, Judy. "One, Two, Three, Four—We Opened Up the Iron Door." *eJewishPhilanthropy.com*, 5 Feb. 2015, https://ejewishphilanthropy.com/one-two-three-four-we-opened-up-the-iron-door/.
Marion, Phillipe. *Traces en cases. Essai sur la bande dessinée*. Louvain-la-Neuve: Académia, 1993.
Massey, Doreen. *Space, Place, and Gender*. University of Minnesota Press, 1994.
McClintock, Anne. *Imperial Leather: Race, Gender, and Sexuality in the Colonial Contest*. Routledge, 1995.
McCloud, Scott. *Understanding Comics: The Invisible Art*. HarperCollins, 1993.
McDowell, Linda. "Place and Space." *A Concise Companion to Feminist Theory*, edited by Mary Eagleton, Blackwell Publishers, 2003, pp. 11–31.
McGlothlin, Erin. *Second Generation Holocaust Literature*. Camden Press, 2006.
"Media Analyst Convicted over France-2 Palestinian Boy Footage." *The Guardian*. 26 June 2013.
Mihăilescu, Dana. "Jewish Identity amid Wars and Migration: Transnational and Transgenerational Itineraries in Julia Alekseyeva's *Soviet Daughter: A Graphic Revolution*." *Literature and Belief*, vol. 40.2 and 41.1, edited by Victoria Aarons, Brigham Young University Press, 2021, pp. 147–172.
Mihăilescu, Dana. "Mapping Transgenerational Memory of the Shoah in Third Generation Graphic Narratives." *Journal of Modern Jewish Studies*, vol. 17, no. 1, Feb. 2018, pp. 93–110.
Mikics, David. "Holocaust Pulp Fiction." *Tablet*, 19 Apr. 2012, https://www.tabletmag.com/sections/arts-letters/articles/ka-tzetnik.
Mironova, Oksana. "Soviet Daughter: An Interview with Julia Alekseyeva." *Lilith*, 24 Feb. 2017.
Modan, Rutu. *Jamilti and Other Stories*. English edition. Drawn and Quarterly, 2008.
Mothers Against Violence Israel. 2020, https://www.mavisrael.com/mavisrael.
Mouly, Françoise. Interview with Nora Krug. "The Bracing Honesty of 'Belonging,' a Graphic Memoir About German Identity." *The New Yorker*. 31 July 2018.
Novick, Peter. *The Holocaust in American Life*. Mariner Books, 2000.
Oksman, Tahneer. *How Come Boys Get to Keep Their Noses?* Columbia University Press, 2016.
Omer-Sherman, Ranen. *Israel in Exile*. University of Illinois Press, 2006.
Panofsky, Ruth. "Memories Seeded in Longing: An Interview with Bernice Eisenstein." *Studies in Canadian Literature*, vol. 42, no. 2, 2018, pp. 132–143.
Pinchevski, Amit, and Roy Brand. "Holocaust Perversions: The Stalags Pulp Fiction and the Eichmann Trial." *Critical Studies in Media Communication*, vol. 24, no. 5, 2007, pp. 387–407.

Pratt, Minnie Bruce, et al. *Feminism and War: Confronting US Imperialism*. Zed Books. 2008.
President's Commission on the Holocaust. *Report to the President*. Sept. 1979, https://www.ushmm.org/information/about-the-museum/presidents-commission.
"The Question of Palestine." *United Nations*, 24 May 2024, https://www.un.org/unispal/document/summary-of-icjs-order-24may24/.
Raab, Alon. "Ben Gurion's Golem and Jewish Lesbians." *The Jewish Graphic Novel*, edited by Samantha Baskind and Ranen Omer-Sherman, Rutgers University Press, 2010, pp. 214–236.
Rahman, Abid. "Jonathan Glazer's Oscar Speech Becomes Latest Battleground in the Israel-Gaza Conflict." *The Hollywood Reporter*, 11 Mar. 2024.
Rajaram, Prem Kumar, and Carl Grundy-Warr, eds. *Borderscapes: Hidden Geographies and Politics at Territories Edge*. University of Minnesota Press, 2008.
Raz-Krakotzkin, Amnon. "Binationalism and Jewish Identity." *Hannah Arendt in Jerusalem*, edited by Steven E. Aschheim, University of California Press, 2001, pp. 165–180.
Reingold, Matt. "Heimat Across Space and Time in Nora Krug's *Belonging*." *Monatshefte*, vol. 111, no. 4, 2019, pp. 551–569.
Reingold, Matt. "Mapping Transformative Spaces: Maps as a Tool for Understanding Rites of Passage in *Flying Couch* and *How to Understand Israel in 60 Days or Less*." *Images*, vol. 14, no. 1, 2020, pp. 40–53.
Ricci, Benedetta. "Lest We Forget: Charlotte Salomon's *Life? or Theatre?*" *Artland Magazine*. https://magazine.artland.com/lest-we-forget-charlotte-salomon-life-or-theatre/.
Rich, Adrienne. "Notes Toward a Politics of Location (1984)." *Blood, Bread, and Poetry: Selected Prose 1979–1985*, Virago Press, 1986, pp. 210–231.
Ringelheim, Joan. "The Split Between Gender and the Holocaust." *Women in the Holocaust*, edited by Dalia Ofer and Lenore Weitzman, Yale University Press, 1998, pp. 340–350.
Rose, Jacquelyn. *The Last Resistance*. Verso, 2007.
Rosello, Mireille, and Stephen F. Wolfe, eds. *Border Aesthetics: Concepts and Intersections*. Vol. 3. Berghahn Books, 2019.
Roskies, David. "What Is Holocaust Literature?" *Studies in Contemporary Jewry*, vol. 21, 2005, pp. 157–212.
Rotbard, Sharon. "Wall and Tower: The Mold of Israeli Architecture." *A Civilian Occupation*, edited by Rafi Segal and Eyal Weizman, Verso, 2003, pp. 39–56.
Rothberg, Michael. *The Implicated Subject: Beyond Victims and Perpetrators*. Stanford University Press, 2019.
Rothberg, Michael. "Memory and Implication at the Limits of the Human: Response to Nathan Snaza." *Parallax*, vol. 23, no. 4, 2017, pp. 412–416.
Rothberg, Michael. *Multidirectional Memory*. Stanford University Press, 2009.
Sacco, Joe. *Footnotes in Gaza*. Metropolitan Books, 2009.
Salomon, Charlotte. *Life? or Theatre?* Translated by Leila Vennewitz. Waanders Publishers, 1998.
Saper, Craig. *Intimate Bureaucracies: A Manifesto*. Punctum Books, 2012.
Schneer, David, and Caryn Aviv. *Queer Jews*. Routledge, 2002.
Schreier, Benjamin. *The Impossible Jew: Identity and the Reconstruction of Jewish American Literary History*. New York University Press, 2015.
Schwab, Gabriele. *Haunting Legacies: Violent Histories and Transgenerational Trauma*. Columbia University Press, 2010.
Segev, Tom. *The Seventh Million*. Henry Holt, 1991.

Segev, Tom. "Who Were You, Karl Zetinski?" *Haaretz*, 27 July 2001, https://www.haaretz.com/2001-07-27/ty-article/who-were-you-karl-zetinski/0000017f-e688-d62c-a1ff-fefbf38b0000.

Sered, Susan. *What Makes Women Sick? Maternity, Modesty, and Militarism in Israeli Society*. Brandeis University Press, 2000.

Siegel, Tatiana, and Alex Ritman. "Controversy Grows After Zone of Interest Director Jonathan Glazer Uses Oscar Speech to Condemn the Israel-Hamas War." *Variety*, 13 Mar. 2024, https://variety.com/2024/film/awards/zone-of-interest-director-jonathan-glazer-oscar-speech-israel-hamas-war-gaza-controversy-1235940637/.

Simmel, Georg. (1903). "The Sociology of Space." Translated by M. Ritter and D. Frisby. *Simmel on Culture: Selected Writings*, edited by D. Frisby and M. Featherstone, Sage, 1997, pp. 137–178.

Soja, Edward. *Postmodern Geographies: The Reassertion of Space in Critical Social Theory*. Verso, 1989.

Soja, Edward. *Third Space: Journeys to Los Angeles and Other Real-and-Imagined Places*. Blackwell Publishers, 1996.

Spiegelman, Art. *Maus*. Pantheon Books, 1973.

Stanczyk, Ewa. Introduction. *Journal of Modern Jewish Studies*, vol. 17, no. 1, February 2018, pp. 1–7.

Steiner, George. *Extraterritorial: Papers on Literature and the Language Revolution*. Atheneum Books, 1971.

Steiner, George. "Our Homeland, the Text." *Salmagundi*, vol. 66, winter–spring 1985, pp. 4–25.

Sternhell, Zeev. *The Founding Myths of Israel*. Princeton University Press, 1998.

Tabachnick, Stephen E. "Of Maus and Memory: The Structure of Art Spiegelman's Graphic Novel of the Holocaust." *Word & Image*, vol. 9, no. 2, 1993, pp. 154–162.

Tuan, Yi-Fu. *Space and Place: The Perspective of Experience*. University of Minnesota Press, 1977.

"UN News: ICC Issues Arrest Warrant for Israel, Hamas Leadership." *United Nations*, 23 Nov. 2024, https://news.un.org/en/story/2024/11/1157406.

"VanCAF Formal Apology." *VanCAF*, https://www.vancaf.org/vancaf-formal-apology/.

Weizman, Eyal. *Hollow Land: Israel's Architecture of Occupation*. Verso, 2007.

Yuval-Davis, Nira. *Unsettling Settler Societies*. Vol. 11. Sage Publications, 1995.

Zertal, Idit. *Israel's Holocaust and the Politics of Nationhood*. Cambridge University Press, 2005.

Zerubavel, Yael. "The Desert and the Settlement as Symbolic Landscapes in Modern Israeli Culture." *Jewish Topographies: Visions of Space, Traditions of Place*, edited by Julia Brauch, Anna Lipphardt, and Alexandra Nocke, Ashgate Press, 2008, pp. 201–222.

Zerubavel, Yael. *Recovered Roots: Collective Memory and the Making of Israeli National Tradition*. University of Chicago Press, 1995.

Index

Page numbers in italics refer to figures.

About the Author

LAINI KAVALOSKI is an associate professor of English and humanities at the State University of New York in Canton, where her research and teaching interests include graphic narratives, digital rhetorics, contemporary American literature, and Jewish literature and culture. Her publications include articles in *Studies on Critical Security*, *Studies in Comics*, *MELUS*, *Comparative Drama*, and *MLA Approaches to Teaching Jewish-American Literature*.